Educators' Discourses on
Student Diversity in Canada

Educators' Discourses on Student Diversity in Canada
CONTEXT, POLICY, AND PRACTICE

Edited by Diane Gérin-Lajoie

Canadian Scholars' Press Inc.
Toronto

Educators' Discourses on Student Diversity in Canada: Context, Policy, and Practice
edited by Diane Gérin-Lajoie

First published in 2008 by
Canadian Scholars' Press Inc.
180 Bloor Street West, Suite 801
Toronto, Ontario
M5S 2V6

www.cspi.org

Copyright © 2008 Diane Gérin-Lajoie, the contributing authors, and Canadian Scholars' Press Inc. All rights reserved. No part of this publication may be photocopied, reproduced, stored in a retrieval system, or transmitted, in any form or by any means, electronic, mechanical, or otherwise, without the written permission of Canadian Scholars' Press Inc., except for brief passages quoted for review purposes. In the case of photocopying, a licence may be obtained from Access Copyright: One Yonge Street, Suite 1900, Toronto, Ontario, M5E 1E5, (416) 868-1620, fax (416) 868-1621, toll-free 1-800-893-5777, www.accesscopyright.ca.

Every reasonable effort has been made to identify copyright holders. CSPI would be pleased to have any errors or omissions brought to its attention.

Canadian Scholars' Press Inc. gratefully acknowledges financial support for our publishing activities from the Government of Canada through the Book Publishing Industry Development Program (BPIDP).

Library and Archives Canada Cataloguing in Publication

    Educator's discourses on student diversity in Canada : context, policy, and practice / edited by Diane Gérin-Lajoie.
Includes bibliographical references.
ISBN 978-1-55130-346-8

          1. Minorities—Education—Canada. 2. Multicultural education—Canada. 3. Inclusive education—Canada. 4. Teaching—Canada. I. Gérin-Lajoie, Diane, date
LC3734.E386 2008   370.1170971   C2008-900276-8

Cover design: Aldo Fierro
Cover art © Kmitu. "Apple Diversity," Dreamstime.com #1587636
Interior design and composition: Em Dash Design

08 09 10 11 12   5 4 3 2 1

Printed and bound in Canada by Marquis Book Printing Inc.

Canadä

Table of Contents

Acknowledgements   7

CHAPTER 1   The Issue of Diversity in the Canadian Educational Context
Diane Gérin-Lajoie, OISE, UNIVERSITY OF TORONTO   9

CHAPTER 2   A Cross-sectional Sketch of a Few Demographic Characteristics of Teachers in Canada
Jean-Guy Blais and Soundiata Diene Mansa Ouedraogo, UNIVERSITÉ DE MONTRÉAL   29

CHAPTER 3   The Discourse on Diversity in British Columbia Public Schools: From Difference to In/Difference
Marianne Jacquet, SIMON FRASER UNIVERSITY   51

CHAPTER 4   "Our School Is Like the United Nations": An Examination of How Discourses of Diversity in Schooling Naturalize Whiteness and White Privilege
Mélanie Knight, OISE, UNIVERSITY OF TORONTO   81

CHAPTER 5   Student Diversity and Schooling in Metropolitan Toronto: A Comparative Analysis of the Discourses of Anglophone and Francophone School Personnel
Diane Gérin-Lajoie, OISE, UNIVERSITY OF TORONTO   109

CHAPTER 6   The Social Function of the School and the Work Performed by Montreal Teachers in the Context of Quebec Student Integration Policies
Louis LeVasseur, UNIVERSITÉ LAVAL   133

CHAPTER 7   Marking Bodies: Inhabiting the Discursive Production of
            Outstanding "Canadian Education" within Globalization
            Christine Connelly, OISE, UNIVERSITY OF TORONTO   163

CHAPTER 8   What Next? Official Discourse and School Reality
            Diane Gérin-Lajoie, OISE, UNIVERSITY OF TORONTO   183

Acknowledgements

On behalf of the contributors to this book and in my role as editor, I would like to thank all the people that made this publication possible. First, my gratitude goes to the teachers and principals across Canada that willingly agreed to take part in the national longitudinal study between 2002 and 2007, which was the source of data for discussion in the chapters. Their multi-year commitment to our study was remarkable, considering their very busy schedules. Their opinions were invaluable to our comprehension of the contemporary educational scene across Canada. We are also grateful to the school boards that allowed our research team to work with these participants.

Thank you also to those who have provided insightful comments on some chapters, in particular my colleagues Diane Farmer and Claude Lessard, as well as Christine Lenouvel, my research assistant. Christine Connelly, a recent PhD graduate, was also instrumental in the production of this book, in addition to providing important feedback. Her contribution to the realization of this project was invaluable. Without her technical skills and constant patience, I would have been lost more than once. A special thanks goes also to my colleague Stephen Anderson for his contribution to the title of the book.

Last but not least, I want to acknowledge the support received from Canadian Scholars' Press Inc. in the person of Rebecca Conolly, publishing manager, whose guidance has made my experience of editing this book very positive. I also want to acknowledge the two external reviewers for their insightful comments.

The data used in the book were gathered as part of a pan-Canadian study funded by the Social Sciences and Humanities Research Council of Canada through its Major Collaborative Research Initiatives program (2002–2007).

CHAPTER 1

The Issue of Diversity in the Canadian Educational Context

Diane Gérin-Lajoie

Over the past decades, Canadian schools have experienced important demographic changes in their student population and have become increasingly diversified. Diversity takes different forms, though, and as explained by Harper (1997), "schools are expected to meet the needs of a population that is racially, culturally and linguistically diverse, to confront gender, racial and economic disparity and discrimination" (p. 192). Although part of the official discourse in education for decades now, notions such as diversity, integration, and inclusion are still vague in the minds of many. For example, the word *multiculturalism* is commonly used but does not always carry the same meaning for everyone. As well, the term *multicultural education* represents a concept that is often interpreted in a variety of ways. As stated by Tator and Henry (1991):

> There is enormous confusion and ambiguity in the language which is used, as well as a lack of clarity with respect to the significant distinction, which underlies the words. The vocabulary includes the labels of multiculturalism, intercultural and cross-cultural education, race relations, racial and ethnocultural equity, and antiracist education. (p. 12)

This vagueness found in the official discourse gives contradictory signals to teachers and principals and might explain the failure of the true integration of student diversity in our system (Jones, 2000). Ministry of Education guidelines in each province are not always clear on how to work with student diversity in the mainstream classroom. The present educational climate is not always conducive to a collective reflection on the need to create more equitable classrooms. In an era where accountability is at the centre of the school personnel's preoccupations, issues of equity are often put on the back burner (Gérin-Lajoie, 2007). In some instances, schools have made concerted attempts to address student differences, as with the recent emphasis on implementing new methods of differentiated pedagogy adapting the curriculum to the individual needs of students. However, often when discussion takes place among school personnel, it is more about finding solutions to make all students fit into the prescribed model developed by school administrators and policy makers than about finding solutions to accomplish the type of inclusion beneficial to students from diverse racial, ethnic, and linguistic backgrounds. Student diversity continues to be interpreted as an individual experience, disconnected from the larger social context. Multicultural education is still about "celebrating differences" (Harper, 1997). Even among teacher candidates, the understanding of multicultural education remains linked mostly to the "celebration of difference" paradigm, as explained by Mujawamariya and Mahrouse (2004) in their comments on a study they performed with pre-service students.

Over the years, criticisms have been made of this approach to student inclusion. As mentioned by Jones (2000), "a paradox that should be noted concerns the lack of progress in addressing the educational problems affecting visible minority adults and children, despite the popularization of multicultural education during the 1970s and the 1980s" (p. 119).[1]

Critical educators claim that it is not enough to celebrate differences among students and that it is necessary "to examine how and when difference is produced and treated" (Harper, 1997, p. 201). This is the goal of anti-racist education. As described by van Dijk (1993):

> Antiracist views hold that lacking access to quality schools, discrimination in the classroom, stereotyping in textbooks, and a host of other factors lead to a position of minority children at school that is usually described as "disadvantaged," but in reality reflect their subordinate position. (p. 200)

Anti-racist education emphasizes the need to look closely at how the school system perpetuates the social order and how power relations are reproduced, for instance, in terms of who is integrating whom, and to what structures. From this perspective, "democratic racism" is still vividly present in schools. On one hand, schools convey liberal values concerned with tolerance and respect. On the other hand, differential treatment based on racial, ethnic, and linguistic backgrounds is also present in schools and can lead to potential discrimination (Henry & Tator, 1999, p. 90). Critical educators notice that the school system demonstrates colour-blindness when it comes to student diversity. For example, it is not uncommon to hear teachers mention that their students are all the same: simply children. This discourse does not acknowledge the impact of race and ethnicity on the students' lived experiences in school as well as outside of the school.

Other studies have pointed out the lack of critical consciousness on the part of the teachers (Solomon & Levine-Rasky, 1996; King, 2004; Sleeter,

2004; Mujawamariya & Mahrouse, 2004). Results presented in these studies demonstrate that the multicultural approach is very much alive in the teachers' discourse when it comes to the inclusion of students from diverse backgrounds. Often, teachers are colour-blind and see the challenges of these students as being individual ones, not the result of a more systemic process of exclusion. King (2004) states that white teachers in particular need to develop a more critical approach to diversity. She insists on the importance of developing a "liberatory pedagogy for the elite" in teacher pre-service and in-service programs. As she explains, "ideology, identity and indoctrination are central concepts I use in my Foundations of Education course to help students free themselves from miseducation and uncritically accepted views that limit their thought and action" (p. 77). As potential agents of change in the school, it is suggested that teachers—and I would add to that, principals—develop anti-racist pedagogical practices (Solomon & Levine-Rasky, 1996). However, while recognizing the need to do consciousness-raising with white teachers and, as a matter of fact, with all teachers, it is also imperative to find a way to give teachers ways of being more "oppositional" to the actual school practices in regard to student inclusion (Giroux, 1997).

To gain a better understanding of the response to racial, ethnic, and linguistic diversity in Canadian schools, the contributing authors of this book asked teachers and principals across the country to talk to them about this issue. From different points of view and different disciplines, we examine the issue of diversity in schools through the discourses of those who spend the most time with students—teachers and principals. The notion of discourse is understood here as being more than simple "talking and speaking practices"; social reality is shaped by discourses that in turn influence social interactions. Meanings are created through social practices and are influenced by history. As expressed by Niesz (2006):

> While discourses are often shared within and across communities, they are also linked to particular historical moments, and they represent interests that are political in nature. Moreover, discourses are not static across time, they are always in competition with contradictory discourses, and, in fact, constitute cultural resources that are used in diverse ways by local agents situated in particular social contexts. (p. 337)

Results from a recently completed national five-year study will be examined in the context of the book. The authors, from across Canada, have all been involved as researchers or research assistants in this national study. The purpose of the book is to analyze how teachers and/or principals make sense of racial, ethnic, and linguistic diversity in the context of their schools and what they have to say in terms of its impact on their daily work. These discourses are located within the context of existing educational policies dealing with student diversity, but they are also influenced greatly by other policies that are presently affecting the working lives of teachers and principals across the country.

Findings Used for the Forthcoming Analyses

As mentioned above, the analyses are based on results obtained from a five-year, pan-Canadian study funded by the Social Sciences and Humanities Research Council of Canada (SSHRC) through its Major Collaborative Research Initiatives program. The aim of this longitudinal study, titled *Current Trends in the Evolution of School Personnel in Canadian Elementary and Secondary Schools*, was to examine the daily work activities of school personnel in primary and secondary schools across Canada and to investigate their working conditions as well as their interactions with students and with other education stakeholders. The research focused on four areas of inquiry: 1) the working conditions and the renewal of teachers; 2) the impact of education reforms and policies on teachers and principals; 3) the training and professionalization of teachers; and 4) the transformation of school practices among teachers and principals. Our program of research analyzed significant changes faced by teachers and principals working in elementary and secondary schools in Canada and followed the evolution of these changes over a period of five years. The intent was to describe, interpret, and understand the dynamics of change, in both areas of education and society, that affect the work of the school personnel. The intent was also to analyze and document these changes in order to understand how teachers and principals adapt according to the resources available and the context in which they find themselves. Four research questions guided the longitudinal study:

1. Who are the teachers and principals working in Canadian schools and what are their working conditions?
2. How do school policies and reforms affect the performance of teachers and principals?
3. How do school personnel perceive their level of competency in regards to the profession and the daily activities associated with their work? Notions of professionalization and teachers' practices, as well as teacher training, were addressed.
4. What are the school practices of teachers and principals on a day-to-day basis and how do they make sense of these activities? In this context, we examined how changes in both policy and demographic

contexts affected the school practices. We also examined, among other things, student diversity and its impact on teaching practices.

In order to answer these questions, we divided the study into four sub-projects:

1. Project 1 had for its objective the creation of a national database of statistical information on teachers and principals in Canada between 1990 and 2005.
2. Project 2 looked at the impact of policies and school reforms—whether local, provincial, or national—on the professional lives of teachers and principals in Canadian schools. A policy analysis was performed that covered the period between 1990 and 2006.
3. Project 3 administered a national survey to teachers and principals across Canada on their conceptions and opinions on the dynamics of change that have occurred in the school setting over the years.
4. Project 4 followed a cohort of 500 participants (teachers and principals) over a period of five years, including 100 teachers and principals recruited in Vancouver, Toronto, and Montreal respectively for a total of 300. The rest of the participants (200) were from Halifax, Moncton, Winnipeg, and Saskatoon. Annual questionnaires were administered to all 500 participants. In addition, the 300 participants from Vancouver, Toronto, and Montreal also agreed to take part in two individual interviews during the program of study. Common interview guidelines were used across the country to facilitate data entry and data analysis.[2]

For analysis purposes, we used N6 software to code the interview transcripts in a uniform manner across the country according to question headings. Finer coding based on emergent ideas and themes was then performed in each of the three regions, according to local needs.[3]

The findings referred to in the book are mostly from Project 4, concerning the professional practices of teachers and principals, where the issue of diversity was addressed in great detail.

The framework for our data analysis can be explained as follows. Our findings point to four pan-Canadian themes when it comes to examining the overall focus of recent educational policies and reforms: inclusion and diversity, accountability, professionalization, and governance. For this book, the main focus of inquiry will be on diversity. However, the issue of diversity can certainly be linked to the three other themes, which represent some of the key contemporary stakes for school personnel. For example, standardized testing, which is associated with the theme of accountability, constitutes a major issue for teachers and principals when results from students of diverse racial, ethnic, and linguistic backgrounds, as well as students with special needs, are taken into account. Finally, while it is understood that analyses presented in the book are drawn mostly from the results of the fourth sub-project (the professional practices of teachers and principals), most of the authors also use some of the results originating from other sub-projects in the national study, such as the analyses of educational policies and the statistical database.

Having provided information on the research context, I will now turn to our object of inquiry: student diversity in Canadian schools.

The Official Discourse on Diversity

When we look at the situation that currently prevails in schools, it is important to consider the history of racial, ethnic, and linguistic homogeneity and heterogeneity. The classroom is now a place where numerous languages and cultures mix, making the school a social milieu where linguistic and cultural borders are routinely crossed by students. Efforts have been made to help schools to become more inclusive through the development of specific policies. Policy responses to differences have taken several forms over the years. Harper (1997) identifies five historical responses, which I summarize as follows:

1. Suppressing difference. This response aims to assimilate subordinate groups into the dominant group through the suppression of the former group's cultures and/or languages. In Canada, this has been the case, for example, for First Nations peoples and for francophones outside of Quebec. This response intended to create uniformity within the Canadian population.
2. Insisting on difference. Recognizing that differences are natural, this response emphasizes the need for accommodation. The notions of separation and segregation become part of the official discourse. Historically, women, blacks, and people with disabilities have been marginalized by this particular approach prevalent at the end of the 19th century and in the early 20th century. However, nowadays, the segregated movement is back in some instances. For example, for some education stakeholder groups, all-black schools, or all-girls schools, are seen as a way to alter power relations and enhance the opportunity for disadvantaged students to excel in schools. This recent call for segregation, however, stands in contrast to the movement of imposed segregation that the country experienced at the turn of the 20th century.

3. Denying difference. This response minimizes rather than highlights differences among students. This approach is associated with the popular notion of meritocracy, which emphasizes that success is an individual responsibility, and that with hard work and perseverance, anyone can succeed. This liberal perspective emphasizes the need to create equal opportunity. Denying difference is a notion that was salient in the 1960s. Again, it is possible to argue that this response to difference has returned, albeit in a different form. In the accountability context in which school personnel and students currently live, expectations are that all students attain common performance standards, as measured by government standardized tests, regardless of the students' background, past performance, and social reality. In this instance, policy makers are seeking to redress inequality by holding all students to common learning outcomes.
4. Inviting difference. This response is concerned with celebrating diversity, where the notion of multiculturalism is central. It is more about tolerance than about change. Canada is commonly perceived as a mosaic, composed of a variety of ethnic groups, which have their own cultural traditions that need to be acknowledged by the host country. This approach invokes a folkloric notion of culture. In the 1970s and 1980s, this response was manifested in multicultural education policies embraced by most Ministries of Education across the country. It is still very much part of the present educational discourse.
5. Critiquing difference. This response is about understanding power relations. How and when difference is produced becomes the main focus of inquiry. Anti-racist education is the best known example of this type of critical inquiry. It examines prejudices and systemic discrimination and emphasizes that the way that society is structured limits some students while placing others at an advantage.

It is in the context of these responses to difference that the ensuing analysis is presented in this book. For example, the celebration of difference was on the policy agenda of the provincial and territorial governments at the beginning of the 1970s, consistent with the 1971 Canadian federal policy on multiculturalism. Ministries of Education across Canada established multicultural committees in order to study the issue and to develop plans to respond to the presence of growing numbers of immigrant students. Referring specifically to the province of Ontario, Harper (1997) explains that this type of committee had the mandate to recommend specific "policies and practices" in order "to invite and celebrate difference" (p. 199). This approach was not unique to Ontario. A quick examination of policies that emerged around the same time across the country indicates a similar approach in other provinces. Although policy discourse with regards to diversity in schools has shifted since the 1970s, the multicultural approach continues to reverberate throughout educational policy, as well as through teachers' and principals' work. In the context of the book, I look briefly at three Canadian provinces that have always received and that continue to receive a large number of newcomers: British Columbia, Ontario, and Quebec. I have chosen to illustrate the situation in these three provinces because most of the findings analyzed in the following pages come from participants living in these three regions.

Historical Context: Policies in British Columbia, Ontario, and Quebec

SETTING THE STAGE

In the 1950s and 1960s, Canada experienced a high rate of immigration. Toward the end of the 1960s, a growing level of dissatisfaction was noticeable among the population in Quebec, and the rise of nationalism in that province brought the federal government to set up the Royal Commission on Bilingualism and Biculturalism (1963–1969). During the commission's public hearings, individuals and groups other than francophones and anglophones voiced their concerns about the way other cultures were portrayed in the new Canadian social mapping, expressing frustration with being marginalized by the notion of Canadian cultural duality. A policy on "multiculturalism within a bilingual framework" was thus elaborated. In 1971, under the federal Liberal government leadership of Prime Minister Pierre Elliot Trudeau, Canada became the first country in the world to adopt an official policy on multiculturalism. The resulting official discourse insisted on the recognition of the value of all Canadian citizens regardless of their racial or ethnic background, language, or religion. The government also recognized the rights of Aboriginal peoples and the status of the Canadian official languages, English and French. There were four themes to the policy:

1. To assist Canadian cultural groups in need, resources permitting.
2. To assist members of all cultural groups in overcoming cultural barriers to full participation in Canadian society.
3. To promote creative encounters and interchange among all Canadian cultural groups in the interest of national unity.
4. To continue to assist immigrants in acquiring at least one of the two official languages.

The policy was eventually enacted into legislation in 1988 in the form of the Canadian Multiculturalism Act—Bill C-93, passed by the federal government, which reaffirmed multiculturalism as a basic characteristic of the Canadian society. This bill still emphasized cultural retention (as in the policy of 1971), but another dimension was added: that of social equality (Li, 1999). Bill C-93 has been criticized by both right- and left-wing opponents. In the case of the former, some Canadians suggest that immigrants should give up their respective cultures to embrace the culture of the host country. In the latter case, critics suggest that the multicultural paradigm affirms the notion that racism is the result of individual racist attitudes and not a systemic reality, and effaces structural changes from the agenda (Henry & Tator, 1999, p. 95). Despite the debate, multiculturalism as an approach to managing diversity was well received in government circles, including ministries. This was especially the case in the area of education.

Since responsibility for setting educational policy and delivering education services is a provincial and territorial responsibility in Canada, the enactment of the policy of multiculturalism in the educational sector was left essentially to the provincial and territorial governments. In this specific policy context and because of the increasing number of students from diverse racial, ethnic, and linguistic backgrounds, particularly in urban settings, Ministries of Education throughout the country put the issue of students' diversity on their political agenda. The policies and measures put in place essentially mirrored those of the federal government, even if in some parts of the country efforts were made to look at student inclusion differently. Discussions on the inclusion of a diverse school population into the mainstream school system resulted in two separate perspectives at the provincial level. In English Canada, multicultural education policies were developed in the spirit of the federal policy on multiculturalism. By contrast, the Quebec government adopted intercultural education. In the early 1990s, Ontario adopted an anti-racist orientation toward the issue of diversity, which emerged as a third perspective. I will briefly describe each of them.

Multicultural Education

Within this perspective, cultures are celebrated and are seen to form what is often called "the Canadian cultural mosaic." Multicultural education insists on respecting and showing comprehension toward the diversity of students' racial, cultural, and linguistic backgrounds. The celebration of these differences is performed mainly through folkloric attributes, such as food, clothing, or traditions. This is often illustrated in schools by the deployment of countries' flags and displays on walls of the number of languages spoken by students in the school (in an ironic twist, the variety of languages spoken by students is usually silenced within the school and relegated to students' lives outside of school).

The official discourse on multiculturalism as enacted through the school perpetuates a "foods and festivals" approach, which, from a critical point of view, constitutes a superficial approach to student inclusion. The issue of equity is not present in this discourse, and critics point out that true integration will be difficult to accomplish until systemic changes take place in schools. Multicultural education, in the Canadian context, is often seen as a means to assimilate minorities into the host society.

Intercultural Education

In Quebec, the government has opted for a different approach to the inclusion of immigrants, which it calls "interculturalism." Interculturalism involves establishing a dialogue among diverse cultural groups and integrating newcomers to the host society, the intent being to define together a new francophone social order where every culture finds its place. As defined by Ouellet (1986), intercultural education refers to

> the systemic effort towards the development, among members of the majority groups as well as minority groups, of a better understanding of the various cultures, a greater capacity to communicate with persons of other cultures, and more positive attitudes towards the various cultural groups of society. (p. 16)

Within this approach, it is mainly by learning the French language that immigrants are integrated in the Quebec society. Intercultural education is considered by its critics to be as assimilative in nature as multicultural education. In order to be truly inclusive, intercultural education would need to raise the issues of discrimination and racism as an important step toward altering the structure of the system. Critics add that it is essential for immigrants to achieve structural inclusion into the host society, not only cultural integration. If the intention is to establish more equitable social relations between newcomers and the host society, intercultural education in its present form is far from attaining this objective (Ghosh et al., 1995).

Anti-racist Education

An attempt to implement an anti-racist education framework took place in Ontario at the beginning of the 1990s with the election of the New Democratic Party (NDP). In 1993, the provincial government published a set of guidelines for the development of policies on anti-racism and ethnocultural equity in Ontario school boards. As stated in the document:

> Antiracism and ethnocultural equity school board policies reflect a commitment to the elimination of racism within schools and in society at large. Such policies are based on the recognition that some existing policies, procedures, and practices in the school system are racist in their impact, if not their intent, and that they limit the opportunity of students and staff belonging to Aboriginal and racial and ethnocultural groups to fulfill their potential and to maximize their contribution to society. (Ontario Ministry of Education and Training, 1993, p. 5)

The objective of this policy was to go further than celebrating differences between students from diverse racial, ethnic, and linguistic backgrounds. Anti-racist education in the context of the NDP document was geared toward eliminating racism in Ontario schools with the goal of creating more equal social relations. Ideally, such a policy would provide equal opportunities to students regardless of their respective backgrounds. This type of policy called for a critical examination of school practices by school personnel as well as by students, representing a language of possibilities (Gérin-Lajoie, 1995). However, with the change in government in 1995, the policy was never fully implemented.

With that very brief overview of approaches toward student inclusion in Canadian schools, we will now look at specific policy contexts that affect the work of school personnel in Vancouver, Toronto, and Montreal.

THE SITUATION IN BRITISH COLUMBIA

At the end of the 1980s, the publication of the Royal Commission on Education report (often referred to as the Sullivan Commission) set the tone for the implementation of a series of policies and reforms in the educational system of British Columbia. The mandate of this commission was to address issues such as the quality of the school system, accountability, teaching and curriculum, and governance. Following the commission's report in 1989, the government published *Policy Directions: A Response to the Sullivan Royal Commission on Education by the Government of British Columbia*. Some of these policy orientations dealt specifically with equity issues, such as gender equity and issues of diversity and inclusion. First Nations education, in particular, was seen as a priority, and initiatives were put in place to better meet the needs of the students (Chan et al., 2004). Cultural diversity was also given priority in relation to other markers of difference. As explained by Chan et al. (2004), "issues of race, ethnicity, gender and special education, were acknowledged and put forward as they related to diversity and inclusion in education" (p. 12).

A review of hiring and promotion practices was recommended to ensure they were equitable. Teaching materials were also marked for review for gender and racial bias. During the 1990s, more money was allocated for the purpose of student inclusion in the areas of English as a Second Language, the promotion of multiculturalism and anti-racism, as well as the learning of a second language (such as Punjabi, Mandarin, and Japanese). French language education was also dealt with. In 1998, the first French language school board was established: the Conseil scolaire francophone.

In 2004, the Ministry of Education of British Columbia selected a more inclusive definition of diversity. Diversity, in the official discourse, became defined as "the ways in which we differ from each other. Some of these differences may be visible (e.g. race, ethnicity, gender, age, ability), while others are less visible (e.g. culture, ancestry, language, religious beliefs, sexual orientation, socio-economic background)" (p. 11).

THE SITUATION IN ONTARIO

Education policy in Ontario has, over the past five provincial governments, reflected a paradigm shift toward a tighter regulation of teacher work and student performance through accountability, teacher professionalization, and governance discourses. Equity issues have been part of the political agenda for a long time, even though they have not been given the same importance by all governments. In early 1970s, an increasing racial, ethnic, and linguistic diversity in Ontario prompted the educational milieu to put forward measures in order to meet the needs of that shifting school population.

Three decades of a Conservative government (1960s–1980s) gave way to Liberal leadership toward the end of the 1980s. In the 1990s, the NDP, the political party in power at the time, commissioned a province-wide report on education. Recommendations from the Royal Commission on Education included, among other initiatives, the compression of the secondary school program to four years, the re-establishment of a core curriculum, the creation of the Education Quality and Accountability Office, the Ontario College of Teachers, school board amalgamation, and the reform of education finances (Anderson and Ben Jaafar, 2006, p. 8). The NDP government implemented some of these initiatives before losing power to the Conservatives in 1995. The Harris Conservative government, with its Common Sense Revolution in the mid- to late 1990s, reduced education spending and implemented widespread reforms associated with accountability and regulation. Equity issues were not a priority for the Conservatives. As explained by Anderson and Ben Jafaar (2006):

> One dramatic reversal in policy concerned the equity policies enacted by the Liberal and NDP governments. The Conservatives shut down an Anti-Racism Secretariat created by the NDP, and its counterpart in

the Ministry of Education, and took steps to remove references to pro-equity goals (e.g., anti-racism, gender) from future curriculum policy documents. (p. 9)

The NDP policy guidelines on equity, *Antiracism and Ethnocultural Equity in School Boards: Guidelines for Policy Development and Implementation* (1993), were discarded by the Harris government. These guidelines had been developed after a 1992 Education Act amendment had been passed by the NDP government that required all Ontario school boards to develop and implement anti-racism and ethnocultural equity policies that would ensure equity in the areas of curriculum, materials, student assessment, staffing, and community relations.

The area of French minority language education also received attention from the Ontario government in the 1990s. In 1994, the Ministry of Education and Training presented the francophone school stakeholders with measures to help maintain the French language and French culture in Ontario. Three documents were produced: *Politique d'aménagement linguistique*, *Investir dans l'animation culturelle*, and *Actualisation linguistique en français/Perfectionnement du français*. The language planning policy was not fully implemented at the time. After a public consultation that took place in 2003, the *Politique d'aménagement linguistique* was significantly reworked, with a particular emphasis on the student's process of identity construction. The policy was launched in October 2004 and is being implemented in the 12 francophone school boards in the province.

THE SITUATION IN QUEBEC

As in the case of Ontario, it was in the 1970s that the Quebec Ministry of Education started to examine the issue of racial, ethnic, and linguistic diversity in its school system. At the time, the Quebec government was trying to find ways to better integrate immigrants into the Quebec society in order to have this new segment of the population contribute to the creation of a new society in this province.

Since Bill 101 in 1977, immigrants have had to enrol in French-speaking elementary and secondary schools by law. Anglophones still have access to English-speaking schools but under specific provisions. In the 1980s, the Ministry of Education created a department to deal with issues related to the education of new immigrants. In the middle of the 1980s, a committee recommended the development of a policy on intercultural education. Following this recommendation, several documents on intercultural education were published (Ghosh et al., 1995).

It was only in 1998 that the first policy was promulgated under the leadership of the Parti Québécois, entitled the *Politique en matière d'intégration scolaire et d'éducation interculturelle* (*Policy Statement on Educational Integration and Intercultural Education* in English). The policy's plan of action has five objectives: 1) to implement the Policy Statement on Educational Integration and Intercultural Education in the schools; 2) to facilitate the integration of all newly arrived students into their school; 3) to learn how to live together in a francophone, democratic, pluralist society; 4) to ensure that school staff receive appropriate initial and ongoing training and to set up an exchange network; and 5) to follow up and evaluate the plan of action (Quebec Ministry of Education, 1998). The policy states that changes need to be brought to the existing curriculum in order to better integrate the newly arrived immigrants, in terms of French language acquisition, but also in terms of acceptance of diverse races, languages, and cultures on the part of the host society as well as on the part of newcomers. It is important to note, however, that in the 1980s, the school boards located in Montreal (Commission des Écoles Catholiques de Montréal and the Protestant School Board of Greater Montreal) had already developed political views on the issue of student inclusion and had implemented specific initiatives. These experiences were in fact drawn upon in the development of the provincial educational policy released in 1998 (Lessard et al., 2004).

In the area of Aboriginal education, Quebec created the Cree and Kativik school boards in 1978, granting the Inuit and First Nations the right to be educated in their native languages in elementary schools as well as the right to administer their own schools. To better meet the needs of students, funding for these school boards was revised in 1998. Support was also provided for the implementation of curriculum reforms in 2001 (Lessard et al., 2004).

FRENCH MINORITY LANGUAGE EDUCATION IN CANADA

Before closing this section on provincial policies, I would like to draw attention to the issue of French minority language education in the context of official language minorities in Canada, especially given that a few of the chapters in this book address the situation of teachers and principals working in francophone minority environments such as Vancouver and Toronto. The situation of French minority language education, in French language schools located outside of Quebec, is not well known. For this reason, I will briefly address the issue.

The Canadian educational system, through the provinces and territories, provides for parallel publicly funded education systems in both official languages. The Canadian Charter of Rights and Freedoms guarantees francophones living outside of Quebec the right to be educated in French. As a result, each province and territory has school boards and schools where the language of instruction is French. In these schools, issues of racial, ethnic, and linguistic diversity are also present.

French language minorities in Canada have an increasingly heterogeneous school population, especially in the area of language use. Students have a tendency to speak English among themselves even though the language in use at school must be French. A large number of French minority language students live mostly in English outside the school setting. Consequently, there is a wide variation in students' proficiency in French. Finally, in the last 15 years, schools located in French minority language settings have also received a significant number of immigrants, which makes schools more diverse in terms of languages and cultures present among students.

The Organization of the Book

Recent changes to the educational system have raised questions about the transformation of the role of the school. As an agent of knowledge transmission, but even more powerfully, as an agent of socialization, the school contributes to the reproduction of values and abilities deemed important to the development of students as "good citizens of tomorrow." However, with an increasingly diverse student population, the school perceives itself as fulfilling a third function, that of inclusion for students who are not part of the mainstream school population. In that category, we find immigrant students or children of immigrants, Canadian official linguistic minorities, and students with disabilities of all kinds. What links can we identify between the social functions of the school, the impact of educational policies and reforms on students and teachers, and the increasing heterogeneity of the school population? These are the types of questions that the authors of this book, who live and work in different parts of Canada, have addressed in examining the findings of our national study. Here is a brief description of what follows.

Before looking specifically at the issue of student diversity, we want to familiarize readers with some demographic data about the teachers working in our Canadian schools. Chapter 2, co-authored by Jean-Guy Blais and Soundiata Diene Mansa Ouedraogo, presents a cross-sectional examination of a few demographic characteristics of teachers in Canada. They describe their analysis as cross-sectional because it examines the data at two and sometimes three different points in time, using different samples of data. Variables such as teachers' age, sex, membership in a "visible minority," religious affiliation, mother tongue, place of birth, and education have been selected for examination. Presently, this information is available through different institutional channels (e.g., Ministries of Education, school boards, and professional associations), but mostly at the provincial or territorial level. The chapter gives a national sketch of the information arising from teachers' surveys conducted as part of our national study, as well as from existing databases, and covers the period between 1991 and 2006.

With Chapter 3, we begin our journey into teacher and principal discourses on student diversity and inclusion across Canada. Author Marianne Jacquet explores the impact of the changes encountered in student demographics and the surrounding policy context on educators' discourse on their school practices. She examines the discourse of school personnel on racial, ethnic, and linguistic diversity in three instructional language contexts in the Vancouver area—the anglophone, francophone, and French immersion school programs. Drawing from the interview results, the findings suggest that teachers and principals are well aware of the important demographic changes in their respective schools and classrooms, yet they report a lack of experience and training with respect to diversity and claim to have limited knowledge of policies and resources on diversity issues in education. The examples they give of inclusive professional practices are generally limited to minor efforts at integrating diverse cultural artifacts into the classroom. The author concludes that, more than ever, the school system must adopt a more critical multicultural perspective when it comes to student diversity and student inclusion.

In Chapter 4, Mélanie Knight focuses on how the current debate on how to best support the racially diverse student population in schools has primarily relied on the multiculturalism model of "inclusivity," a model that superficially addresses issues of power and oppression. Using the literature on whiteness and white privilege, the author examines the interview results from white teacher discourses in Toronto on the increasing racial diversification of the student body. She discusses how whiteness as a system of domination is sustained and how white privilege is naturalized. In her data analysis, she outlines five strategies of whiteness found in the teacher discourses: the first strategy involves looking at diversity as foreignness/diversity as Other. The second sees the world as raceless and perpetuates the myth of sameness. The third strategy is to exoticize the Other. The fourth strategy refers to the notion of "becoming friends" with the Other, which she describes as the "Driving Miss Daisy Syndrome." The last strategy refers to the notion of the bourgeois decorum. The chapter concludes with possible strategies for equity and social justice that move beyond the notion of equal representation and essentialist characterizations of marginalized groups.

In Chapter 5, I present a comparative analysis of school personnel discourses on the notion of diversity in English and French language schools in Ontario. In both systems, the diversity of the school population has altered the social mapping of the schools. Based on an analysis of the interview results from school personnel working in Toronto, I show that in both types of schools, findings indicate that teachers' and principals' views on inclusion reflect those of the official policy discourse, which emphasize acceptance and celebration of diversity in recognizing diverse students' cultural and religious backgrounds. My analysis examines three main areas. The first is concerned with teacher and principal discourses on students' racial, ethnic, and linguistic diversity and the inclusion of these students into their classrooms. The second presents the teachers' and principals' views on the impact of students' racial, ethnic, and linguistic diversity on their work and how prepared they feel they are to accomplish that work. Finally, I focus my attention on teacher and principal discourses on the notion of language. Results show that there exist similarities between discourses on the first two issues discussed within the two linguistic school systems, although anglophones and francophones work in very different school realities. However, differences in the participants' views occur on the issue of language. I conclude, nevertheless, that the notion of Otherness remains present in the participants' discourses, in both linguistic groups.

In Chapter 6, Louis LeVasseur examines the ways that teachers in Montreal make sense of the inclusion process taking place in their schools. Beginning with a discussion of the functions played by the school in our society, he describes the educational policies in Quebec pertaining to the inclusion of two types of students: immigrants and students with disabilities (either physical, intellectual, or emotional). In his analysis, an intriguing point is made regarding the process of inclusion in school settings and the impact of policies promoting the decentralization of schools on this process of inclusion. The author argues that instead of working toward the inclusion of all students, decentralization can lead to greater differentiation, where schools become more selective about who they serve. Through his analysis of teachers' views, LeVasseur concludes that the implementation through school policy of inclusive measures that contribute to increased student heterogeneity have an impact not only on teachers' daily work in the classroom, but also on teachers' sense of professional identity.

In Chapter 7, Christine Connelly examines how teachers and principals engage in the work of schools within a framework of education based on two competing processes of globalization: reproduction of uniformity and standardization, and diversification and difference. Through her analysis, she tries to understand how these educators make sense of their responsibilities and of the possibilities of engaging students in socially transformative ways in the context of a diverse student population. The author looks at how teachers and principals in Vancouver, Toronto, and Montreal make sense of the work that they do in relationship to the terms of recent educational reforms that emphasize excellence. The chapter examines how social difference in this context is subject to particular processes of cultural production such as erasure or neutralization of difference, assimilation/integration, norm-referenced, remediation-oriented schooling, the gentrification of schools, and the exercise of school authority. The chapter also discusses the implications of new structures of accountability in education for students and their families, as well as for the school personnel.

My concluding remarks in Chapter 8 take the form of a question: What next? What more can we do to make sure that student diversity is constructively taken into account by the educational system? Our findings suggest that the participants' discourse regarding racial, ethnic, and linguistic diversity among students is, for the most part, in line with the government discourse. How can the findings and insights about responses to diversity in Canadian schools highlighted in this book inform the ongoing efforts of school personnel and other education stakeholders to ensure that students from all backgrounds are fully and positively integrated into the education process and schools across Canada? The type of integration we are witnessing in schools today now is still failing the students. Perhaps it is time to shift the focus and interrogate the type of actions taken in the past to meet the needs of an increasingly diverse school population. It is time to ensure student empowerment. In order to do so, however, school personnel must be prepared to inquire critically about what needs to be changed for schools to become truly inclusive of all students.

Notes

1. Although the term *visible minority* is commonly employed, it is important to note that the use of this term is not unproblematic. The designation of particular social groups as "visible minorities" has been defined by the majority who decides who is an insider or an outsider. In the official discourse, this term remains central to the construction of difference.
2. I would like to mention that there were three main questions that were asked about student diversity and inclusion in our second interview guidelines. These questions were first conceptualized in French and then translated into English. The following question did not reflect the exact meaning that it had in French. *Au quotidien, comment composez-vous avec la diversité ethnoculturelle de vos élèves?* was translated into "On a daily basis, what helps you to deal with the ethno-cultural diversity of your students?" The use of "deal with" was understood by many participants as referring to problematic situations with their students, which was not the intent of the question.
3. Information on the four sub-projects is available on our website at www.teachcan.ca.

References

Anderson, S. & Ben Jaafar, S. (2006). *Policy trends in Ontario education—1990–2006*. Toronto, Canada: Centre for Educational Change, OISE, University of Toronto.

British Columbia Ministry of Education. (1989). *Policy directions: A response to the Sullivan Royal Commission on Education by the Government of British Columbia*. Victoria: British Columbia Ministry of Education.

Chan, A., Fisher, D. & Rubenson, K. (2004). *Policy narrative for British Columbia*. Vancouver: Centre for Policy Studies in Higher Education and Training, University of British Columbia.

Gérin-Lajoie, D. (2007). Effets des politiques scolaires dans la pratique du métier d'enseignante et d'enseignant au Canada. In R. Malet (Ed.), *L'école, lieu de tensions et de médiations: Quels effets sur les pratiques scolaires? Actes du colloque international de l'AFEC, 22, 23 et 24 juin 2006* (pp. 395–405). Lille: Association francophone d'éducation comparée.

Gérin-Lajoie, D. (1995). Les écoles minoritaires de langue française canadiennes à l'heure du pluralisme ethnoculturel. *Études ethniques au Canada/Canadian Ethnic Studies*, 27(1), 32–47.

Giroux, H.A. (1997). Rewriting the discourse of racial identity: Towards a pedagogy and politics of whiteness. *Harvard Educational Review*, 67(2), 1–29.

Ghosh, R., Zimman, R. & Abdulaziz, T. (1995). Policies relating to the education of cultural communities in Quebec. *Études ethniques au Canada/Canadian Ethnic Studies*, 27(1), 18–31.

Harper, H. (1997). Difference and diversity in Ontario schooling. *Canadian Journal of Education*, 22(2), 192–206.

Henry, F. & Tator, C. (1999). State policy and practices as racialized discourse: Multiculturalism, the Charter and employment equity. In P.S. Li (Ed.), *Race and ethnic relations in Canada* (pp. 88–115). Toronto: Oxford University Press.

Jones, B.M. (2000). Multiculturalism and citizenship: The status of "visible minorities" in Canada. *Études ethniques au Canada/Canadian Ethnic Studies*, 32(1), 111–125.

King, J.E. (2004). Dysconscious racism: Ideology, identity, and the miseducation of teachers. In G. Ladson-Billings & D. Gillborn (Eds.), *The Routledge-Falmer Reader on Multicultural Education* (pp. 71–83). London: Routledge-Falmer Publishing Company.

Lessard, C, Henripin, M. & Larochelle, M. (2004). *Les politiques d'éducation au Québec: Introduction*. Montreal: Faculty of Education, Université de Montréal.

Li, P.S. (1999). The Multiculturalism Debate. In P.S. Li (Ed.), *Race and ethnic relations in Canada* (pp. 148–177). Toronto: Oxford University Press.

Mujawamariya, D. & Mahrouse, G. (2004). Multicultural education in Canadian pre-service programmes: Teacher candidates' perspectives. *The Alberta Journal of Educational Research*, 50(4), 336–353.

Niesz, T. (2006). Beneath the surface: Teacher subjectivities and the appropriation of critical pedagogies. *Equity and Excellence in Education*, 39, 335–344.

Ontario Ministry of Education and Training. (2004). *Politique d'aménagement linguistique pour l'éducation en langue française*. Toronto: Government of Ontario.

Ontario Ministry of Education and Training. (1994). *Aménagement linguistique en français: Guide d'élaboration d'une politique d'aménagement linguistique*. Toronto: Government of Ontario.

Ontario Ministry of Education and Training. (1994). *Actualisation linguistique en français et perfectionnement du français*. Toronto: Government of Ontario.

Ontario Ministry of Education and Training. (1994). *Investir dans l'animation culturelle*. Toronto: Government of Ontario.

Ontario Ministry of Education and Training. (1993). *Antiracism and ethnocultural equity in school boards: Guidelines for policy development and implementation*. Toronto: Government of Ontario.

Ontario Royal Commission on Learning. (1994). Equity considerations. In *For the love of learning, Volume IV: Making it Happen* (chap. 16). Toronto: Queen's Printer for Ontario.

Ouellet, F. (1986). Teachers' preparation for intercultural education. In R.J. Samuda & S.L. Kong (Eds.), *Multicultural education: Programmes and methods* (pp. 15–24). Toronto: Intercultural Social Sciences.

Quebec Ministry of Education. (1998). *Policy statement on intercultural integration and intercultural education*. Quebec City: Government of Quebec.

Sleeter, C.E. (2004). How white teachers construct race. In G. Ladson-Billings & D. Gillborn (Eds.), *The Routledge-Falmer Reader in Multicultural Education* (pp. 163–178). London: Routledge-Falmer Press.

Solomon, R.P. & Levine-Rasky, C. (1996). Transforming teacher education for an antiracism pedagogy. *Canadian Review of Sociology and Anthropology, 33*(3), 337–359.

Tator C. & Henry, F. (1991). *Multicultural education: Translating policy into practice*. Ottawa: Multiculturalism and Citizenship Canada.

van Dijk, T.A. (1993). *Elite discourse and racism*. Newbury Park, CA: Sage Publications.

CHAPTER 2

A Cross-sectional Sketch of a Few Demographic Characteristics of Teachers in Canada

Jean-Guy Blais and Soundiata Diene Mansa Ouedraogo

Thanks to concerted efforts on the part of university researchers and the agencies that collect and compile statistics in certain industrialized nations, several socio-demographic databases have become accessible to researchers in recent years. In addition, user-friendly procedures have been developed that make these databases easier to work with. Taking advantage of these advances, one sub-project of the national study has set itself the goal of exploring and using the data that has become available in order to document and compare the situations of elementary and secondary school teachers in Canada from 1990 to 2006.[1]

Obviously, this type of undertaking depends upon the availability of high-quality, relevant data for the target description. At the present time, data that match this description—cross-sectional national data—are hard to come by. They are mainly to be found in the national census that is conducted every five years and in various national surveys conducted by Statistics Canada. In the context of the cross-sectional sketch developed for this monograph, and from all of the data that are available, we chose the data from the 1991 and 2001 censuses. From time to time, and as circumstances permitted, these data were complemented by the results of a survey conducted in 2006 in the context of our national study in which a questionnaire was administered to more than 4,000 teachers in Canada. Thus the points in time at which the provinces are compared are the years 1991 and 2001 and, from time to time, 2006.

A few preliminary remarks about the data from the 1991 and 2001 censuses and the 2006 survey are in order. The data that we have used and that we associate with the censuses are not derived from statistical operations involving the general population. They were collected at the time of the census from a sample of the population (more than 800,000 respondents in 2001). In this context, the elementary and secondary teacher population—the population that is of particular interest to our research project and that was targeted in our survey in 2006—is not the Census Canada population that was sampled. In the census operation questionnaires, the data on the type of employment are grouped according to the National Occupational Classification. One of the categories in this system of classification is "teacher," although the level taught (i.e., elementary, secondary, college, or university) is not specified. Consequently, elementary and secondary school teachers are surveyed on the same basis as any other individual who could be selected in the national survey conducted during a census and a national or provincial sample that is "representative" of the teacher population is not available at this time.

For these reasons, the category of "teacher" may be underrepresented or overrepresented in the samples, compared to its actual weight in the population. This phenomenon may also contribute to fluctuations in the cross-sectional profiles proposed in this chapter. Furthermore, given the number of individuals in the occupational category of teacher, it is sometimes difficult to cross the variables that we are interested in with the variables initially chosen in order to create a cross-sectional national portrait, that is, the year and the province.

Thus, for the analysis of the data from the 1991 and 2001 census operations, generalizations about the characteristics of elementary and secondary school teachers in Canada are simply hypotheses that are difficult to test, given the time at which these data were collected and the possibility that they are not representative of the target population.

The situation is different where the questionnaire administered in 2006 is concerned. The data are more "representative" of the target population—elementary and secondary school teachers in Canada. A stratified, national, random sample of more than 15,000 teachers was created and used to collect data from more than 4,000 individuals, with a response rate of more than 25 percent. However, in this type of survey, the number of questions that can be asked does not compare to what can be done during the census operation. Thus, for a variety of reasons, several variables for which the census operations provide data do not have counterparts in the survey questionnaire administered in 2006 (for our purposes, the variables in the 2006 questionnaire that are used are age, sex, and place of birth).

As the title indicates, our objective in this text is to present a cross-sectional sketch of certain demographic characteristics of teachers in Canada. We have called it a sketch because it would be presumptuous to claim that it is either complete or precise. We have described it as cross-sectional because it examines the data at two and sometimes three different points in time, using different samples. It attempts to describe the population of a certain category of teachers; in fact, however, it is difficult to say that it represents just elementary and secondary school teachers. As we have mentioned, the number of variables that we could have used is very high, and certain choices were inevitable. Lastly, the constraints of the publication format limit the inclusion of tables and figures that were the analytical tools we used for the analysis.

From all of the information currently extracted from the various Statistics Canada databases and the operations that accompanied the 1991 and 2001 censuses, we have selected the following variables: age, sex, membership in a visible minority, religious affiliation, mother tongue, place of birth, and level of education. Our objective was not to provide a complete and precise portrait; it was to provide a foretaste or sketch in the hopes that readers will want to explore the program's website (at www.teachcan.ca); we also wanted researchers to discover the quantity, diversity, and limitations of the data presented and to consult the Statistics Canada databases directly to find data on the variables relevant to their specific projects. The database on the website is not the only database in Canada with a specific interest in education. The EDUDATA website (at www.edudata.educ.ubc.ca) is also interested in data on education, but with a focus on other issues, such as grade retention and student achievement in British Columbia schools and British Colombia school district expenditures.

Presentation of a Few Demographic Characteristics

Presenting a large number of data is always somewhat problematic when there are space constraints. In this text, we have chosen to present and comment on the data with respect to numbers and percentages, providing tables and figures to illustrate our description. For ease of reading, we placed these tables and figures directly in the running text, rather than in a separate appendix. The descriptions are fairly consistent from variable to variable, and they present the number of teachers in percentages, to ensure that the differences between the provinces do not make the comparisons any more complicated than necessary. We look at the main differences in the situation in 1991 and in 2001 and then compare these differences. When the data allow, we add a description of the 2006 data and compare them to 1991 and 2001. Whenever possible, the profile takes the specificity of the provinces into account. However, for certain crossed descriptions using the variable "membership in a visible minority," given the limited number of respondents, we provide a portrait for Canada as a whole.

AGE

Table 2.1 and Figure 2.1 provide the data for the variable "age" that are available for the three points in time used. These data are divided into five age groups: under 30 years of age, 30 to 39 years of age, 40 to 49 years of age, 50 to 59 years of age, and 60 years of age and over.

For the 1991 operation, the two categories with the highest concentration of teachers were those of teachers 30 to 39 years of age and 40 to 49 years of age; these two categories accounted for 62 percent and 66 percent of teachers respectively. Quebec had the highest concentration of teachers in the 40 to 49 years of age group (38 percent of teachers), as did Nova Scotia (with 37 percent of teachers). This age group also had the highest concentration of teachers in British Columbia and Ontario, with 34 percent of teachers. The 30 to 39 years of age group was also very well represented. It was the largest age group for Newfoundland and Labrador, Prince Edward Island, Manitoba, Saskatchewan, and Alberta, accounting for 33 percent, 34 percent, 32 percent, 34 percent, and 35 percent of teachers respectively. The category with the lowest concentration of teachers is the category of teachers 60 years of age and over; percentages ranged from 2 percent to 8 percent. The second lowest category is the category of teachers from 50 to 59 years of age; these percentages ranged from 9 percent in Newfoundland and Labrador to 17 percent in Quebec. When all of the provinces are combined, these two categories account for between 10 percent and 21 percent of teachers. "Young" teachers—teachers under 30 years of age—account for 15 percent (Prince Edward Island) and 25 percent (Newfoundland and Labrador). Thus, in 1991, many of the respondents were between 30 and 49 years of age, a smaller percentage of teachers were over 50 years of age, and approximately 20 percent on average were under 30 years of age.

By 2001, the situation had changed considerably. Whereas in 1991 the dominant categories (30 to 39 years of age and 40 to 49 years of age) had been the same in all of the provinces, in 2001, there was a larger concentration in the 50 to 59 years of age category. In fact, in Quebec, this category had become the largest. However, it would be more accurate to say that, in 2001, teachers were divided almost equally in the categories 30 to 39 years, 40 to 49 years, and 50 to 59 years and that a few provinces differed in this regard. We see that Newfoundland and Labrador, Nova Scotia, and Prince Edward Island did not follow this distinct trend. The 50 to 59 years of age group became the largest in Quebec, Prince Edward Island, Ontario, and British Columbia with 27 percent, 31 percent, 26 percent, and 27 percent of teachers respectively. However, the increase in this category is easier to see when we compare the numbers for 1991 and 2001. The differences for this age group and for the two census periods range from +8 percent for Newfoundland and Labrador to +18 percent for Prince Edward Island. The group of teachers under 30 years of age remained fairly stable between 1991 and 2001, except in Newfoundland and Labrador where it decreased by 10 percent. There was little change in the 60 years of age and over group, except in Prince Edward Island where, in 2001, it decreased by approximately 7 percent. Thus, from 1991 to 2001, we see an overall shift from the 30 to 39 years of age group and the 40 to 49 years of age group toward the 50 to 59 years of age group. We also see relative stability in the under 30 years of age group and the 60 years of age and over group.

TABLE 2.1 Distribution of Teachers by Age Group (1991–2001–2006)

1991	NL	PEI	NS	NB	QC	ON	MB	SK	AB	BC
-30	0.25	0.19	0.15	0.18	0.17	0.19	0.22	0.20	0.18	0.16
30–39	0.33	0.34	0.30	0.30	0.24	0.27	0.32	0.34	0.35	0.31
40–49	0.31	0.28	0.37	0.32	0.38	0.34	0.30	0.27	0.31	0.34
50–59	0.09	0.13	0.14	0.15	0.17	0.16	0.12	0.13	0.12	0.13
60+	0.02	0.08	0.04	0.04	0.04	0.05	0.05	0.06	0.04	0.06

2001	NL	PEI	NS	NB	QC	ON	MB	SK	AB	BC
-30	0.15	0.19	0.13	0.15	0.19	0.18	0.16	0.18	0.18	0.16
30–39	0.28	0.23	0.22	0.26	0.25	0.25	0.24	0.26	0.25	0.25
40–49	0.37	0.26	0.33	0.28	0.25	0.26	0.30	0.31	0.29	0.26
50–59	0.17	0.31	0.28	0.27	0.27	0.26	0.25	0.22	0.23	0.27
60+	0.03	0.01	0.04	0.04	0.04	0.05	0.05	0.03	0.05	0.05

2006	NL	PEI	NS	NB	QC	ON	MB	SK	AB	BC
-30	0.03	0.04	0.06	0.12	0.08	0.03	0.12	0.08	0.13	0.03
30–39	0.33	0.41	0.20	0.34	0.18	0.24	0.19	0.29	0.24	0.21
40–49	0.38	0.27	0.27	0.29	0.14	0.35	0.25	0.28	0.28	0.27
50–59	0.25	0.28	0.44	0.24	0.52	0.35	0.42	0.33	0.33	0.44
60+	0.00	0.01	0.02	0.01	0.08	0.04	0.03	0.01	0.02	0.06

The portrait that emerges for 2006 underscores the value of cross-sectional and national studies. Even though the results for 2006 cannot be compared directly to those of 1991 and 2001, this comparison may stimulate dialogue on the aging teacher population and the impact of the declining birth rate for individuals considering a career in teaching. It is important to bear in mind that the 2006 data are probably more precise and reliable than the data from the 1991 and 2001 census operations.

FIGURE 2.1 Distribution of Teachers by Age Group (1991—2001—2006)

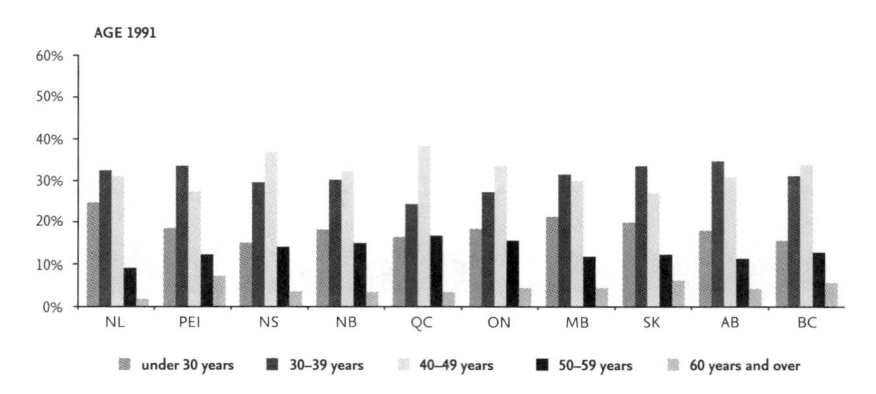

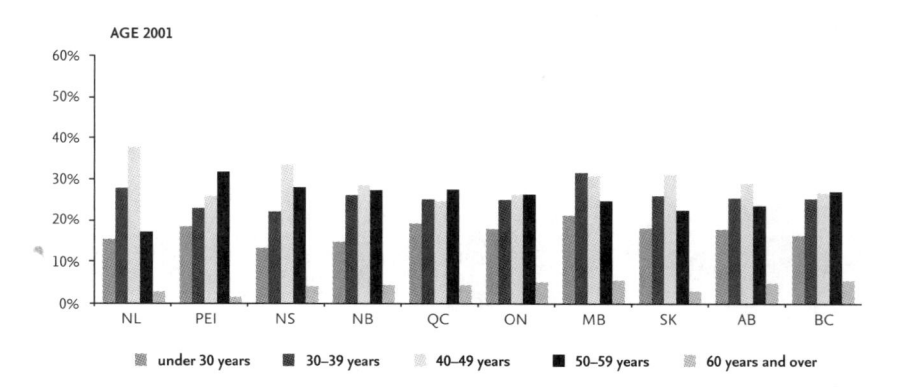

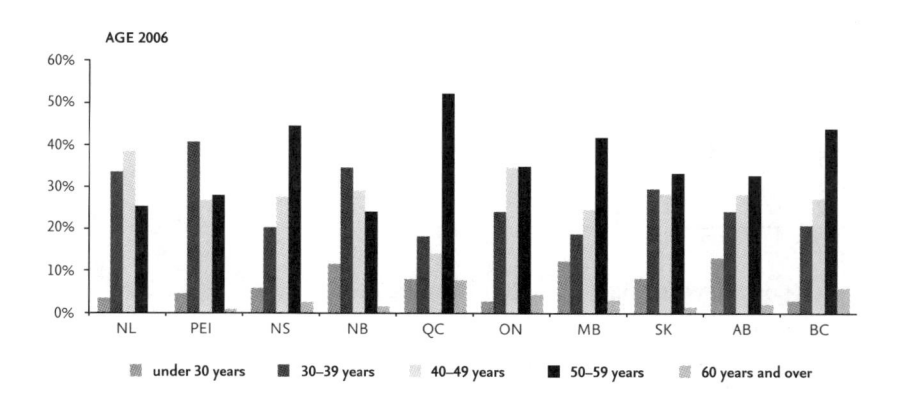

From the 2006 survey, we see that the 50 to 59 years of age group is now the largest in seven out of 10 provinces. The greatest difference is clearly in Quebec where, in 2006, more than 50 percent of teachers were in this age group (compared to 17 percent in 1991 and 27 percent in 2001). In this age group, the percentages in British Columbia, Manitoba, and Nova Scotia were 44 percent, 42 percent, and 44 percent respectively. In 2006, the two largest groups are the 40 to 49 years of age group and the 50 to 59 years of age group. The two categories combined represent as many as 71 pecent of teachers in British Columbia and Nova Scotia. The under 30 years of age group lost the largest number of teachers to the older age groups; in 2006, there was a big decrease in the number of teachers under 30 years of age in every province except New Brunswick. The percentage of teachers in this age group went from 25 percent to 3 percent in Newfoundland and Labrador, from 19 percent to 4 percent in Prince Edward Island, from 15 percent to 6 percent in Nova Scotia, from 17 percent to 8 percent in Quebec, from 19 percent to 3 percent in Ontario, from 22 percent to 12 percent in Manitoba, from 20 percent to 8 percent in Saskatchewan, and from 16 percent to 3 percent in British Columbia.

TABLE 2.2 Percentage of Teachers in the Under 30 Years of Age Group and the 50 to 59 Years of Age Group (1991–2001–2006)

	TEACHERS UNDER 30 YEARS OF AGE									
	NL	PEI	NS	NB	QC	ON	MB	SK	AB	BC
1991	0.25	0.19	0.15	0.18	0.17	0.19	0.22	0.20	0.18	0.16
2001	0.15	0.19	0.13	0.15	0.19	0.18	0.16	0.18	0.18	0.16
2006	0.03	0.04	0.06	0.12	0.08	0.03	0.12	0.08	0.13	0.03

	TEACHERS 50–59 YEARS OF AGE									
	NL	PEI	NS	NB	QC	ON	MB	SK	AB	BC
1991	0.09	0.13	0.14	0.15	0.17	0.16	0.12	0.13	0.12	0.13
2001	0.17	0.31	0.28	0.27	0.27	0.26	0.25	0.22	0.23	0.27
2006	0.25	0.28	0.44	0.24	0.52	0.35	0.42	0.33	0.33	0.44

Table 2.2 and Figure 2.2 make it possible to more directly compare the categories that experienced the largest losses or gains—the under 30 years of age group and the 50 to 59 years of age group. Once again, these data demonstrate the shift from "younger" teachers to "older" teachers, reflecting perhaps the greying of teachers in the workforce. The lowest percentages for the under 30 years of age group are found in 2006; this is true for all of the provinces. There was a pronounced increase from 1991 to 2006 for the 50

to 59 years of age group and a notable increase from 2001 to 2006 in nine of the 10 provinces (Newfoundland and Labrador, Prince Edward Island, Nova Scotia, Quebec, Ontario, Manitoba, Saskatchewan, Alberta, and British Columbia). Thus, it is not an exaggeration to say that, during the period from 1991 to 2006, the population of teachers in almost all of the provinces aged. Over the next decade, we will likely see huge numbers of teachers retire and many new teachers arrive, with all of the benefits and unknowns that such a transformation brings.

FIGURE 2.2 Percentage of Teachers in the Under 30 Years of Age Group and the 50 to 59 Years of Age Group (1991–2001–2006)

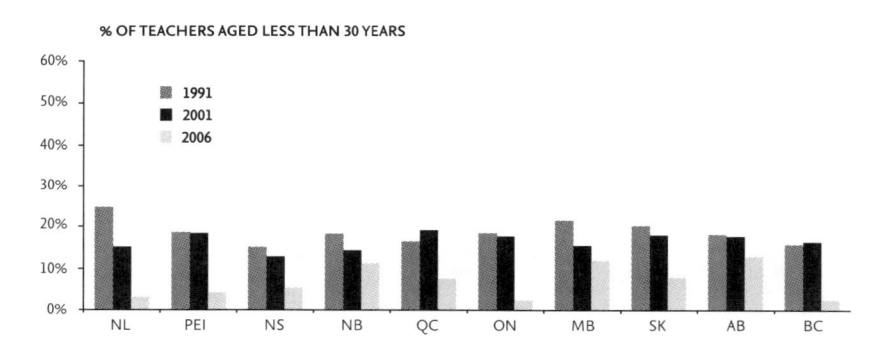

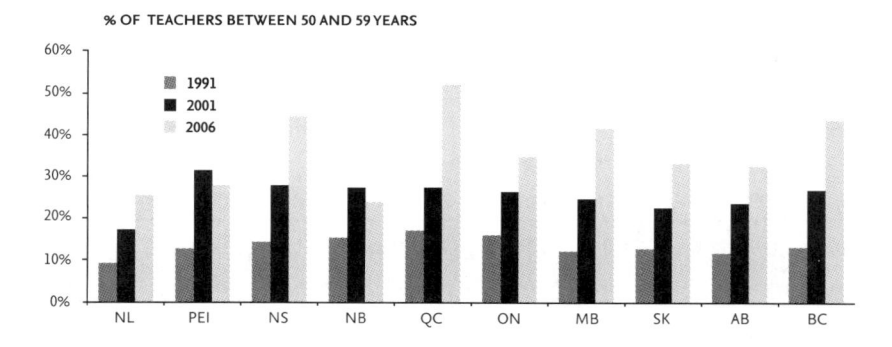

SEX

Table 2.3 and Figure 2.3 show the distribution of men and women in the occupational category of "teacher" in the 1991 and 2001 censuses and the 2006 survey. In fact, only the percentages for female teachers are presented; the percentages for male teachers can easily be extrapolated.

First, we note that, except for New Brunswick, the percentages are almost identical in 1991 and 2001. The percentages range between 61 percent (Newfoundland and Labrador) and 71 percent (Prince Edward Island) for 1991 and between 60 percent (Nova Scotia) and 71 percent (Prince Edward Island) for 2001. The difference between the data from the 2001 Census and the 2006 survey is greater for Ontario (+16 percent female), followed by Nova Scotia (+14 percent), Manitoba (+10 percent), Alberta (+9 percent), and Quebec (+9 percent). There are various explanations for the differences seen at the three times of data collection. They may be partly due to fluctuations related to the sampling; however, they may also reflect a gradual exodus of men from the teaching profession over a 15-year period. It is unfortunate that the data from the census operations do not make it possible to distinguish between teaching levels, thereby limiting our ability to perform cross-sectional comparisons of the distribution of the sexes based on this variable. In 2006, according to the survey, more than 60 percent of teachers were female in all of the provinces; more than 70 percent of teachers were female in five of the provinces; and more than 80 percent of teachers were female in one province.

TABLE 2.3 Percentage of Female Teachers (1991–2001–2006)

	NL	PEI	NS	NB	QC	ON	MB	SK	AB	BC
1991	0.61	0.71	0.63	0.68	0.63	0.65	0.65	0.67	0.66	0.65
2001	0.62	0.71	0.60	0.61	0.63	0.65	0.64	0.67	0.64	0.62
2006	0.63	0.77	0.74	0.69	0.72	0.81	0.74	0.67	0.73	0.68

FIGURE 2.3 Percentage of Female Teachers (1991–2001–2006)

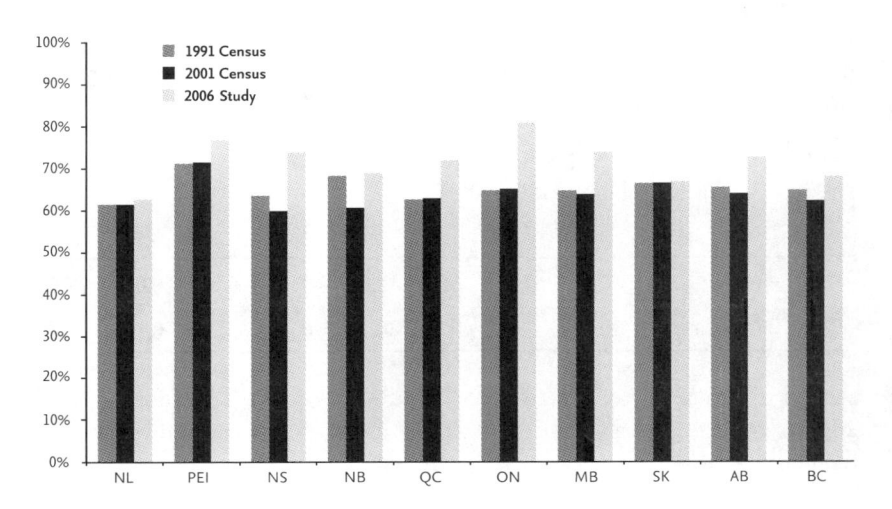

MEMBERSHIP IN A VISIBLE MINORITY

A Portrait of the Provinces

Several census questions relate to ethnic origin, immigration status, or membership in a visible minority. We chose the latter variable to illustrate, albeit partially, some of the characteristics of the "ethnic" composition of individuals who reported that they were teachers. In the 2001 census database, there are five possible responses to the question on membership in a visible minority: Chinese, South Asian, Black, Other Visible Minority, and Not a Member of a Visible Minority.[3] For the purposes of this presentation, the data are divided into two categories: member of a visible minority or not a member of a visible minority.

The data in Table 2.4 and Figure 2.4 reveal that few respondents who reported that their occupational category was "teacher" also reported that they were members of a visible minority (at least, this is what they reported about themselves on the census). For the 1991 operation, these percentages are 8 percent in Ontario and British Columbia; for the 2001 operation, these percentages are 10 percent and 12 percent respectively. These two Canadian provinces traditionally receive the largest number of individuals who are likely to belong to this category. It will also be noted that the number of individuals reporting that they belonged to a visible minority doubled in Alberta between 1991 and 2001. This may reflect the increased demand for labour due to developments in the oil and gas industry in that province. The same observation may also be made, although to a lesser degree, for Saskatchewan, where the number of individuals reporting that they belonged to a visible minority increased from 3 percent to 5 percent. By contrast, very few teachers reported that they belonged to a visible minority in the Atlantic Provinces; virtually no teachers reported this in Prince Edward Island in 2001. In Quebec, the percentage of individuals who identified themselves as belonging to a visible minority was 5 percent in 1991 and 5 percent in 2001.

TABLE 2.4 Percentage of Teachers Surveyed Who Reported Belonging to a Visible Minority (1991–2001)

	NL	PEI	NS	NB	QC	ON	MB	SK	AB	BC
1991	0.01	0.03	0.04	0.02	0.05	0.08	0.06	0.03	0.05	0.08
2001	0.02	0.00	0.04	0.03	0.05	0.10	0.05	0.05	0.10	0.12

FIGURE 2.4 Percentage of Teachers Surveyed Who Reported Belonging to a Visible Minority (1991–2001)

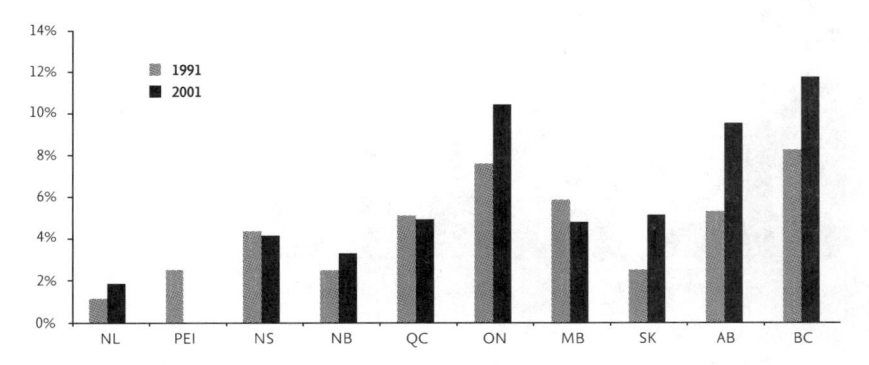

Visible Minority and Age

Table 2.5 and Figure 2.5 present the results of a cross between the variable "membership of a visible minority" and the variable "age" for the 1991 and 2001 census data, irrespective of province. For 1991, we see a general trend that we have already noted, that teachers tend to be in the 30 to 39 years of age and 40 to 49 years of age categories. However, respondents who reported that they were members of a visible minority also tended to be well represented in the under 30 years of age category, with approximately 25 percent. This is six percentage points higher than the percentage of those who reported that they did not belong to a visible minority. In 2001, this trend is even stronger and the distance between the two groups is even greater in the under 30, 30 to 39, and 50 to 59 years of age groups. Further in-depth analyses would clarify the meaning of these tendencies; however, this trend could mean that the average age of teachers who belong to a visible minority is lower than that of teachers who do not belong to a visible minority. Relatively speaking, in 2001, there are more young teachers who report that they belong to a visible minority.

TABLE 2.5 Age of Teachers and Membership in a Visible Minority (1991–2001)

1991	UNDER 30	30–39	40–49	50–59	60+
Member of a visible minority	0.24	0.29	0.25	0.17	0.05
Not a member of a visible minority	0.18	0.29	0.35	0.15	0.04
2001	UNDER 30	30–39	40–49	50–59	60+
Member of a visible minority	0.28	0.32	0.21	0.14	0.06
Not a member of a visible minority	0.17	0.24	0.27	0.27	0.05

FIGURE 2.5 Age of Teachers and Membership in a Visible Minority (1991–2001)

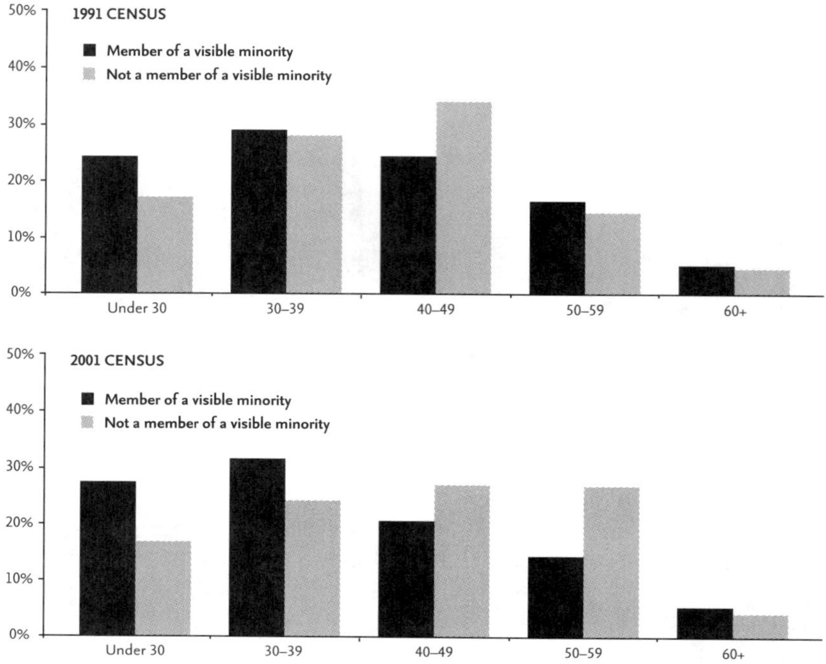

Visible Minority and Sex

Table 2.6 and Figure 2.6 present the results of a cross between the variable "membership in a visible minority" and the sex of the respondents in the census operations. First, it is interesting to note that the respective percentages by sex in 1991 and 2001 are virtually unchanged. Individuals reporting that they belong to a visible minority are approximately 53 percent female and 47 percent male in 1991 and 2001. Individuals reporting that they do not belong to a visible minority are approximately 65 percent female and 35 percent male; this represents a 10 percent difference compared to the group of teachers who reported belonging to a visible minority. A look at the 2006 census data would tell us whether this trend is continuing and enable us to make observations about the future mix of teachers in Canada. Unfortunately, these data were not available at the time this chapter was written.

TABLE 2.6 Sex of Teachers and Membership in a Visible Minority (1991–2001)

		MALE	FEMALE
Member of a visible minority	1991	0.525	0.475
	2001	0.530	0.470
Not a member of a visible minority	1991	0.653	0.347
	2001	0.650	0.350

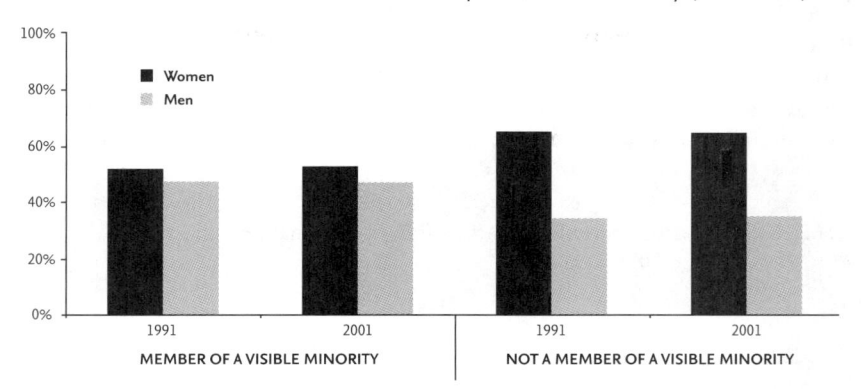

FIGURE 2.6 Sex of Teachers and Membership in a Visible Minority (1991–2001)

RELIGIOUS AFFILIATION

Table 2.7 and Figure 2.7 show that the religious affiliations of teachers who took part in the 1991 census reflect what has probably been a characteristic of Canada since its founding. The Protestant and Catholic faiths represent the lion's share of religious affiliation in most of the provinces, with combined percentages ranging from 80 percent (Alberta) to 94 percent (Newfoundland and Labrador and Prince Edward Island). Once again, however, there is an exception to this observation. In British Columbia, the combined percentages for Protestants and Catholics represent only 66 percent of all teachers in 1991. The Catholic faith is predominant in Quebec and New Brunswick at 83 percent and 53 percent respectively; the Protestant faith is predominant in the other eight provinces. Teachers reporting no religious affiliation represent 29 percent of teachers in British Columbia and 16 percent, 12 percent, and 12 percent in Alberta, Manitoba, and Ontario respectively. In 1991, few respondents chose the category "other" religions: 7 percent (Ontario), 6 percent (Alberta and Manitoba), and 5 percent (British Columbia and Quebec). In the Atlantic Provinces, very few respondents chose this category (i.e., fewer than 2 percent of respondents).

The data for 2001 reveal that the situation did change somewhat in the intervening 10-year period. The Catholic and Protestant faiths are still reported by the highest number of teachers, with combined percentages of between 69 percent and 89 percent. British Columbia continues to stand out with only 53 percent of respondents reporting an affiliation with one of these two religions, down 13 percent from 1991. In five out of 10 provinces—the provinces in Eastern and Central Canada—we see a slight decrease in these two categories combined: -3 percent in Newfoundland and Labrador, -5 percent in Prince Edward Island, -6 percent in Nova Scotia, -5 percent in Quebec, and -5 percent in Ontario. The percentages remained substantially the same in New Brunswick, and were lower in the three other western provinces at -9 percent in Manitoba, -8 percent in Saskatchewan, and -10 percent in Alberta. Quebec and New Brunswick continued to have proportionally more teachers reporting that they belong to the Catholic faith. In 2001, more respondents in Prince Edward Island also reported belonging to the Catholic faith (50 percent) than the Protestant faith (39 percent).

TABLE 2.7 Distribution of Teachers by Religious Affiliation Reported on the 1991 and 2001 Censuses

1991										
	NL	PEI	NS	NB	QC	ON	MB	SK	AB	BC
PROTESTANT	0.56	0.50	0.51	0.37	0.06	0.47	0.53	0.54	0.52	0.49
CATHOLIC	0.38	0.44	0.38	0.53	0.83	0.34	0.29	0.32	0.27	0.17
NONE	0.05	0.06	0.08	0.08	0.07	0.12	0.12	0.10	0.16	0.29
OTHER	0.02	0.00	0.02	0.02	0.05	0.07	0.06	0.04	0.06	0.05
2001										
	NL	PEI	NS	NB	QC	ON	MB	SK	AB	BC
PROTESTANT	0.50	0.39	0.45	0.31	0.05	0.36	0.45	0.45	0.40	0.36
CATHOLIC	0.41	0.50	0.38	0.59	0.79	0.37	0.28	0.33	0.29	0.17
NONE	0.08	0.09	0.12	0.08	0.10	0.15	0.18	0.14	0.21	0.35
OTHER	0.02	0.03	0.05	0.03	0.06	0.11	0.09	0.08	0.10	0.12

Given the decreases in the percentage of teachers who reported that they were Protestant or Catholic, it should not be surprising that the values in the categories "None" and "Other" increased in 2001. In British Columbia in 2001, 35 percent and 12 percent of teachers surveyed reported belonging to these two categories—an increase of 7 percent over 1991. The increases were higher in Western Canada than in Central or Eastern Canada, probably reflecting (at least for British Columbia and Alberta) the demographic changes that have occurred in these two provinces since the early 1990s.

FIGURE 2.7 Distribution of Teachers According to Religious Affiliation Reported on the 1991 and 2001 Censuses

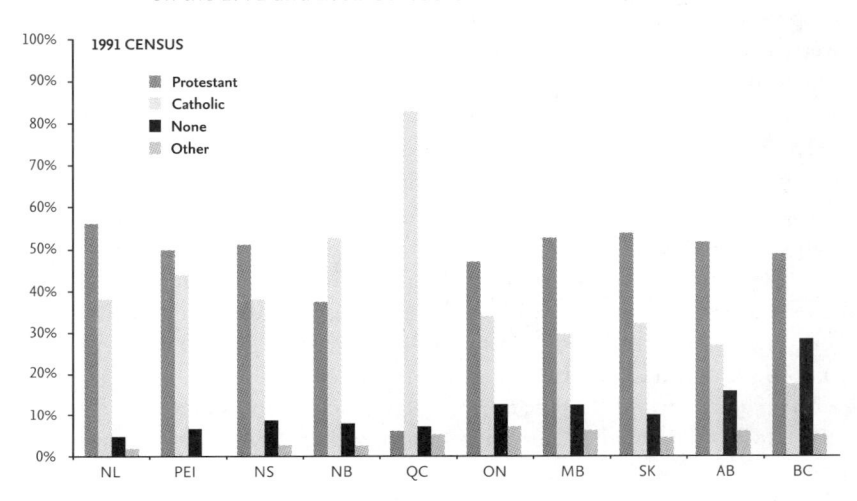

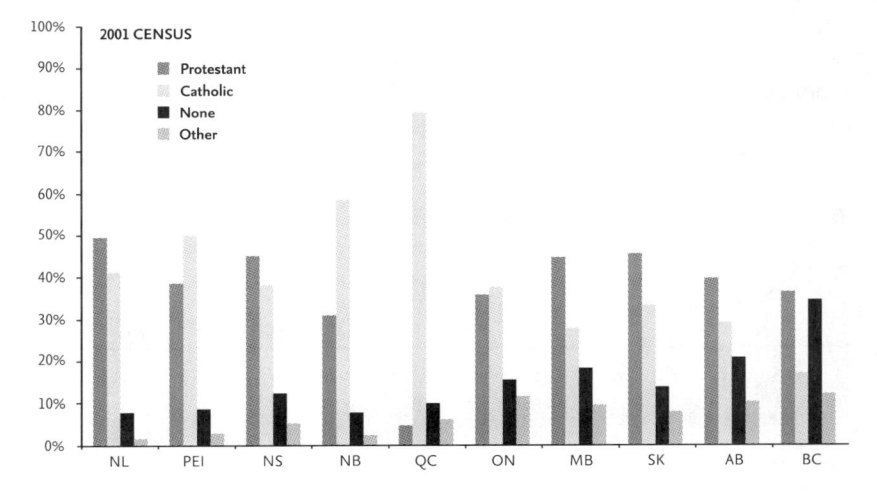

1991 CENSUS
- Protestant
- Catholic
- None
- Other

2001 CENSUS
- Protestant
- Catholic
- None
- Other

MOTHER TONGUE

Table 2.8 and Figure 2.8 show that, with the exception of teachers in Quebec, English was the mother tongue of the overwhelming majority of teacher-respondents in 1991. This was the case for 97 percent of teachers in Newfoundland and Labrador, 90 percent of teachers in Prince Edward Island, and 89 percent of teachers in Nova Scotia. The situation was somewhat different in New Brunswick where 60 percent of respondents reported that their mother tongue was English and 38 percent reported that their mother tongue was French. In Quebec, these percentages were very different: 10 percent and 83 percent respectively. For Ontario and British Columbia, the percentages were respectively 77 percent and 81 percent for English and 7 percent and 3 percent for French. Other languages were reported as mother tongues primarily in Ontario (16 percent), British Columbia (15 percent), Alberta (15 percent), Manitoba (19 percent), and Saskatchewan (13 percent).

In 2001, there were very few differences with what was observed in 1991 irrespective of having French, English, or another language as a mother tongue. The fluctuations were no doubt the result of the sampling and, in light of these data, we can conclude that the distribution of mother tongues among teachers surveyed in 1991 and 2001 remained fairly stable. This is well illustrated in the data for Ontario and British Columbia where 73 percent and 80 percent declared English as their mother tongue in 2001, compared with 77 percent and 81 percent in 1991. Quebec stood out once again in 2001, with 80 percent of teachers reporting that French was their mother tongue and 10 percent reporting that English was their mother tongue. New Brunswick also differed from the other provinces, although to a lesser extent with 58 percent and 37 percent of teachers reporting English and French respectively as their mother tongue. In Ontario, 20 percent of respondents reported a mother tongue other than English or French, as did 17 percent of respondents in British Columbia; these percentages had increased by 4 percent and 2 percent respectively over 1991.

TABLE 2.8 Distribution of Teachers by Mother Tongue Reported on the 1991 and 2001 Censuses

1991	NL	PEI	NS	NB	QC	ON	MB	SK	AB	BC
ENGLISH	0.97	0.90	0.89	0.60	0.10	0.77	0.72	0.84	0.81	0.81
FRENCH	0.00	0.09	0.06	0.38	0.83	0.07	0.09	0.03	0.04	0.03
OTHER	0.03	0.01	0.05	0.03	0.07	0.16	0.19	0.13	0.15	0.15

2001	NL	PEI	NS	NB	QC	ON	MB	SK	AB	BC
ENGLISH	0.97	0.84	0.87	0.58	0.10	0.73	0.75	0.84	0.81	0.80
FRENCH	0.02	0.13	0.07	0.37	0.80	0.07	0.08	0.04	0.04	0.03
OTHER	0.02	0.03	0.06	0.05	0.09	0.20	0.16	0.11	0.15	0.17

FIGURE 2.8 Distribution of Teachers by Mother Tongue Reported on the 1991 and 2001 Censuses

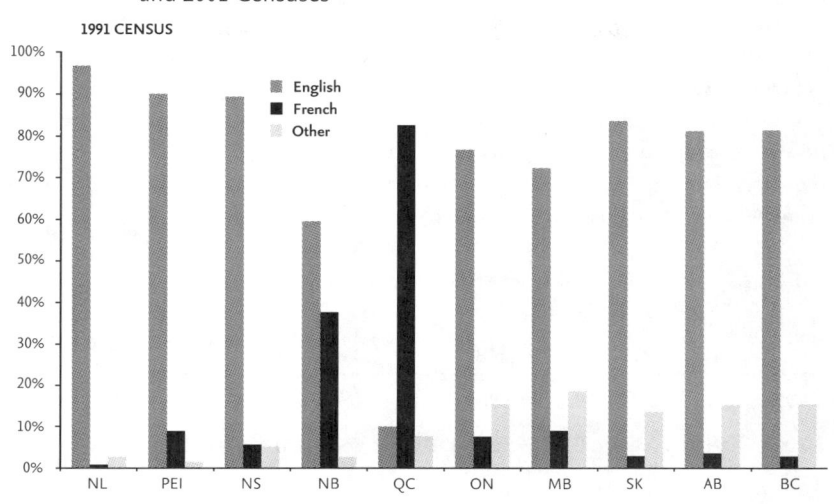

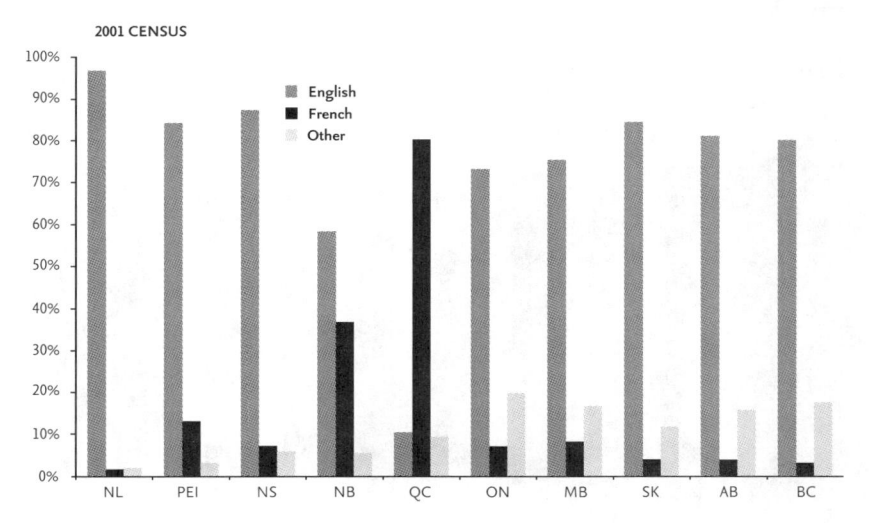

PLACE OF BIRTH

Table 2.9 and Figure 2.9 reveal that the percentage of teachers reporting that they were born in Canada is almost identical for the census operations in 1991 and 2001, but different for the survey in 2006. In 1991 and 2001, British Columbia and Ontario had the lowest percentages with approximately 75 percent of teachers being Canadian-born. Newfoundland and Labrador and Prince Edward Island had the highest percentages with approximately 95 percent of teachers in this category having been born in Canada. For the 2006 survey, the percentages increased somewhat; several values were close to 100 percent (99 percent in New Brunswick and 98 percent in Newfoundland and Labrador, Prince Edward Island, Nova Scotia, and Saskatchewan) and values close to 90 percent in Ontario (89 percent) and British Columbia (86 percent). It is difficult to find a justification for some of these increases, particularly for the time period considered (+5 years). Between 2001 and 2006, British Columbia and Nova Scotia experienced a 10 percent increase; Alberta experienced a 12 percent increase; and Ontario experienced a 13 percent increase.

TABLE 2.9 Percentage of Teachers Reporting Being Born in Canada (1991–2001–2006)

	NL	PEI	NS	NB	QC	ON	MB	SK	AB	BC
1991	0.95	0.94	0.89	0.92	0.87	0.77	0.86	0.90	0.82	0.74
2001	0.94	0.94	0.88	0.91	0.87	0.76	0.88	0.89	0.82	0.76
2006	0.98	0.98	0.98	0.99	0.95	0.89	0.91	0.98	0.94	0.86

FIGURE 2.9 Percentage of Teachers Reporting Being Born in Canada (1991–2001–2006)

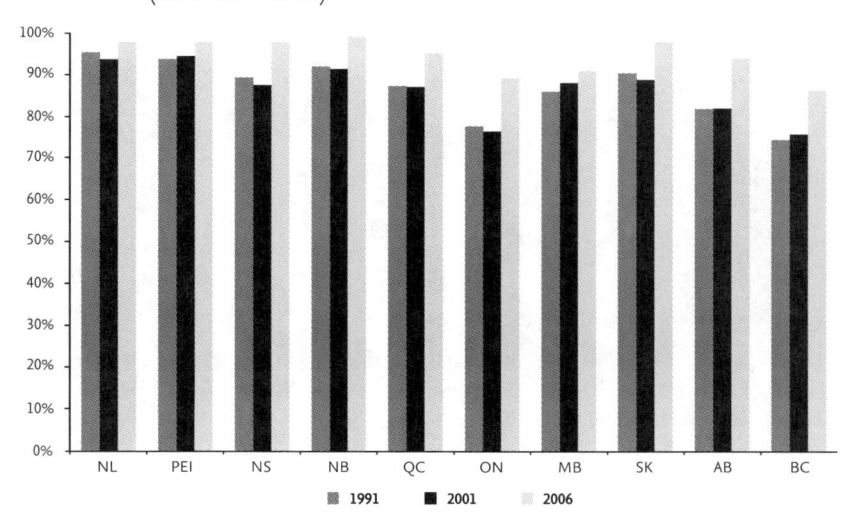

EDUCATION

Bachelor's Degree as a Minimum Level of Education

In 1991, the majority of respondents in the teacher category declared that they had at least a bachelor's degree (see Table 2.10 and Figure 2.10). However, the percentage varied from province to province. The percentages observed ranged from 56 percent in Prince Edward Island to 72 percent in British Columbia and Newfoundland and Labrador, which is a spread of 16 percent. In 2001, the percentage of teachers reporting that they had at least a bachelor's degree had increased considerably, probably illustrating an improvement in the formal qualifications for individuals working as teachers. In 2001, teachers in this category represented more than 80 percent of respondents for each of the provinces. The disparities between the provinces seem to disappear; there was only a 5 percent difference between the lowest percentage—80 percent in Prince Edward Island—and the highest percentage—85 percent in British Columbia. The largest increase was in Prince Edward Island (+24 percent) and Nova Scotia and British Columbia (+19 percent).

TABLE 2.10 Percentage of Teachers Reporting Having at Least a Bachelor's Degree

	NL	PEI	NS	NB	QC	ON	MB	SK	AB	BC
1991	0.72	0.56	0.65	0.65	0.66	0.68	0.67	0.66	0.72	0.66
2001	0.84	0.80	0.84	0.82	0.81	0.82	0.83	0.82	0.84	0.85

FIGURE 2.10 Percentage of Teachers Reporting Having at Least a Bachelor's Degree

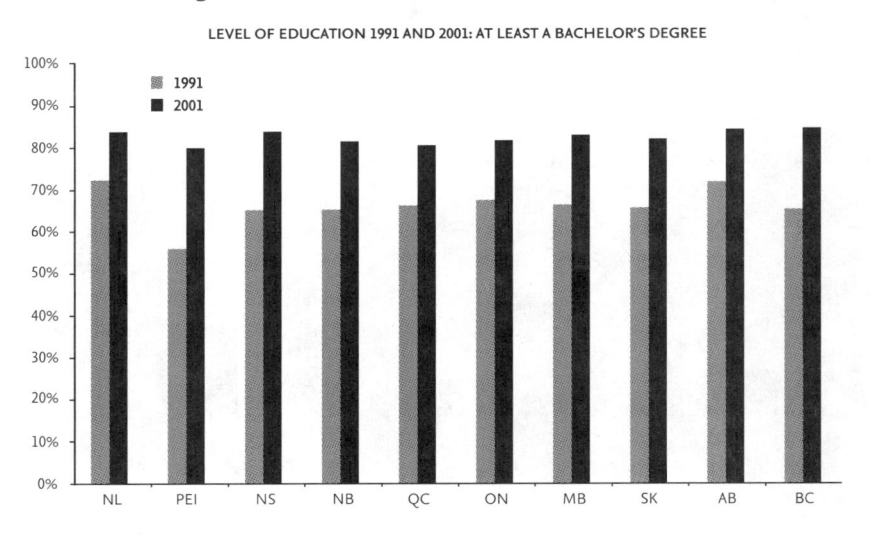

LEVEL OF EDUCATION 1991 AND 2001: AT LEAST A BACHELOR'S DEGREE

Number of Years of Education and Membership in a Visible Minority

In terms of the number of years of university education completed, Table 2.11 and Figure 2.11 show that there is a difference between the category "member of a visible minority" and "not a member of a visible minority" in terms of percentages of individuals reporting having completed six or more years. In 1991, the percentages were 34 percent and 18 percent respectively; in 2001, they were 43 percent and 27 percent respectively. Relatively speaking, once again, it would appear that a higher percentage of individuals reporting that they belonged to a visible minority had also completed more than six years of university. This suggests a hypothesis for testing, namely that individuals belonging to a visible minority (whether long-time residents of Canada or newcomers) do not find employment commensurate with their university education and turn to teaching for a livelihood.

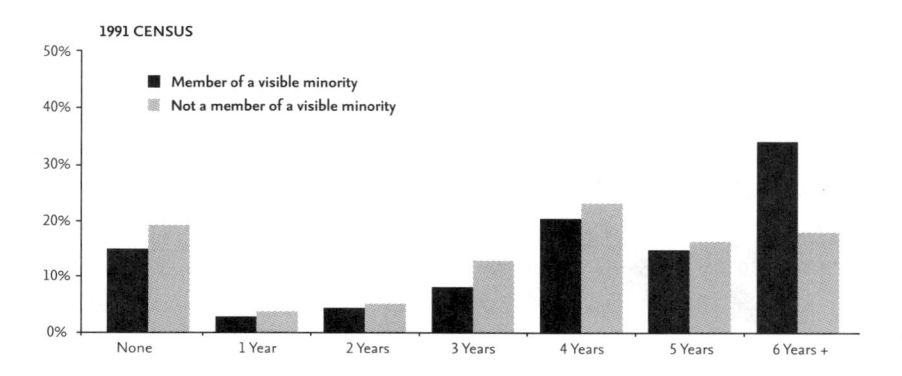

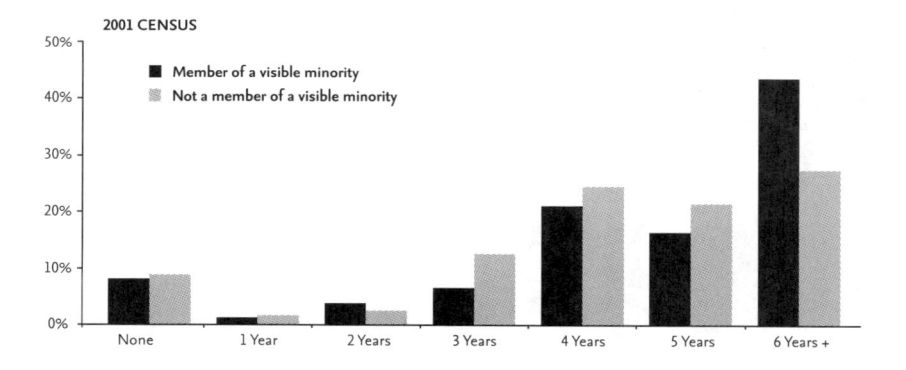

FIGURE 2.11 Number of Years of University Completed and Membership in a Visible Minority

TABLE 2.11 Number of Years of University Completed and Membership in a Visible Minority

1991	None	1 year	2 years	3 years	4 years	5 years	6 years +
Member of a visible minority	0.15	0.03	0.04	0.08	0.20	0.15	0.34
Not a member of a visible minority	0.19	0.03	0.05	0.13	0.23	0.16	0.18

2001	None	1 year	2 years	3 years	4 years	5 years	6 years +
Member of a visible minority	0.08	0.01	0.04	0.07	0.21	0.15	0.43
Not a member of a visible minority	0.09	0.02	0.03	0.12	0.24	0.21	0.27

Conclusion

The primary objective of this cross-sectional sketch was not to present an interpretative analysis of the results but to present a descriptive analysis of certain data on the characteristics of teachers in Canada. Even though the goal was not to provide a viable interpretation in an elaborate conceptual framework, the data do suggest a number of avenues that some readers will want to pursue.

These include possibilities for age, sex, and membership in a visible minority. For example, if the teaching population is aging and enters a cycle of renewal, what does this mean in terms of succession planning, especially when it has been announced that in most Canadian provinces fewer students will be attending school? In terms of the sex of teachers, the differences between the 1991 and 2001 census data in terms of the percentage of women in teaching were small; however, when the comparison included the data from the 2006 survey, they were more pronounced for some provinces. It would be useful to pursue this comparison, including the data from the 2006 census. Also for 2006, it would be interesting to look at the percentage of teachers who reported belonging to a visible minority to determine whether there is a trend underlying the increases observed and whether this trend is continuing.

A second objective of this cross-sectional sketch was to stimulate interest in the educational research community in data with good potential for documenting or completing analyses, embarking on more advanced research, and developing cross-sectional descriptions of a population. In this presentation, only data from the 1991 census and the 2001 census were used. Other Statistics Canada surveys are described and analyzed on the website www.teachcan.ca. The number of variables is very high, as is the potential;

however, certain pitfalls, such as getting lost in a sea of available information, must be avoided and researchers should rely on markers in order to identify the inferential limitations of this type of data.

Notes

1. Several Statistics Canada surveys have been explored and used in the context of the research project. These surveys are available on the research program website at www.teachcan.ca.
2. The data are strictly from the 10 provinces; the low number of respondents from the three Canadian territories made it impossible to incorporate them into the description.
3. For Canada as a whole, approximately 87 percent of respondents reported that they did not belong to a visible minority.

References

www.edudata.educ.ubc.ca (EDUDATA)
www.teachcan.ca (Major Collaborative Research Initiatives in Canada)

CHAPTER 3

The Discourse on Diversity in British Columbia Public Schools
FROM DIFFERENCE TO IN/DIFFERENCE

Marianne Jacquet

Attempting to address issues of inclusion related to ethnocultural diversity in schools is like opening a Pandora's box. In taking into consideration the nuances and intersections of diversity (social class, culture, race, language, religion, gender, age, ability, etc.) as well as the different disciplines and perspectives from which issues of diversity are addressed, the apparently innocuous word *diversity* quickly develops into a morass. In times of rapidly changing demographics in Canada, the challenges involved in developing inclusive schools and professional practices are complex and sometimes contradictory. It is not surprising that even those teachers and principals who are most dedicated to social justice and equity in education are at times overwhelmed by what needs to be done. In British Columbia, the diversity framework in education (BC Ministry of Education, 2004) offers broad orientations for the inclusion of diversity in school that are supported by concepts such as multiculturalism, human rights, equity, and social justice. However, this framework does not offer any specific guidelines for addressing conflicting values in education, which are bound to emerge in the praxis of inclusion of diversity in school, nor does it take into account the complex and contextual issues of language, culture, and identity. Comparing the discourse on ethnocultural diversity in three different language programs (anglophone, francophone, and French immersion) in British Columbia provides opportunities for understanding the impact of shifting power relations in different contexts (majority/minorities and official minority/minorities) and for understanding the dynamic of inclusion/exclusion of difference. In this chapter, I explore the impact of changing student demographics and the BC diversity policy imperative on educators' professional practice. In particular, I examine the discourse of elementary school teachers and principals in British Columbia on ethnocultural diversity and the way they meet—or do not meet—the challenges of inclusion of diversity in their schools and professional practice.

Contexts of Diversity in British Columbia

Four important contexts inform my study of the discourse on diversity of school staff: the demographic context, the school context, the context of education policies, and approaches to diversity in education.

DEMOGRAPHIC CONTEXT OF BRITISH COLUMBIA

The 2001 census reveals that Canadian society is becoming increasingly multi-ethnic, multilingual, and multi-confessional, with more than 200 different ethnic origins[1] and 100 languages[2] reported, as well as an increase in visible minorities[3] and in religions other than Catholic and Protestant (Statistics Canada, 2003). In particular, one million people, or 26 percent of the population of British Columbia, were born outside of Canada according to the 2001 census (Statistics Canada, 2003). In contrast, only 22 percent of the BC population was born outside of Canada in 1996 (Statistics Canada, 2003). Visible minorities in British Columbia represent 22 percent (836,400) of the total population, which is well above the national average of 13 percent. The three predominant visible minority groups in this province in 2001 were Chinese (9.4 percent), followed by South Asian (5.4 percent) and Filipino (1.7 percent) (Statistics Canada, 2003).

British Columbia's changing demographics are mirrored in the diversity of the school population in the Vancouver Metropolitan Area, where the majority of migrants to the province settle. Immigration to British Columbia in 2005 stood at approximately 45,000 immigrants. Of these, 86 percent settled in the Vancouver Metropolitan Area and 40 percent were identified as children and youth (Friesen, 2006). Recent statistics for the school year 2005–2006 indicate that for 126,872 students (21.2 percent of the total population of the elementary and secondary public schools) the primary language[4] spoken in the home is not English. This number represents a substantial increase since the 1996–1997 school year, when only 16.2 percent of the students came from homes in which the primary language was not English (BC Ministry of Education, 2006).

SCHOOL CONTEXTS IN BRITISH COLUMBIA

There are many school programs that aim to address the varied needs of the student population in British Columbia. In this chapter, I focus mainly on the anglophone, the French immersion, and the francophone programs. In the anglophone program, the language of instruction is English. This program, which is the "regular" program offered in the BC school system, has by far the highest enrolment and serves the vast majority of the province's students.

There are 1,662 public schools across the province (BC Ministry of Education, 2006).[5] Most of these schools serve anglophone students and deliver all instruction from Kindergarten to Grade 12 in English. As Table 3.1 shows, student enrolment in the anglophone program has dropped over the last few years, while enrolment is up in both the French immersion and francophone programs. At the same time, the number of English as a Second Language (ESL) students in these schools has increased from 56,676 in 2001–2002 to 59,103 in 2005–2006 (BC Ministry of Education, 2006).

TABLE 3.1 Number of Students Enrolled in Each Language Program in the Public School System

SCHOOL YEAR	ANGLOPHONE PROGRAM	FRANCOPHONE PROGRAM	FRENCH IMMERSION PROGRAM
2001–2002	589,201.6	2,914	31,669
2002–2003	581,924.0	2,930	32,471
2003–2004	575,901.9	3,146	33,860
2004–2005	570,927.3	3,455	35,985
2005–2006	565,471.7	3,632	38,389

Source: BC Ministry of Education (2006)

In British Columbia, French immersion programs are generally offered in dual-track schools, which provide the option for students to enrol in either the regular English language instruction program or the French immersion program. French immersion provides non-francophone students with the opportunity to be bilingual in French and English by the end of Grade 12. Students may enter the program in Grade 1 (early immersion) or in Grade 6 (late immersion). Bilingualism is achieved by delivering 100 percent of the instruction in French in the early years, then gradually decreasing instruction in French to two courses by Grade 12, while gradually increasing instruction in English (BC Ministry of Education, 1997).

Since the first French immersion program was offered in 1963 in St-Lambert near Montreal, interest in this format has exploded and it is now offered across Canada to a diverse linguistic population. French immersion was first introduced in British Columbia in 1973, just outside Vancouver, in the city of Coquitlam. It has been very popular in the province, with enrolment increasing every year in the last six (Table 3.1). As of 2006, French immersion is offered in 248 public schools; most of these schools are dual track. French immersion is offered in 44 of British Columbia's 59 school districts (Canadian Parents for French, 2006).

The French immersion program was initially designed for anglophone students as an alternative to Core French teaching (Rebuffot, 1993). Over the years, however, French immersion has gained popularity among other linguistic groups, and enrolment of ethnic minority students has increased (Swain & Lapkin, 2005). Qualitative studies conducted with immigrant families in British Columbia who enrolled their children in this program indicate that parents view French immersion very positively in terms of greater academic challenges provided to their children and better access to linguistic capital, as represented by official French-English bilingualism (Dagenais & Day, 1998; Dagenais & Jacquet, 2001).

French language education for francophone minority children in British Columbia is enshrined in section 23 of the Canadian Charter of Rights and Freedoms, which guarantees specific language of instruction rights for official minorities, wherever they reside in Canada[6] (Martel, 1997). In British Columbia, the francophone program was formerly known as the *Programme-cadre*; it was implemented and administered by the English language school boards. The province's francophone minority has progressively gained control over French language education and French language schools. In 1995, the Conseil scolaire francophone (CSF) was created to manage and deliver the francophone program in public schools in the Vancouver Metropolitan Area. In 1997, the CSF obtained full governance of French language education, and, since 1998, it has had jurisdiction over the province-wide delivery of the francophone program to students who are entitled to instruction in French.

The children of Canadian citizens are entitled to French language instruction if they meet certain criteria: 1) one of the parents' first language learned and still understood is French; 2) one of the parents received his or her elementary education in French; or 3) one sibling in the family has started or is receiving an education in French in an elementary or secondary school in Canada. In 2006, 3,640 students were registered in the francophone program (2,936 in Grades K to 7; and 704 in Grades 8 to 12), which is offered in 39 schools across the province. Eighteen of these schools are French only. Due to low enrolment, in particular in rural areas, 21 "schools within schools" share a building with an anglophone school (CSF, 2006).

Historically, francophone schools have been located in more rural areas where they served a population that was fairly homogeneous in terms of language, culture, and religion (Gérin-Lajoie, 1996; Heller & Jones, 2002; Tardif, 1993). They are now well established in urban areas, such as the Vancouver Metropolitan Area, serving a population that reflects the current trends of interprovincial and international migration. Today, francophone schools in minority settings are diverse not only in terms of language but also in terms of culture. According to the CSF (2006), ethnocultural diversity is an important characteristic of francophone schools in the Vancouver Metropolitan Area. Families arrive from the province of Quebec, but also from francophone countries around the world and, in some cases, from non-francophone countries, after initially settling in Quebec. About 52 languages are represented in the schools and 80 percent of the students are from exogamic families, where another first language (mostly English) is spoken by one of the parents in addition to French. Thus, although French is the language of reference for all students attending francophone schools, their level of competency in French varies. Some students speak French fluently, while others had little, and in some cases, no knowledge of French prior to attending a francophone school.

In light of historic and unequal power relations between anglophones and francophones, education has always been a source of contention between the majority and the minority (Heller, 2002). As a result, francophone schools in minority settings have played—and continue to play—an important role in the reproduction of French language and culture. The teachers in these schools are expected to actively promote the construction of a francophone identity and are considered role models for both language and culture (Gérin-Lajoie, 1996, 2006; Gilbert et al., 2004; Tardif, 1993). Neither the anglophone program nor the French immersion program has this explicit ideological mission to maintain and develop a community of speakers for generations to come.

The linguistic and cultural diversity in francophone schools in the Vancouver Metropolitan Area adds another layer of complexity to the role of the teachers. Like their colleagues in the anglophone and French immersion programs, teachers in the francophone program are expected to promote the inclusion of diversity in school and in their professional practice. However, in this program, the diversity policy imperative is promoted within a different power structure. In the anglophone and French immersion programs, the power imbalance is between the (anglophone) majority and other ethnic minorities. In this context, inclusion of diversity does not necessarily challenge the legitimacy of British Columbia's anglophone majority. Conversely, in the francophone program, power relations are played out between an official francophone minority (mostly historically French Canadian) and other francophone minorities (mostly new francophone immigrants). With a student population that is diverse in terms of language, culture, and religion, what is at stake here are competing discourses on legitimacy—who has the right to define what constitutes a francophone identity. Being a very small community, the intrinsic diversity of the student population in the francophone program leads inevitably, if not intentionally, to a challenge of the implicit, historic assumption of a homogeneous francophone identity.

EDUCATION POLICIES ON DIVERSITY IN BRITISH COLUMBIA

Following the adoption of the bilingualism and biculturalism policy in 1969, minority leaders in Canada started to advocate for an official policy of "multiculturalism," rather than "biculturalism," to give equal status to everyone in Canada, regardless of ethnic origin. The federal multiculturalism policy was adopted in 1971 by Prime Minister Pierre Elliott Trudeau. The intent of this policy was to support ethnic groups wishing to develop their cultural heritage beyond assimilation to either English-Canadian or French-Canadian culture (Breton et al., 1980, pp. 379–380). Thus, the multiculturalism policy represented a shift from the prevalent ideology of assimilation to an ideology of integration into a pluralistic society (Pietrantonio et al., 1996). It has since paved the way for the recognition of cultural and linguistic pluralism in Canada. Although the provinces have responded to cultural diversity in different ways, most provincial governments have expressed a commitment to multicultural education, intercultural education, and, in some cases, race relations programs (Moodley, 1995).

Since the adoption of the provincial Multiculturalism Act in July 1993 (Bill 39), the BC government has fostered cross-cultural understanding, anti-racism, and the removal of systemic barriers to equality. The BC Multicultural Advisory Council, appointed by the government in October 2003 to develop future directions for the province in the area of multiculturalism and anti-racism, made six recommendations in its *Strategic Framework for Action* (BC Multicultural Advisory Council, 2005) and identified opportunities for improving the quality and effectiveness of British Columbia's approaches to the promotion of multiculturalism and the elimination of racism. The six recommendations aim to

1. promote an understanding and a celebration of the concept of Canadian multiculturalism;
2. build leadership capacity and systems to prevent and resolve acts of bias, hate, prejudice, and discrimination;
3. provide incentives to the private and public sectors to create economic and educational opportunities for disadvantaged groups and individuals;
4. ensure multiculturalism and anti-racism resources and services are available and accessible to all;
5. support research and community forums on the incidence of bias and hate and the effectiveness of training and intervention techniques; and
6. monitor and support the role of other ministries in promoting and role-modelling multiculturalism and anti-racism. (BC Multicultural Advisory Council, 2005, p. 3)

A recent provincial education policy, *Diversity in BC schools: a framework*, is grounded in the values expressed in various federal and provincial statutes. The policy outlines four core values to be followed in schools: 1) multiculturalism; 2) human rights; 3) employment, equity, and social justice; and 4) respect of the rights of individuals under the law. Implementation of this policy requires a strong commitment from the BC school system, which is expected "to create and maintain conditions in school that foster success for all students and that promote fair and equitable treatment for all" (BC Ministry of Education, 2004, p. 8). Six conditions are listed in the policy for attaining social justice and equity within multicultural school settings:

1. equitable access to, and participation in, quality education for all students;
2. school cultures that value diversity and respond to the diverse social and cultural needs of the communities they serve;
3. school cultures that promote an understanding of others and respect for all;
4. learning and working environments that are safe and welcoming and free from discrimination, harassment, and violence;
5. decision-making processes that give a voice to all members of the school community; and
6. policies and practices that promote fair and equitable treatment. (BC Ministry of Education, 2004, p. 8)

In this policy, the Ministry of Education adopts a global and overarching definition of diversity, which is grounded in the concepts of both individual and group difference. Diversity, then,

> refers both to our uniqueness as individuals and to our sense of belonging or identification within a group or groups. Diversity refers to the ways in which we differ from each other. Some of these differences may be visible (e.g., race, ethnicity, gender, age, ability), while others are less visible (e.g., culture, ancestry, language, religious beliefs, sexual orientation, socio-economic background). (BC Ministry of Education, 2004, p. 11)

The Ministry of Education recognizes the ongoing challenges of addressing the needs of an increasingly diverse student population and fosters action at both the teaching and modelling levels. Responsibility for the BC school system entails working on students' attitudes by teaching understanding and respect for all persons, and by modelling understanding and respect in educators' practices. Modelling involves taking into account the beliefs, customs, practices, languages, behaviours, and physical differences of individuals and cultural groups and fostering understanding, mutual respect, and inclusion (BC Ministry of Education, 2004). However, this policy does not give specific guidelines for what school boards, principals, or teachers are supposed to do in situations in which different—and sometimes conflicting—values are at stake, nor does it take into consideration the variable dynamic of power relations in different language contexts.

In the Vancouver Metropolitan Area, some school organizations such as the British Columbia Teachers' Federation and the long-established Vancouver School Board have developed policies or guidelines to address social justice, multiculturalism, and anti-racism in schools (VSB, 1995). The Conseil scolaire francophone (CSF) addresses, more specifically, the reproduction of French culture and identity (CSF, 2006). As explained above, this ideological position results, in part, from the historical power balance between the anglophone majority and Quebec francophone minority in Canada that has tinted the issue of identity within francophone minorities outside Quebec (Heller, 2002). This position does not preclude the recognition of cultural diversity or the implementation of anti-racism strategies in school; however, it is a powerful filter through which the issue of inclusion of diversity is assessed. Also, given the fact that the CSF is a fairly new organization, and given the ethnocultural diversity in its schools, it is not surprising that CSF policy is less well-developed in this regard.

Needless to say, irrespective of the language program, providing culturally responsive instruction is not an easy task for educators who lack the training and expertise to deal with the complex and sometimes contradictory values that are an inherent part of pluralism in the schools (Bourgeault et al., 1995; Jacquet, 2002). Wideen and Barnard (1999) point out the lack of systematic in-service and pre-service training on diversity in British Columbia for school staff. They argue that the lack of support from the Ministry of Education to the school boards for implementing such policies means they are at best loosely coupled in practice. Furthermore, faced with serious professional constraints (e.g., bigger class sizes, bigger workloads, and limited resources) and a greater demand for accountability (D'Amico et al., 2005), principals and teachers often lack the time to reflect critically on their own practice with respect to ethnocultural diversity in schools. In today's multi-ethnic society, teaching and school leadership practices that are sensitive to, and appropriate for, diversity in school are more important than ever. However, in the face of the complex and sometimes contradictory demands that educators face, they are not always easy to implement.

APPROACHES TO DIVERSITY

There is an extensive, interdisciplinary literature on difference in education. This body of work encompasses different and overlapping perspectives, such as multicultural education, anti-racism education (the two often complementing each other), and intercultural education in Quebec, all intended to support the needs of diverse learners. Each approach has its drawbacks and critics.

Multicultural Education

Multicultural education is a polymorphous, ambiguous, evolving notion that defies a straightforward definition. According to Moodley:

> What is understood by the term multicultural education is indeed varied, both in terms of theory and practice. Since its inception, it has evolved through a range of interpretations as to what it is and what it should be. Multicultural education has been said to have the potential for reinforcing or challenging hegemony (Sleeter, 1989). It has been extolled as a practicable alternative to current educational practices or dismissed as a palliative for the cultural and social inequalities in Canadian society. (Moodley, 1995, p. 808)

Multicultural education is usually viewed from one of two basic and contrasting perspectives: the social-pathological and the anthropological. This is still the case in many places. The first perspective identifies the cultural background of minority students as the source of a "problem" that needs to be fixed, while the second emphasizes equal respect for all cultures, based on the anthropological notion of relativism. Critics of the latter perspective point out that it reduces culture to "song and dance" activities; others point to the negative impact of fostering cultural differences in light of "social cohesion." Both perspectives overlook the complex interrelationship between the economic, social, and political factors that transcend the cultural framework (Helly, 1994; McAll, 1991a; 1991b; Moodley, 1988, 1995).

Intercultural Education

In Canada, the intercultural education approach is prevalent in Quebec. This approach was developed in opposition to the multiculturalism model, which was thought to treat the francophone community on the same level as other ethnic minorities and to reinforce difference (McAndrew, 1995). Intercultural education aims to foster a "dialogue between cultures," while promoting integration into the dominant French culture of Quebec (Conseil supérieur de l'éducation, 1983, 1987; Ministère de l'Éducation du Québec (MEQ), 1995,

1988). Initially, intercultural education, like multicultural education, was grounded in an anthropological and relativistic perspective of culture.

However, the ambiguity surrounding this concept and contradictory educational practices conducted under the umbrella of intercultural education led to pitfalls similar to those attributed to multicultural education: the marginalization of the Other, an overemphasis on the cultural dimension to explain issues of inequality in education (McAll, 1991a; 1991b), and the reification of cultural and racial attributes, in particular in school textbooks (Blondin, 1990; Jacquet, 1996; McAndrew, 1986, 1987). McAndrew (1995) argues that simple inclusion of information about minorities (e.g., a description of a Chinese New Year festival) or their representation in the curriculum (e.g., photos of black students) constitutes "additive multiculturalism."

Anti-racism Education

By contrast, anti-racism education seeks to address systemic racism experienced by an individual or group within institutional and power structures by examining the ways in which racist ideology and individual actions become entrenched and (consciously) supported in institutional structures (Dei, 1996, p. 27). Anti-racism education is a critical discourse of race and racism in society that has emerged largely in opposition to multicultural education (Sleeter and Delgado-Bernal, 2004). Although race is an important signifier of difference, the anti-racism perspective seeks to include other forms of social oppression. Thus, "anti-racism education may be defined as an action-oriented strategy for institutional systemic change to address racism and the interlocking systems of social oppressions" (Dei, 1996, p. 25). In their discussion of anti-racism education, Moodley (1995) and Sleeter and Delgado-Bernal (2004) point out some of the limitations of anti-racism education. Anti-racism education reduces racism to a question of colour discrimination; it tends to overlook racism based on other ethnic markers; it portrays racism as exclusively perpetrated by whites against blacks or another visible minorities; it reifies the essentialist focus on "race" that may exacerbate the very stigmatization that anti-racism aims to de-stigmatize; and lastly, it blames "institutional racism" exclusively for the difficulties experienced by minorities in schools, and therefore blinds itself to other causes of inequity such as group-specific histories and traditions.

Critics of multicultural and intercultural education policies and practices have set a course for addressing systemic issues in education such as racism and discrimination. Under An Act for the preservation and enhancement of multiculturalism in Canada (Government of Canada, 1988), multicultural education and anti-racism education are no longer parallel perspectives; rather, they complement each other. The focus has changed from cultural difference to social difference; with this focus, equality, anti-racism, and the participation of all citizens are important priorities. Similarly, criticism of the intercultural education approach in Quebec has led to a discussion of issues of systemic discrimination and of the best way to support minorities (McAndrew, 1993; MEQ, 1985, 1988). Intercultural education in a recent education policy (*La politique d'intégration scolaire et d'éducation interculturelle*) (MEQ, 1998) is tied to citizenship education. Together, these approaches aim to foster the development of a democratic, francophone, pluralist society in Quebec.

Difference, Power, and Identity

Just as our understanding of the complexities of diversity in schools has deepened, the notion of multicultural and intercultural education has also evolved. A critical approach to multiculturalism aims to address the weaknesses of multicultural education, intercultural education, and anti-racism education by shifting the focus from culture and a narrow interpretation of racism to the politics of difference. This approach includes a broader concern for different forms of racism and disadvantage, as well as a postmodern understanding of identity as hybrid, dynamic, and rapidly shifting. Critical multicultural education is defined as an anti-racist, egalitarian, inclusive process that is embedded in all aspects of school life: program, pedagogy, social interactions between school actors, and notions of learning and teaching. Based on the philosophy of critical pedagogy, critical multicultural education focuses as much on the process of knowledge construction as on the process of praxis (McLaren, 2007; Nieto, 2000).

Recent developments in the literature on multicultural education focus on the composite nature of multicultural education (Ladson-Billings, 2004), whereby complex issues of race, social class, gender, and so forth are addressed at their intersection, rather than in isolation (Banks, 2004; Garcia, 2002; Ghosh & Abdi, 2004; Gollnick & Chinn, 2002; Ladson-Billings, 2004; Nieto, 2000). Recognition of multiple intersections of difference adds to the inherent complexity of multicultural education theory and practice and brings the question of identity to the forefront.

> It is no longer solely race, or class, or gender. Rather, it is the infinite permutations that come about as a result of the dazzling array of combinations human beings recruit to organize and fulfill themselves.... The variety of "selves" we perform have made multicultural education a richer, more complex, and more difficult enterprise to organize and implement than previously envisioned. (Ladson-Billings, 2004, p. 50)

Ghosh and Abdi (2004) acknowledge the complex intersections of difference, as well as the differences both within and between groups. They argue that power and identity are the operative concepts in theorizing difference. Thus, difference is taken as a process of construction of meanings embedded in the interplay of power and identity, where groups interact on the basis of their subordination. They address three questions illustrating the interplay of power and identity in the construction of difference: Difference from what? Different in what way? Different for whom?

> The answer to the first question—difference from what—requires a definition of the norm, or dominant groups who enjoy dominance over others and are the depositories of power. Those who are not from the norm are different, and this in itself may be the underlying factor for discrimination.... The second question—different in what way—brings issues of identity of the other into the portrayal of the category of otherness. Those who are different (they, the outsiders) are defined by the dominant group (we, the insiders). Both we and they are artificially constructed in unitary fashion, disregarding the differences within each construct. The physical and economic differences that are used to categorize groups and define people also reproduce inequalities through relations of domination and subordination.... Finally, different from whom? By remaining invisible—because whites do not give themselves a racial identity—the dominant group remains outside the hierarchy of social relations and in that way is not part of the politics of difference. (Ghosh & Abdi, 2004, pp. 27–28)

In his discussion about multiculturalism and recognition of difference, Taylor (1994) argues that the construction of identity is partially dependent on recognition, non-recognition, and/or misrecognition by others. The non-recognition or/misrecognition of a person or group of people may have a serious negative impact on their identity: "it can inflict harm and literally can be thought of as incarcerating people or oppressing them in a false, deformed, and existentially reduced mode of being" (Taylor, 1994, p. 42).

A postmodern criticism of cultural identity brings another layer of complexity to the attempt to theorize difference at the interplay between power and identity. Identity here is understood as a process that is fluid and dynamic rather than static and homogenous (Bhabha, 1996). The discourse of hybrid identity emphasizes "the contingent, the complex, and the contested aspect of identity formation. Multiple, shifting, and, at times, non-synchronous identities are the norm for individuals. This position highlights the social and historical constructedness of culture and its associated fluidity and malleability" (May, 1999, p. 22).

In the contested field of multicultural education, some scholars, in particular Banks (2004) and Sleeter and Grant (2007), argue that in order to implement multicultural education successfully, institutional changes must be made at various levels, such as "the teaching material; the teaching and learning styles; the attitudes, perceptions, and behaviours of teachers and administrators; the goals, norms, and culture of the schools" (Banks, 2004, p. 4). Banks's (1992) model of multicultural education includes five intertwined dimensions: content integration; the knowledge construction process; prejudice reduction; equity pedagogy; and an empowering school culture and social structure. Content integration refers to the teachers' use of examples and content from different cultures and groups in order to illustrate key concepts, principles, generalizations, and theories in their subject areas or discipline. The knowledge construction process refers to the teachers' facilitation of the students' development of a critical perspective and the ways in which implicit cultural assumptions, frames of reference, perspectives, and biases within a discipline influence the construction of knowledge. Prejudice reduction focuses on the characteristics of students' racial attitudes and the way they can be modified by appropriate teaching methods and materials. Equity pedagogy requires that teachers modify their teaching practice in order to facilitate the academic achievement of students from diverse groups (i.e., from groups that differ in terms of race, culture, and social class). Finally, an empowering school culture and social structure promotes structural changes in the school and in society. At the level of the school, it requires a critical examination of school practices that create barriers to the full participation of minority students (Banks, 2004).

My theoretical framework is informed by both critical multiculturalism and hybridity; this allows me to include a critical, non-essentialist approach to cultural difference. The former highlights the complexity and intersected dimensions of difference, and locates the question of difference, its recognition, non-recognition, and/or misrecognition, within the wider nexus of power relations. The latter emphasizes the contested identities and the cultural and historic "situatedness" of difference. The discourse of hybrid identity opens up an "interstitial" agency where power is both unequal and equivocal. This third space "refuses the binary representation of social antagonism" (Bhabha, 1996, p. 58). The reference to James Banks's model of multicultural education helps to link critical multiculturalism theory and school practice. In this chapter, school staffs' discourse on diversity in three school language contexts is interpreted as part of a close examination of the interplay of power and identity.

Despite the profusion of literature on multicultural education, there is a tremendous gap between theory and practice in the field. According to Gay (1992), "theory development has outpaced development in practice, and a wide gap exists between the two" (quoted in Banks, 2004, p. 3). In light of demographics, policy imperatives on the inclusion of diversity, and professional constraints on teaching, what does it mean to educators to teach a population that is diverse in terms of language, culture, race, and social class? In the context of the present study, what meanings do participants attribute to diversity in the three language programs studied? How does difference play out in their professional practices? What policy resources and publications are available to school staff from the school district or the Ministry of Education? These questions lead us to the heart of the politics of difference in school because they highlight how teachers and principals respond to the complex, and at times contradictory, issue of inclusion of difference.

Methodology

In this chapter, I discuss a subset of qualitative data from interviews with 100 teachers and school administrators from both Vancouver elementary and secondary schools. These data were gathered in the context of the national study on the evolution of school personnel in Canada (see Chapter 1). In this analysis, only the discourse of staff in elementary schools is discussed. Further analysis will be conducted to compare this discourse with the discourse of staff in secondary schools. Thus, my subset of participants consists of 38 respondents (27 teachers and 11 principals) from elementary schools in the three language programs (anglophone program: 20 participants; francophone program: 7 participants; French immersion program: 11 participants).

During the interviews, teachers and principals were asked to respond to four questions about ethnocultural diversity: 1) the existence and characteristics of ethnocultural diversity; 2) experience, training, and policy supports for managing ethnocultural diversity; 3) examples of inclusion of ethnocultural diversity in professional practice; and 4) the use of languages other than the language of instruction in the school.

Discussion

In this section, I discuss the responses of elementary teachers and school administrators to three of these four questions. First, I discuss their descriptions of ethnocultural diversity in schools and highlight three emerging dynamics with respect to difference and identity: inclusion, exclusion, and avoidance. Second, I compare the extent of preparedness and support school staff's claim for dealing with diversity in schools, and underscore some similarities and differences in the three programs. Third, I discuss the extent of recognition, non-recognition, or misrecognition of difference in the professional practices described by the participants.

DIVERSITY IN SCHOOL: INCLUSION, EXCLUSION, AND "IGNORANCE"

The respondents in elementary schools were first asked two questions aimed at describing the ethnocultural profile of the student population in their schools. Analysis of the data indicates that the majority of respondents in the anglophone, francophone, and French immersion programs acknowledge the extent of ethnocultural diversity in their respective schools. However, when prompted to elaborate on the diversity of the school population, their description varied according to the program.

In the francophone schools, participants stressed linguistic and cultural diversity; very few acknowledged the social and educational disparities between families. Nor did they mention other forms of diversity such as racial or religious diversity. They described their students as sharing French as a common language and coming from various francophone countries around the globe and more recently from non-francophone countries, such as the East European countries, Russia, Spain, India, and Asia.[7]

> There are people who are from all over the world but whose language of origin is French. People may be from Europe, France, Switzerland, or Belgium. There are people from Haiti. There are people from Vietnam, Lebanon, and North Africa. Then there are many immigrant groups, in particular Hispanophones, which immigrated to Quebec before moving to British Columbia. So they started their education in French and they continue in the francophone school here as well. (Interview #1008, francophone program, translated from French)

This excerpt illustrates how language plays an important role in a francophone minority setting by allowing for a more fluid identity that crosses national borders. Due to recent shifts in international migration, the demographic profile of francophone schools in minority settings is rapidly changing (Gérin-Lajoie, 2005). These changes bring complexity to the interplay between power and identity in francophone minority settings. They open up a space in which the traditional francophone identity, which was "homogeneous" in terms of language, culture, and religion, may be contested. What emerges from the first level of discourse is a more malleable power relation between "us" and "them," with diversity (difference) becoming more and more an inherent dimension of francophone schools in minority contexts. In the long run, recognition of diversity within francophone schools may result in a more fluid sense of francophone identity or what Bhabha (1996) calls a hybrid identity.

By comparison, in the anglophone program, respondents discussed diversity in broader terms, referring to linguistic, ethnic, cultural, racial, and, in few cases, religious diversity. One respondent mentioned the socio-economic dimension of diversity. As in the francophone schools, ethnic diversity is extensive, with many students coming from locations outside of Canada, such as Africa, Asia, the Middle East, and Eastern Europe. However, the teachers and principals report that most students are from countries in Asia, South Asia (China and India), and Southeast Asia (the Philippines, Vietnam, Taiwan, and Laos). The two groups mentioned most frequently were Chinese and Indo-Canadian. This observation reflects current trends in migration to British Columbia. Only two respondents out of 20 included First Nations students in their portrait of ethnic diversity in the school; two other respondents briefly mentioned white English-speaking Canadians. The discourse about diversity of the respondents in the anglophone program clearly reflects their position as members of the majority. Except for two respondents who included students from "traditional white English Canada" in their discourse on the diversity of the school population, they focused mainly on students from minority groups.

> Indo-Canadian cultures and Punjabi cultures are strongly represented; to a lesser extent, there are other Asian cultures and religions, a few Muslims, lot of Sikhs, a few Hindus, a few Southeast Asian cultures and religions. Traditional Canadian, white Canadian, they're there too. (Interview #1051, anglophone program)

The process of visibility/invisibility is central to the construction of difference and underlines the interplay of power and identity in the portrayal of Otherness. Ghosh and Abdi (2004) point out that the majority group remains outside the hierarchy of social relations and excludes itself from the politics of difference. As they elaborate on the profile of ethnocultural diversity in their schools, the discourse of teachers and principals shows a similar pattern. The study participants attribute diversity in the school to the presence of different minority groups. As a result, students from minority groups (they, the outsiders) are rendered highly visible in terms of race, language, culture, and religion, while students from the dominant group (we, the insiders) are invisible. Ghosh and Abdi (2004) suggest that the artificially constructed "we" and "they" disregard differences within each construct. If entrenched, the dichotomy insiders/outsiders may lead to further marginalization of groups and obstruct their inclusion within the locus of power.

Although diversity per se does not seem to be problematic for the majority of participants, there is a distinct focus on linguistic diversity in their discourse. They frequently mention ESL students and talk about facilitating communication with their families. Only two participants expressed concern about linguistic diversity by referring to the extra one-on-one attention needed by international students[8] who do not master English well enough to follow the regular program.

In addition, some participants raised concerns about ethnic tensions in their school when a single minority such as Indo-Canadians or Chinese students forms the majority in the school. Participants noted that, in this case, the "majority" minority "doesn't mingle together" with the other students.

In the French immersion program, participants are less explicit in their characterizations of diversity in their schools. Their discussion is mainly around bilingual French/English diversity, with some reference to other languages spoken by the families. There is no discussion about other dimensions of diversity, such as ethnicity, socio-economics, culture, or religion. The emphasis on French and English is not surprising in light of the historical development and objectives of French immersion programs in Canada. Presented as an alternative to the Core French program for anglophone students, this program was designed with two main objectives in mind: 1) to enable students to develop proficiency in both official languages; and 2) to foster intercultural dialogue between the two solitudes, anglophone and francophone. In practice, most of the French immersion programs in British Columbia are delivered in dual-track schools. Thus, the most salient "difference" to teachers in these schools has to do with the programs that are delivered—French immersion versus English instruction. Here is how one vice-principal in a dual-track school describes diversity in his school:

> [We have] some cultural diversity, but it's mostly French or English. However, we do have more students coming into the school that have an ESL background. There's Spanish, Korean, Asian, I believe Vietnamese, Chinese, and some Japanese too that I know of, to round out the diversity of cultures in the school. But still we're a fairly, if I may say, homogenous school. (Interview #1080, French immersion program)

In this excerpt, the participant acknowledges the shift in the linguistic background of students in French immersion programs in British Columbia. French immersion no longer attracts only anglophone students, as was the case when the program was developed in the 1960s; it is now very popular with other ethnic groups in Canada (Swain & Lapkin, 2005). However, compared to the other two programs, the description of the characteristics of diversity is subsumed under the structural dichotomy anglophone/francophone that characterizes this program.

As with respondents in the anglophone program, when respondents from the French immersion program do mention students from different backgrounds, one of their key concerns is facilitating communication with parents in languages other than English.

SUPPORT FOR DIVERSITY IN THE PROGRAMS: SIMILARITIES AND DIFFERENCES

Two questions in the interview probed teachers and principals about their experience with, training about, and knowledge of the diversity policy. The first question asked them to identify what kind of support they have for handling ethnocultural diversity in their class or school. Data analysis shows important similarities between the three programs. Most of the teachers and principals in these programs rely for the majority of the time on their personal values and experiences (e.g., travel, interest in other cultures, and the experience of immigrating or being a member of a visible minority themselves). Some respondents also rely on their peers, special education specialists, and, minimally, on students. Finally, in the anglophone and French immersion programs, some members of the staff speak other languages and often provide translation for communication with parents. One teacher, in an anglophone context, describes the significance of her personal experiences:

> Int.: Okay. On a daily basis, what helps you to deal with the ethnocultural diversity of your school or classroom? That could be personal experience, training, whatever. What do you use?
> Resp.: Personal experience and training.
> Int.: What personal experience? Or what training?
> Resp.: Well, I've done a lot of travelling, so I know a lot about the different cultures that I'm teaching. (Interview #1045, anglophone program)

A minority of respondents in the anglophone and French immersion programs report that professional training (ESL training, pre-service training) and experience (years of teaching, knowledge of classroom management strategies) support their professional practice with respect to issues of diversity in school. In the francophone schools, teachers describe their lack of professional experience of, and training in, ethnocultural diversity in education; for example:

> Int.: In your daily practice, what helps you to deal with ethnocultural diversity in your school? In terms of personal experience, do you have a specific training?
> Resp.: No, I don't have any specific training with respect to ethnic diversity. (Interview #1003, francophone program, translated from French)

This relative lack of institutional support and knowledge with respect to diversity in francophone schools is well documented in the research on the challenges of francophone schooling in minority settings (Gérin-Lajoie, 2006; Gilbert et al., 2004).

In the three programs, and in particular in the anglophone and French immersion programs, a few respondents appeared clearly surprised by the question on support for diversity and showed some hesitation before responding. The expression of surprise may suggest that the teacher did not understand the question and, in particular, the wording "ethnocultural diversity," which is more frequently used in Quebec than in Western Canada. It may also suggest that the verb phrase *to deal with* combined with the term *ethnocultural diversity* may have implicitly suggested that diversity is a "problem" to be solved or dealt with, which would explain why some participants felt obliged to assert that diversity is not "a problem," that "we don't really see it," or that it is "something natural," as in the following excerpts:

> Int.: On a daily basis, what would you say helps you to deal with the ethnocultural diversity of your school or classroom?
> Resp.: What helps me?
> Int.: Uh hmm.
> Resp.: I—I don't really see it as a problem. (Interview #1071, French immersion program)

> Int.: On a daily basis, what helps you to deal with ethnocultural diversity in your school or class?
> Resp.: It's probably just being actually exposed to it. After a while you don't really see it, they're just kids. (Interview #1034, anglophone program)

> Int.: On a daily basis, what helps you to deal with ethnocultural diversity in school?
> Resp.: For us, it is frankly something that is part of our daily practice. It has always been like that since I am here, since the francophone program. I have been teaching for 20 years in the francophone program and it has always been the case. So, I think that it is not something that is notice-

able; it is just natural in our school. There is nothing particular. (Interview #1009, francophone program, translated from French)

In the last two excerpts, the expression of surprise may suggest that they didn't think about taking diversity into account in their professional practices as a daily requirement for social justice and equity in education. However, because the question was not very well formulated, it is difficult to draw tangible conclusions, even though the literature often talks about "blindness to difference" as a way for teachers to portray themselves as "unbiased." Taylor (1994) argues that non-recognition of difference is a form of discrimination that can incarcerate people in "a false, deformed, and existentially reduced mode of being" (p. 42). The concept of "blindness to difference" refers to treating every student as the same, irrespective of their cultural, racial, or socio-economic background.

The following excerpt raises the question as to whether inclusion of diversity is truly woven into the curriculum:

> Int.: Would you say there's any issues of ethnocultural diversity that you have to deal with—address—in your teaching, and if so, what resources do you draw on?
> Resp.: I think it's more weaving it into your classroom management and a personal planning aspect of school. Just because we've had to have conversations that something might be acceptable in one culture and it might be not acceptable in another culture, and so you have to come to a common understanding. That's probably the only place that it's really talked about; otherwise, you have to follow the curriculum. So, it sort of goes into that but not really. It's more of your classroom management. It's more dealing with different issues if something arises outside of the classroom. Dealing with it that way, it doesn't sort of get woven into your standard curriculum. (Interview #1058, anglophone program)

In silencing difference, school staff run the risk of reinforcing social inequity in education, as well as their own positioning at the locus of power (Ghosh & Abdi, 2004). The issue is not merely acknowledging difference, but enabling difference to be expressed in other ways—"going beyond the equality concept that remains within the existing traditional structure to a configuration that would encompass differences" (Ghosh & Abdi, 2004, p. 39). In other words, in order to foster social changes in education, one has to go beyond acknowledging diversity in schools and challenge school practices that are based on the presumption that treating all children as being the same leads to equitable conditions in learning.

LIMITED KNOWLEDGE OF POLICIES AND RESOURCES ABOUT DIVERSITY

The third question in the interview probed study participants' knowledge of diversity policies. Respondents in all three programs demonstrated a limited knowledge of policies and resources specifically designed to support professional practices that are sensitive to an appropriate approach to diversity in their schools and classrooms. Their responses focused more on teaching resources than on policies. This lack of awareness of policies is particularly acute in the francophone schools where, except for two teachers who mentioned ESL resources and a specific program for Aboriginal students, the majority did not know about any policies or specific resources available in French. Those who did know of such resources did not consult them.

> Int.: Do you have any official documents from the school or the school board that can support you in dealing with ethnocultural diversity?
> Resp.: Well, I wouldn't say that there aren't any, but none that I was aware of. I know that in the area of Native studies, there are some documents, if that interests you, there is a professor that is in charge of that, but regarding people coming from other countries, the diversity outside of Canada, I don't know of any. (Interview #1015, francophone program, translated from French)

In francophone schools in British Columbia, there is no policy on diversity. The school board has only been in existence for 10 years; so far, its priority has been the implementation of a French curriculum across the province.[9] The lack of teaching and learning resources in French has been widely discussed in the literature (Gilbert et al., 2004). Teachers have difficulty finding resources adapted to the context of teaching in a francophone minority setting. This situation is quite different in the well-established anglophone program, where teachers are well aware of teaching materials relevant to the issues of teaching in diverse contexts made available either through publishers or the school district, but they don't necessarily find them useful. However, like teachers in the francophone program, respondents in the anglophone and French immersion programs have limited knowledge of policies on diversity. For example, only one teacher in an anglophone program talked about the general diversity policy of the school district. One participant working in a francophone school mentioned having seen a pamphlet about anti-racism. In the French immersion program, half of the teachers and principals were aware of the existence of "-ism" policies, such as anti-racism and multiculturalism policies. One teacher specifically referred to the multiculturalism policy. Some assumed that such a policy and documents on diversity existed at the district or provincial level, but they either did not read them or did not use them. At least three respondents were explicitly skeptical about the usefulness of such a policy.

> They're probably out there, but it would probably be more theory-based and we need more paper/pencil type awareness. (Interview #1084, French immersion program)

This skepticism was shared by two administrators who discussed the lack of specific guidelines when dealing with different cultural norms in schools. This position is explicit in the following excerpt in which a vice-principal questions the usefulness of the multiculturalism policy:

> Int.: And are there official documents from the district or the province or other kinds of teaching or leadership materials that help you when you're taking into account ethnocultural diversity in your work?
> Resp.: Well, there is a document—a policy followed with regard to respecting other people. But there's no particular document that guides one—if your question is, Are we taught how to deal with the cultural customs, for example, of people coming from different areas? No, we aren't. We just try to use our own Canadian decorum and, hopefully, we treat people correctly. (Interview #1109, anglophone program)

In the three programs, none of the respondents mentioned the recent policy of the Ministry of Education (2004): *Diversity in BC schools: a framework*. The lack of awareness and/or use of policy guidelines as expressed in the discourse of participants may be an indication of the loose coupling between diversity policy and professional practice in schools (Wideen & Barnard, 1999). In all three language programs, teachers are largely left to their own personal resources and initiatives to face the challenges. Thus, we must ask why institutional support for adapting professional practices in light of diversity seems to be lacking.

Surfing over Diversity in Professional Practices

With the final set of questions, school staff were asked to provide concrete examples of how they take ethnocultural diversity into account in their professional practices. Respondents in the francophone schools were less explicit than respondents in the other two language programs about the ways in which they adapt their practices to accommodate diversity. The few concrete examples given by francophone respondents were mainly about content integration and were tied to specific themes or lesson plans rather than to all subjects, as illustrated in the excerpt below. Content integration focused on the extent to which teachers provided examples and content from different cultures and groups in order to support understanding of concepts, principles, generalizations, and theories in their subject areas or discipline (Banks, 2004).

> In social studies, there is a chapter on community and cultural diversity, culture and religion. We focused on it so that we could ask everyone what was their ethnic origin, and then we did an assignment about it to address these issues. But, you know, we are not always talking year-round. (Interview #1017, francophone program, translated from French)

To some extent, the same can be said about participants from the French immersion and anglophone programs. However, they provided more varied examples of integration of content, such as presenting different holiday celebrations, discussing students' cultures, and engaging in activities around languages. They also presented examples of activities geared toward equity pedagogy (support for ESL students and adapted resources, work with peers, use of visual aids, activities relating to multiple intelligence, or students who are physically, mentally, or emotionally challenged). However, in these programs, equity pedagogies focus mainly on language issues, and other differences such as race, culture, social class, or gender are not discussed.

Banks (2004) argues that practitioners often restrict multicultural education to curriculum reforms involving integration of content from various ethnic, cultural, or gender groups, rather than implementing a multi-dimensional and critical approach to social justice and equity. In that sense, critical multicultural education brings a broader approach to social justice and equity in education, as these issues are embedded in all dimensions of the school—program, pedagogy, social interactions between school actors, and conceptions of learning and teaching (McLaren, 2007; Nieto, 2000)—rather than being boxed into one dimension.

Ghosh and Abdi (2004) agree that one important dimension of multicultural education is to teach "dominant groups to challenge oppression, especially because their privileged position tends to make it difficult for them to see the world critically" (p. 39). Thus, addressing knowledge construction helps to reveal assumptions, biases, and frames of reference entrenched in a particular discipline (Banks, 1992). This discussion is missing from the discourse of participants in the three programs, as is a discussion about prejudice reduction. Two teachers in the anglophone program said they addressed issues of racism and discrimination when it was relevant to the curriculum or when a specific issue came up in class (i.e., stereotypes about Muslim students after the events of 9-11). However, they also mentioned that discussing these issues is not part of their regular teaching practices.

> Well, I have addressed ethnocultural differences. The most kind of tension I can remember having in the class was after 9-11. I had a couple Muslim kids in my class, they were [Punjabi] speakers, Northern Pakistan area. They were born in Canada, live in Canada, but they were feeling a lot of stress from just being Muslim. A lot of it was perceived from the media and a general sense of what they were seeing on TV. But they were getting a lot of it from in the classroom too.... I had a lot of kids who were aware, quote-on-quote, that Muslim people were terrorists, and things along those lines. Those kind of superficial stereotypes. I actually had to go in and deal with that in a very concrete way.... I had to talk about the culture and the religion, what Islam was really about and its traditions. I had to talk about the feeling somebody might have being in that kind of hot seat, so I had to deal with that on a lot of different levels. It was a really good experience for the kids because they were actually quite relieved that this is the way it was rather than feeling, I guess pressured from home or something like that and it didn't feel right to them. They felt they were between a rock and a hard place. (Interview #1051, anglophone program)

There is some evidence of an empowering school culture in the three programs. In the French immersion and anglophone programs, examples of religious and cultural accommodation were reported, such as a flexible dress code for Muslim girls in physical education, accommodating Jehovah Witness students' beliefs with respect to non-participation in holiday activities, celebrating diversity during Multicultural Week, and fostering a culture of respect for cultural diversity in school. Other frequent examples of empowerment in these two programs relate to building effective communication with non-English speaking immigrants by using "multicultural staff" in the school district. These examples of accommodation help to empower students from minority groups as they open up a space where different norms—not just those of the dominant group—are included in the culture and social structure of the school. Fostering inclusion of diversity in school requires a critical examination of school practices that create barriers to the full participation of minority students (Banks, 2004). Accommodating student diversity is one key element in fostering inclusive social practices in school.

Finally, the discourse of the school staff in the francophone, anglophone, and French immersion programs illustrates some awareness of the question of diversity in professional practice. However, there is no evidence in the discourse to indicate that school staff understand difference as a complex concept that intersects on levels such as race, gender, social class, culture, and so forth. In addition, the lack of discussion about knowledge construction may be an indication of the difficulties that school staff have in de-centring themselves from their day-to-day teaching activity in order to critically address how difference is historically and culturally situated and how power is unequally distributed (Ghosh, 1996; Ghosh & Abdi, 2004; May, 1999; Sleeter & McLaren, 1995).

Conclusion

In this chapter, the analysis of teachers' and principals' discourse about ethnocultural diversity in their school shows some of the complexity and paradoxes of the multiculturalism policy and the ways it is played out in the different language programs. Teachers and principals in the francophone, anglophone, and French immersion programs all agree that ethnocultural diversity exists in their schools. At the same time, they have more difficulty going beyond the praxis of teaching to account for the political dimension of education. With respect to the limits of the set of qualitative data analyzed, the school staff's discourse does not clearly illustrate a critical understanding of the interplay between power and identity (Ghosh & Abdi, 2004; McLaren, 2007; Sleeter & McLaren, 1995). To some extent, it also shows the difficulties that educators have in de-centring themselves in order to critically examine their professional practices and position of power in light of fostering social justice and equity. At this point in my analysis, there is no evidence of a critical understanding of the concept of difference that would allow teachers and principals to account for the complexity and multi-dimensionality of this concept.

The lack of training on policies and issues of diversity in education, and the lack of knowledge in this area, seem to be a major deterrent to fostering professional practices sensitive to, and appropriate for, diversity in schools. After more than three decades of a multiculturalism policy in Canada, an abundant literature about multicultural, intercultural, and anti-racism education, and numerous educational initiatives, the effect on practice is still largely limited to the superficial integration of contents. Other important dimensions of a critical multicultural education that are rarely discussed by the participants need to be examined; these dimensions include the production of knowledge, prejudice reduction, and the empowerment of all students.

Furthermore, the respondents' obvious lack of knowledge about policies on diversity, as well as the skepticism expressed by some respondents about the usefulness of such "-ism" policies, indicate that principals and teachers need professional development targeted at implementing such policies in school. The professional constraints that educators face in a time of multiple policy changes (Grimmett et al., 2005) add to the complexity of developing inclusive professional practices. Moreover, it may well be unrealistic and, at times, contradictory to require school staff to take the diversity of beliefs, customs, practices, languages, behaviours, and physical differences of individuals and cultural groups into account (BC Ministry of Education, 2004).

Training on the complex issues of diversity is needed to help teachers to develop a critical approach to difference, to see the interplay between power and identity, and to examine controversial issues (Jacquet, 2007). Longitudinal studies are needed to investigate the transfer from pre-service training to professional practices in school. In the francophone program in particular, addressing the challenge of teaching in a minority setting in the absence of a policy on diversity and training in this area is a critical issue.

Notes

1. As defined in the census, "ethnic origin" refers to the ethnic or cultural group(s) to which an individual's ancestors belonged.
2. "Mother tongue" is defined as the first language a person learned at home in childhood and still understood at the time of the census. The list of languages reported includes languages long associated with immigration to Canada such as German, Italian, Ukrainian, Dutch, and Polish, as well as languages such as Chinese, Punjabi, Arabic, Urdu, Tagalog, and Tamil and many others that recorded the largest gains between 1996 and 2001.
3. Statistics Canada defines "visible minority" as persons, other than Aboriginal people, who are identified as being non-Caucasian in race or non-white in colour.
4. The language spoken most often or on a regular basis at home by individual students at the time of the September 30 data collection (BC Ministry of Education, 2006).
5. This number excludes Independent Schools, Federal Band Schools, Yukon Schools, and Independent Offshore BC Programs.
6. Three types of educational rights are recognized for francophone minorities: 1) the right to French language instruction for their children; 2) the right to enrol their children in homogeneous linguistic schools; 3) the right to governance of their schools.
7. Some families from non-francophone countries lived in Quebec before coming to British Columbia, and therefore their children are entitled to instruction in French.
8. International students are neither Canadian citizens nor residents; they are studying in BC public schools in the way that international students study at post-secondary institutions.
9. The Conseil scolaire francophone is currently developing a new policy, *Pédagogie 2010*, which includes a cultural dimension (CSF, 2006).

References

Banks, J.A. (2004). Multicultural education: Historical development, dimensions, and practice. In J.A. Banks, C.A. McGee Banks (Eds.), *Handbook of research on multicultural education* (pp. 3–29). San Francisco: Jossey-Bass.

Banks, J.A. (1992). Multicultural education: Approaches, developments and dimensions. In J. Lynch, C. Modgil, S. Mogdil (Eds.), *Cultural diversity and the schools: Education for cultural diversity: Convergence and divergence* (1) (pp. 83–94). London: The Falmer Press.

Bhabha, H. (1996). Culture's in-between. In S. Hall & P. du Gay (Eds.), *Questions of cultural identity* (pp. 53–60). London: Sage.

Blondin, D. (1990). *L'apprentissage du racisme dans les manuels scolaires*. Montreal: Agence D'ARC.

Bourgeault, G., Gagnon, F., McAndrew, M., & Pagé, M. (1995). L'espace de la diversité culturelle et religieuse à l'école dans une démocratie de tradition libérale. *Revue des migrations internationales, 11*(3), 79–103.

Breton, R., Reitz, J., & Valentine, V. (1980). *Cultural boundaries and the cohesion of Canada*. Montreal: Institute for Research on Public Policy.

British Columbia Multicultural Advisory Council. (2005). *Strategic framework for action: A strategy to stimulate joint action on multiculturalism and the elimination of racism in British Columbia*. Submitted to the Honourable Murray Coell, Minister of Community, Aboriginal and Women's Services. Retrieved November 7, 2006, from www.ag.gov.bc.ca/sam/framework/pdf/framework.pdf.

British Columbia Ministry of Education. (2006, February). *2005/2006 Summary of key information*. Retrieved October 24, 2006, from www.bced.gov.bc.ca/reporting.

British Columbia Ministry of Education. (2004). *Diversity in BC schools: A framework*. Retrieved October 24, 2006, from www.bced.gov.bc.ca/sco/resources.htm.

British Columbia Ministry of Education. (1997). *Language education policy*. Retrieved November 7, 2006, from www.bced.gov.bc.ca/policy/policies/language_educ.htm.

Canadian Parents for French. (2006). *Annual report 2005–2006. & Yukon branch*. Retrieved December 12, 2006, from www.cpf.bc.ca/bc_html/Other/FramePages/f_annualrprts.shtml.

Conseil scolaire francophone. (2006). *Pedagogies 2010*. Retrieved November 8, 2006, from www.csf.bc.ca/projets_speciaux/pedagogie_2010.php.

Conseil supérieur de l'éducation. (1987). *Les défis éducatifs de la pluralité. Avis au ministre de l'Éducation*. Quebec City: Government of Quebec.

Conseil supérieur de l'éducation. (1983). *L'éducation interculturelle. Avis au ministre de l'Éducation*. Quebec City: Government of Quebec.

D'Amico, L., Dagenais, D., Grimmett, P., & Jacquet, M. (2005). *British Columbia regional report. General background questionnaire (Questionnaire 1). Longitudinal study of teaching agents (Project 4)*. Unpublished technical report. Burnaby, BC: Faculty of Education, Simon Fraser University.

Dagenais, D., & Jacquet, M. (2001). Valorisation du multilinguisme et de l'éducation bilingue dans des familles immigrantes. *Journal of International Migration and Integration, 1*(4), 389–404.

Dagenais, D., & Day, E. (1998). Multilingual children and classroom processes in French Immersion. *La revue canadienne des langues vivantes 54*, 376–393.

Dei, G.J.S. (1996). *Anti-racism education: Theory and practice*. Halifax: Fernwood.

Friesen, C. (2006). *Presentation at the National Dialogue on Students at Risk—The learning partnership, Vancouver, BC*. Retrieved October 24, 2006, from www.thelearningpartnership.ca/policy_research/studentsatrisk_conference2006.html.

García, E. (2002). *Student cultural diversity. Understanding and meeting the challenge*, 3rd Edition. Boston: Houghton Mifflin Company.

Gérin-Lajoie, D. (2006). Identité et travail enseignant dans les écoles de langues française situées en milieu minoritaire. *Éducation et francophonie, 34*(1), 162–176.

Gérin-Lajoie, D. (2005). *Teachers as agents of linguistic and cultural reproduction in minority language schools*. Paper presented at the American Education Research Association in Division G, Section 4. Social Contexts of Educational Policy, Politics, and Praxis. Montreal, April 15, 2005.

Gérin-Lajoie, D. (1996). L'école minoritaire de langue française et son rôle dans la communauté. *The Alberta Journal of Educational Research, 42*(3), 267–279.

Ghosh, R., & Abdi, A.A. (2004). *Education and the politics of difference: Canadian perspectives.* Toronto: Canadian Scholars' Press Inc.

Ghosh, R. (1996). *Redefining multicultural education,* 2nd Edition. Toronto: Harcourt Brace.

Gilbert, A., LeTouzé, S., Thériault, J.Y., & Landry, R. (2004). *Le personnel enseignant face aux défis de l'enseignement en milieu minoritaire francophone. Rapport final de la recherche.* Fédération canadienne des enseignantes et des enseignants. Retrieved April 5, 2007, from www.ctf-fce.ca/fr/Issues/Francaise/LesdéfisdeenseignementRapportfinalfrançais.pdf.

Gollnick, D.M., & Chinn, P. (2002). *Multicultural education in a pluralistic society,* 6th edition. Upper Saddle River, NJ: Merrill Prentice Hall.

Government of Canada. (1988). An Act for the preservation and enhancement of multiculturalism in Canada (1988), c. 31.

Grimmett, P., Dagenais, D., Jacquet, M., & Llieva, R. (2005). *The contrasting discourses in the professional lives of educators in Vancouver,* British Columbia. Paper presented at the Annual Meeting of the American Educational Research Association in Montreal, April 14, 2005.

Heller, M. (2002). *Éléments d'une socio-linguistique critique.* Collection Langue et Apprentissage des Langues. Paris: Didier.

Heller, M., & Jones, M.C. (2002). *Voices of authority: Education and linguistic difference.* Westport, CT: Ablex.

Helly, D. (1994). Politique québécoise face au pluralisme culturel et pistes de recherche: 1977–1990. In J.W. Berry & J.A. Laponce (Eds.), *Ethnicity and cultures in Canada* (pp. 81–93). Toronto: University of Toronto Press.

Jacquet, M. (2007). La formation de maîtres à la pluriethnicité: Pédagogie critique, silence et désespoir. *Revue des sciences de l'éducation, 33*(1), 25–45.

Jacquet, M. (2002). *Analyse de la prise de décision des directions d'écoles lors des demandes d'adaptation des normes et pratiques scolaires à la diversité culturelle et religieuse.* Unpublished doctoral dissertation, University of Montreal.

Jacquet, M. (1996). Les formes claires-obscures de l'altérité dans le matériel d'éducation interculturelle au primaire. In K. McLeod, et Z. de Koninck (Eds.), *L'éducation multiculturelle: état de la question. Rapport 3. L'éducation multiculturelle: école et société,* (pp. 122–143). Winnipeg: Canadian Association of Second Language Teachers.

Ladson-Billings, G. (2004). New directions in multicultural education: Complexities, boundaries, and critical race theory. In J. Banks & C.A. McGee Banks (Eds.), *Handbook of research on multicultural education,* 2nd edition (pp. 50–65). San Francisco: Jossey-Bass.

Martel, A. (1997). Droit éducatif et aménagement des langues. L'article 23 de la Charte canadienne des droits et libertés (1982) est-il réparateur? *Études ethniques au Canada 29*(1), 59–80.

May, S. (Ed.). (1999). *Critical multiculturalism. Rethinking multicultural and antiracist education.* Philadelphia: Falmer Press.

McAll, C. (1991a). *Au-delà de la culture: Le Québec et l'immigration.* Document de travail no 25. Ottawa: Economic Council of Canada.

McAll, C. (1991b). L'analyse sociologique des inégalités sociales et de l'ethnicité dans la formation des maîtres. In F. Ouellet & M. Pagé (Eds.), *Pluriethnicité, éducation et société, construire un espace commun* (pp. 275–291). Quebec City: Institut québécois de recherche sur la culture.

McAndrew, M. (1995). Multiculturalisme canadien et interculturalisme québécois: Mythes et réalités. In M. McAndrew, R. Toussaint, O. Galatanu (Eds.), *Pluralisme et éducation: Politiques et pratiques au Canada en Europe et dans les pays du sud, l'apport de l'éducation comparée* (pp. 33–52). Montreal: Publications de la faculté des sciences de l'éducation, Université de Montréal.

McAndrew, M. (1993). *L'intégration des élèves des minorités ethniques quinze ans après l'adoption de la Loi 101: Quelques enjeux confrontant les écoles publiques de langue française de la région montréalaise.* Montreal: Ministère des Communautés culturelles et de l'Immigration, Direction Études et Recherches.

McAndrew, M. (1987). *Le traitement de la diversité raciale, ethnique et culturelle et la valorisation du pluralisme dans le matériel didactique au Québec.* Rapport final soumis au Conseil des communautés culturelles et de l'immigration. Montreal.

McAndrew, M. (1986). *Études sur l'ethnocentrisme dans les manuels scolaires de langue française au Québec.* Les publications de la faculté des sciences de l'éducation, Université de Montréal.

McLaren, P.L. (2007). *Life in schools,* 5th edition. Boston: Pearson Education Inc.

Ministère de l'Éducation du Québec. (1998). *Une école d'avenir. Intégration scolaire et éducation interculturelle.* Quebec City: Government of Quebec.

Ministère de l'Éducation du Québec. (1995). *La prise en compte de la diversité culturelle et religieuse en milieu scolaire: Un module de formation des gestionnaires.* Quebec City: Government of Quebec.

Ministère de l'Éducation du Québec. (1988). *L'école québécoise et les communautés culturelles.* Le Rapport Latif. Quebec City: Government of Quebec.

Moodley, K. (1995). Multicultural education in Canada: Historical development and current status. In J.A. Banks, & C. McGee Banks (Eds.), *Handbook of research on multicultural education* (pp. 801–820). New York: MacMillan Publishing.

Moodley, K. (1988). L'éducation multiculturelle au Canada: Des espoirs aux réalités. In F. Ouellet (Ed.), *Pluralisme et école* (pp. 187–221). Quebec City: Institut québécois de recherche sur la culture.

Nieto, S. (2000). *Affirming diversity: The sociopolitical context of multicultural education,* 3rd edition. New York: Longman.

Pietrantonio, L., Juteau D., & McAndrew, M. (1996). Multiculturalisme ou intégration, un faux débat. In K. Fall, R.H. Moussa, & D. Simeoni (Eds.), *Convergences culturelles dans les sociétés multiethniques* (pp. 147–158). Chicoutimi: Presses de l'Université du Québec.

Rebuffot, J. (1993). *Le point sur l'immersion au Canada.* Montreal: Centre éducatif et culturel.

Sleeter, C.E., & Grant, C.A. (2007). *Making choices for multicultural education: Five approaches to race, class, and gender,* 5th edition. Hoboken, NJ: John Wiley & Sons.

Sleeter, C.E. & Delgado-Bernal, D. (2004). Critical pedagogy, critical race theory, and antiracist education. In J.A. Banks & C.A. McGee Banks (Eds.), *Handbook of research on multicultural education* (pp. 240–258). San Francisco: Jossey-Bass.

Sleeter, C.E., & McLaren, P.L. (Eds.). (1995). *Multicultural education, critical pedagogy and the politics of difference.* Albany: State University of New York Press.

Statistics Canada. (2003). Canada's ethno-cultural portrait: The changing mosaic. Retrieved October 25, 2006, from www12.statcan.ca/english/census01/products/analytic/companion/etoimm/contents.cfm.

Swain, M., & Lapkin, S. (2005). The evolving socio-political context of immersion education in Canada: Some implications for program development. *International Journal of Applied Linguistics, 15*(2), 169–186.

Tardif, C. (1993). L'identité culturelle dans les écoles francophones minoritaires: Perceptions et croyances des enseignants. *Canadian Modern Language Review 49*(4), 786–798.

Taylor, C. (1994). *Multiculturalisme, différence et démocratie.* (D.A. Canal, Trans.). Paris: Aubier (Original work published 1992).

Vancouver School Board. (1995). *Multiculturalism and anti-racism policy.* Vancouver.

Wideen, M., & Barnard, K.A. (1999). *Impacts of immigration on education in British Colombia: An analysis of efforts to implement policies of multiculturalism in school.* Working Paper Series. Retrieved September 11, 2001, from www.riim.metropolis.net/frameset_f.html.

CHAPTER 4

"Our School Is Like the United Nations"

AN EXAMINATION OF HOW DISCOURSES OF DIVERSITY IN SCHOOLING NATURALIZE WHITENESS AND WHITE PRIVILEGE

Mélanie Knight

It is virtually impossible to talk about schools nowadays without entering into some discussion on the ethnic and racial diversification of the student body. This diversity as it pertains to research has primarily been discussed in relation to how teaching personnel can best "manage" the influx of students coming from outside our borders. This is not surprising since inherent in the discourse[1] of diversity is the notion that these newcomers, as Bannerji (2000) notes, "create accommodational difficulties for white Canadians, both at the level of civil society, of culture, and economy, and also for the ruling practice of the state" and as such need to be contained and managed (p. 43). The containment and management of this diversified student body primarily operates through celebratory practices that display narrow understandings of culture. The pervasiveness and seductiveness of discourses of diversity, multiculturalism, and "United Nationism" must, however, continuously be challenged and problematized. Absent in these celebratory discourses is a critical focus on racism, whiteness, and white privilege. Those who dare take up these issues quickly recognize the perilous and paralyzing nature of doing this work. The investment in the myth of sameness on the part of whites renders any discussion of race and difference, at the very least, a highly contested struggle (hooks, 1992). Many are quick to utter the phrases that race is irrelevant, a non-existent and empty category, or, even more disturbing, that race has now been overly exhausted. To make these supposedly innocent claims is to negate Canada's colonial history and history of slavery and indentured labour. Equally problematic is the idea that systemic racism and white privilege can simply be subverted through the increasing ethnic and racial diversification of students.

It is precisely within these understandings of diversity in the schooling context that I wish to examine how whiteness, as a "*historical systemic structural race-based superiority,*" and white privilege are upheld (Wander, Martin &

Nakayama, 1999, p. 15, emphasis in original). I analyze data collected from a national project entitled *Current Trends in the Evolution of School Personnel in Canadian Elementary and Secondary Schools*. Although a variety of data exists from this five-year project, I focus on interviews collected with white teaching personnel in Ontario schools. In the first part of this chapter, I briefly discuss the various theories of whiteness and then detail the research project, methodology, and key findings. I conclude the chapter by discussing several ways in which school personnel and researchers can begin to de-normalize whiteness and interrogate white privilege in schools as well as in research.

My analysis of the data, although informed by a variety of works, relies more specifically on those by Nakayama and Krizek (1999) and Moon (1999), who both outline strategies of the discourse of whiteness. What the interview data primarily reveals, which will be examined in greater detail in the chapter, is that the increasing representation of racialized students in schools produces the notion that festive celebrations and displays of culture are key elements to fighting oppression. This chapter will show that it is precisely in these moments that whiteness as a system of power is upheld and manifested in what I identify as five strategies: 1) Diversity as Foreignness/Diversity as Other (Karim, 1993); 2); Racelessness and the Myth of Sameness (hooks, 1992); 3) Exoticizing the Other (hooks, 1992); 4) the Driving Miss Daisy Syndrome (duCille, 1994); and 5) Bourgeois Decorum (Moon, 1999).

Whiteness and White Privilege

Much of the research to date that seeks to denaturalize whiteness and white privilege does so by specifically interrogating whites' understandings of these systems (Nakayama & Krizek, 1999; Schick, 2002; Solomon, Portelli, Daniel & Campbell, 2005). Since whites are often invisible in discussions of race, it is only when they are confronted about their whiteness and privilege that we are then able to see how these systems are sustained and reproduced (Nakayama and Krizek, 1999). Studies that focus specifically on how whites understand their power and privilege are essential since we, as researchers and educators, are less likely to focus on how those who oppress conceptualize, describe/define, make sense, rationalize, and sustain their power and privilege over others, or how they denounce this very power (Hurtado, 1999). I, however, enter this discussion from a slightly different perspective. I rely on interview data from teaching personnel collected from the *Current Trends in the Evolution of School Personnel in Canadian Elementary and Secondary Schools* research project. The reason why my approach is slightly different is that this research project did not look to examine whiteness and white privilege but ethnocultural diversity.[2] I believe, however, that the nuanced ways in which whiteness operates must be interrogated from different perspectives. In looking at how white teaching personnel talk about diversity in schools, we are able to see how whiteness, as a hegemonic position, is continually re-secured (Nakayama & Krizek, 1999).

When doing critical work on race and racism, it is imperative that we expose whiteness and the strategies/practices that sustain and reproduce its normalcy and centrality in which Other differences are calculated and organized (Nakayama & Krizek, 1999). If we are unable to denaturalize/destabilize its invisibility, we risk "reifying whiteness" (Harper, 2002, p. 273). Levine-Rasky (2002) provides a model that posits the essentiality of studying whiteness from three perspectives: critical, relational, and contextual. A critical approach emphasizes a position on issues of social injustice, and a focus on changing inequitable social relations. The everyday normative position is described as when whites deny racism and give contradictory explanations for social inequalities to preserve their power, resources, and what Levine-Rasky (2002) defines as their "dysconsciousness" (p. 321). A critical approach looks to change these social relations. To examine whiteness from a relational perspective is to demonstrate the symbolic and material dependence of whites and others. Therefore, the marginalization of a particular group cannot be examined outside of the privileges that are simultaneously being retained by a dominant majority group. The two perspectives are related to one another. Finally, a contextual analysis situates whiteness historically and must also be considered in relation to other identities, such as, class, gender, and sexual orientation.

As mentioned above, my analysis in this chapter more specifically focuses on two key works by Nakayama and Krizek (1999) and Moon (1999), who examine the communicative and micro-level ways in which whiteness is performed. For Nakayama and Krizek (1999), exposing whiteness's universality can be accomplished by looking at its everydayness. Since the Other is most often marked against the experiences and communication patterns of whites who are often taken as the norm, particularizing white experience or assessing the "everydayness of whiteness" will displace whites from a universal normalized and naturalized position. They, too, will be confronted with questions and challenges that are often faced in relation to other social locations. Rather than search for an essentialized nature to whiteness, Nakayama and Krizek (1999) look to understand "the ways that this rhetorical construction makes itself visible and invisible, eluding analysis yet exerting influence over everyday life" (p. 91).

In order to challenge the universality of whiteness, Nakayama and Krizek (1999) map a strategic rhetoric of whiteness, obtained from a variety of sources, by grouping discourses into a discursive formation. Throughout this chapter, I employ a number of their six outlined discursive strategies and discuss them in greater detail later on. The authors describe the first strategy as one in which the category *white* is identified by whites as being tied to the majority, an identity that is not only de-historicized but rarely critically analyzed. The second strategy is the defining of the category *white* through a negative association as opposed to a positive definition. Here authors observed that the category/identity *white*, although not explicitly named as such, symbolized for instance "not being black." A third strategy is the naturalization of the identity/category *white* as a scientific one. Whiteness, according to authors, is once again de-historicized and rendered invisible. The fourth strategy is where whiteness is confused with nationality, what authors define as "a legal status conferred by social institutions" (p. 99). The fifth strategy is the refusal to use labels. Examples of this would be when people say "I don't see race or ethnicity, I just see people." There is an emphasis on the ideology of individualism over subjectivity that once again erases the social location of whiteness and any claims to history. The sixth and final strategy identified by authors is one where whiteness is defined in relation to European ancestry. Although the identification of a social location shows some recognition of history, this observation does not indicate whether there is an understanding of the power relations that are embedded in that history.

The second study that I rely on more specifically is Moon (1999), who examines the enculturation and performance of whiteness. She adapts Frankenberg's (1993) concept of the "evasion of Whiteness" and Rich's (1979) concept of "white solipsism," two contradictory yet interrelated ideological discourses that frame whiteness. The evasion of whiteness is defined as when whites experience a "disconnection with issues of race" where they do not "'see' that issues of race, racism, racial formation, or the power relations surrounding race as related to their lives. On the other hand, white solipsism configures the world as a white space wherein 'whiteness' is perceived as a normative and universal condition" (p. 178). It is within this configuration that Moon sees whiteness as being performed. More specifically, the performance is enacted through what she defines as *bourgeois decorum*, a practice where whites present a publicly united racial front, which is specifically performed in two ways: through euphemizing white racism and hyperpoliteness. She further defines the euphemizing of white racism as Whitespeak, a type of coded speech, a "racialized form of euphemistic language in which what is *not* said—or the absences in language ... is often far more revealing than what *is* said" (p. 188, emphasis in original). There are three manifestations of Whitespeak: the subjectification of racism and race, the erasure of agency (passive voice), and the disembodiment of subjects. I discuss all of these in more detail further on in the chapter. The second way in which bourgeois decorum is particularized and performed is through hyperpoliteness that "signifies an excessive concern with language forms, similar to what the Right calls 'political correctness,' an ahistorical and decontextualized approach to language use" (p. 192). There was insufficient data to support the theory of bourgeois decorum of hyperpoliteness and therefore this is not discussed in this chapter. Both Nakayama and Krizek (1999) and Moon (1999) enable me to examine the nuanced ways in which whites perform whiteness. Before delving into the findings, the following section outlines the focus of the research project and the methodology.

Research Project and Methodology

As mentioned in the first chapter of this book, data for this chapter comes from the *Current Trends in the Evolution of School Personnel in Canadian Elementary and Secondary Schools* five-year national research project that began in 2002.[3] Although the study took place in several sites across Canada, only results from the Greater Toronto Area, and in particular Project 4, will be examined in this chapter. More specifically, my focus will be on the information obtained from the second interview since it had a specific section on ethnocultural diversity. I only take up the first three questions, as the fourth question on language primarily yielded discussions around the challenges of teaching ESL students that falls outside the scope of this chapter. The questions are as follows: 1). Existence and form of ethnocultural diversity: 1a. Does ethnocultural diversity exist in your class/school? 1b. What characterizes this diversity? Can you describe this diversity? 2). Guideposts for ethnocultural diversity: 2a. On a daily basis, what helps you to deal with the ethnocultural diversity of your school or classroom? (personal experience, training, etc.) 2b. Are there official documents from the school, the school district, or the government or other teaching material that help you in taking into account ethnocultural diversity in your teaching? 3). Accounting for ethnocultural diversity in practice: 3a. Could you talk about a recent event in which you adapted your practice due to ethnocultural diversity?

Out of the 87 interviews conducted for the second interview, I focus only on 73 of those interviews, those conducted with white teaching personnel. This identified number of white participants, however, is only an estimate because as I mentioned earlier, this study did not formally ask participants to identify themselves by race or ethnicity, therefore this estimation is purely based on the recollection of face-to-face interviews. In order to identify participants by race, I enlisted the help of our research officer who had a greater level of contact with every participant. The main reason why I chose to focus specifically on white participants as opposed to everyone is because I am specifically interested in looking at how whiteness and white privilege is communicated and performed by whites.

In terms of the analysis of the interviews, I use critical discourse analysis that, according to van Dijk (1993), is not a homogenous method but one that relies on doing linguistic, semiotic, or discourse analysis. This method of analysis "aims to show *non-obvious ways* in which language is involved in social relations of power and domination, and in ideology" (Fairclough, 2001, p. 229, emphasis added). This consists of the examination of language, social identities, power, domination, and ideology. In terms of the more intricate ways in which this approach works, Luke (1995) contends that the principal unit of analysis for critical discourse analysis is the text, and defines text as "language in use … any instance of written and spoken language that has coherence and coded meanings" (p. 13). All texts are located in social institutions like schools and workplaces. Not only do humans use these texts to make sense of their everyday life but texts also construct individuals. Again, I believe that this approach is most appropriate in this case since text, located in the social institution of the school, constructs and is used to construct whiteness and white privilege as natural and invisible. The following section outlines five strategies of whiteness that emerged from interviews with teaching personnel.

Diversity as Foreignness/Diversity as Other

When participants were asked the first question of whether ethnocultural diversity existed in their school or class, most, if not all, answered yes. When asked what characterized this diversity, many described the different groups based on their ethnicity, race, or nationality.

> Well, in our school, it's very diverse. We have students from various cultures and backgrounds. I think the most prominent in this school is Jamaican, and then Ghana is probably the second. There's quite a few Spanish. A few students maybe from China, a few Italian, a wide variety. (Interview #4124 / W-F)[4]

> We've got a lot of Middle Easterners, a lot of Indians, a lot of Vietnamese, a lot of Chinese, not many Japanese, not many Jewish kids at all. So it's mainly Arabic, Indian, Vietnamese, Chinese, a smattering of new Canadians from Eastern Europe, Yugoslavia, some from Poland, and some from Russia. (Interview #4202 / W-M)

I do not dispute the fact that schools are seeing an increase of recent immigrant children, but it is important to examine how diversity is conceptualized by the interview participants. Although some did include the category *white* or *white ethnics* as part of this diversity, the majority, however, spoke of ethnocultural diversity in terms of non-white groups. Not only was the question of ethnocultural diversity interpreted to mean non-white, many of these students were either described as having just arrived, as having been in Canada for a few years, as being transients, and in some instances as being apartment dwellers. Although there was no specific question formulated around citizenship status, when some participants were asked the citizenship status of the identified students, many did acknowledge that a fair number were Canadian-born but made it clear that their parents were not.

The categorizing of different groups is not an inconsequential act. The term *diversity*, even when used as a purely descriptive term that symbolizes heterogeneity, is not without what Bannerji (2000) describes as "implied power relations, ulterior aim or use" (p. 35). It is a loaded concept that carries a great deal of significance in terms of political and organizational practices. Therefore, to speak of the diversity of students primarily as newcomers and recent immigrants is not a mere descriptive practice but one that is produced (Ng, 1988). Diversity's paradox is that it ensures a level of "realness" to cultural descriptions yet simultaneously negates any understanding of difference as being tied to power relations (Bannerji, 2000). We are made aware that differences do exist between students, but how this difference is produced and the potential effects of this production are obscured.

The practice of linking the notion of diversity to racialized students is not only practised by these participants but is in fact part of a larger discourse. If we look at an Ontario school board's (SB) website, for instance, under the heading of "Equity in Education: Diversity at [SB]," the description notes that "The School Board is proud to be one of the most diverse and multicultural school systems in the world." It describes what "diverse and multicultural" mean. There are four "facts and figures" that then follow this statement. According to this School Board:

> Approximately 53 per cent of SB secondary students have English as their first language. In elementary schools, 41 per cent of students have a language other than English as their first language. More than 80 languages are represented in our schools. Languages from all over the world, such as Urdu, Serbian, Spanish, Swahili, and Cantonese, are spoken by students in the SB. More than 47,000 students or 24 per cent of elementary students were born outside of Canada in more than 175 different countries. More than 11,500 secondary students (11.8 per cent) have been in Canada for three years or less.[5]

Diversity and multiculturalism are therefore linked to students with English as a second language, as speaking a language other than French and English, having been born outside of Canada, or as having been in Canada for a short period of time.

Very early on when the government adopted the policy of "multiculturalism within a bilingual framework," multiculturalism meant that no particular culture was more official than another (Karim, 1993). Furthermore, the concept of multiculturalism in the 1960s and 1970s attempted to deconstruct the notion of two "founding" nations by depicting the entire population as constituting "the multicultural community." Over the years, however, multiculturalism has increasingly come to symbolize "others" (Karim, 1993). When looking at how ethnocultural diversity is conceptualized by participants, it once again becomes clear who is implied when notions of diversity and multiculturalism are invoked.

> It [the population of the school] was about 200 before the amalgamation and it was all kids in the area. Very middle class, very—I think from what I understand—white and European middle class, and then once we had some amalgamation, it opened up into different areas and it's very multicultural. (Interview #4132 / W-F)

> Yes, we have something like 60 different nationalities. It is funny because when I was in [a small town in Ontario] in teachers college and you talked about multiculturalism, that was one thing that was so foreign to a lot of the student teachers who were there and even the professors because a lot of them came from these small towns, very rural. (Interview #4142 / W-M)

Very rarely are French and Scottish Canadians described as "the diversity" (Karim, 1993). If the notion of diversity stands for "the others," what is it held up against? For Bannerji (2000), this superficial non-politicized understanding of difference is marked against a "homogeneous national, that is, a *Canadian cultural self* with its multiple and different others" (p. 37, emphasis added). The core or the "we," which these multiple and different others are positioned against, is often described in cultural or linguistic terms and in relation to the discourse of two "founding" nations. This national mythology, and the individuals who are associated with it, are not defined along cultural, linguistic, or religious lines but defined by the body and skin colour and represent the European/North American physical origin (Bannerji, 2000).

In describing and associating diversity as Other, two things happen: whiteness, which the Other is held against, remains invisible and normalized, and the white settler mythology remains intact. Razack (2002) defines a white settler society as one established by Europeans on non-European soil. Its origins lie in the dispossession and near extermination of Indigenous populations by the conquering Europeans. As it evolves, a white settler society continues to be structured by a racial hierarchy. In the national mythologies of such societies, it is believed that white people came first and that it is they who principally developed the land; Aboriginal peoples are presumed to be mostly dead or assimilated. European settlers thus *become* the original inhabitants and the group most entitled to the fruits of citizenship. A quintessential feature of white settler mythologies is, therefore, the disavowal of conquest, genocide, slavery, and the exploitation of the labour of peoples of colour. (pp. 1–2, emphasis in original)

The problem with this national white settler myth is that "if Aboriginal peoples are consigned forever to an earlier space and time, people of colour are scripted as late arrivals, coming to the shores of North America long after much of the development has occurred. In this way, slavery, indentureship, and labour exploitation ... are all handily forgotten in an official national story of European enterprise" (Razack, 2002, p. 3). Although the following participant's comment was discussed in relation to the second question of how diversity is dealt with, it nonetheless relates to the point I am trying to make here.

> Now we're doing medieval and we haven't touched the Crusades yet, but like I say, we're talking about Europe now. We're not talking about Asia. We're not talking about China. We're not talking about what happened here or we're not talking about what's happening in what's now called Arabia, we're talking about Europe and we're talking about specifically Britain, because a lot of people who came to Canada originally were from there… I started off talking about Tigris and Euphrates and all that and how ideas came and so on, without making a big deal out of it, but at least acknowledging those things and giving the kids opportunities to explore on their own, different sites. Particularly we're interested in finding out what the history was in the middle, what was going on in your country or your area of origin, where your parents or grandparents came from. (Interview #4203 / W-F)

Here we see that racialized peoples' histories as they relate to Canada are positioned as being outside of it. Although I do not discuss curriculum in this chapter, this response demonstrates how white settler national mythology renders racialized peoples in Canada as non-existent. This non-existence has implications for people of colour. Diversity, as an ideological concept that has come to be defined in very specific ways, dictates the ways in which particular groups, namely racialized peoples, are constructed vis-à-vis the nation. This construction of racialized people's place in Canada creates limits on the kinds of claims that can be made in relation to the nation. Those that are defined as newcomers, foreigners, or outsiders can only make particular, if any, claims on the nation as they are deemed less entitled. The only claims they are able to retain, to some extent, are those generated as a result of the generosity of the Canadian state (Shadd, 1991). When racialized groups are predominantly discussed as being non-existent or outsiders in the white settler national mythology, it does nothing to denaturalize this system as racially hierarchically organized. We leave untouched the system itself and how it has been produced as a white space. Also, although the discourse of diversity may result in some form of recognition, a level of tolerance, and some form of advocacy for the rights of particular groups, some question the actual difference that such practices actually have on the lives of people of colour (Bannerji, 2000). Here I have brought forth the issue of what conceptualizations of diversity reveal about our understandings of Canada's colonial history as well as what groups are identified as belonging to the category of diversity. We must always interrogate the discourse of diversity as being more than descriptive in nature and ask who benefits from these conceptualizations and how whiteness is upheld and more importantly normalized in these instances.

Although many participants were able to describe diversity in great detail, a second strategy of whiteness that emerged was what Dei (2000) calls the denying and discounting of difference, what Kendall (2001) outright calls the discounting people of colour on the part of whites, or what hooks (1992) has defined as the discourse of racelessness or myth of sameness.

Racelessness and the Myth of Sameness

When participants were asked the second question of what helped them to deal with the ethnocultural diversity in their school or classroom and whether they knew of any official documents that could help in taking into account ethnocultural diversity in their teaching, many replied that they did not know of any materials offered but would welcome them. Let me say at the onset that I do recognize that the wording of the question is problematic, as it inherently implies that diversity is something that needs to be dealt with. It is not surprising, therefore, that participants overwhelmingly said that it was not something that needed to be dealt with as there were no evident problems among students. Even with the inherent problem with the question, two strategies of whiteness emerged in discussions on "dealing" with diversity, one being through the discounting of difference and the myth of racelessness or sameness. As a subset to this, participants noted that addressing or taking diversity into consideration would only need to take place in times of conflict. This reveals that power and oppression are understood primarily in individualistic overt forms as opposed to systemic and covert ones. The invisibility of conflict meant that oppression was non-existent. I begin, however, by discussing the second strategy/performance of whiteness, which is the belief of the myth of sameness.

When participants were asked this second question, many explained that dealing with diversity was an unnecessary practice as this ethnocultural diversity was non-existent in their eyes. Nakayama and Krizek (1999) identify as their fifth strategy of whiteness when whites refuse to label themselves as such. They give this example: "I don't agree with using ethnic terms. I'm an American and that's all" (p. 100). It is difficult for whites to acknowledge seeing difference because they often believe that highlighting difference is somehow a form of marginalization. Most readily espouse to liberal beliefs of a universal subjectivity that ultimately declares all individuals as being "just people." The belief, very often, is that this philosophy will somehow make racism disappear. Whites are therefore deeply invested in what hooks (1992) describes as "the myth of 'sameness'" (p. 167), as this participant expressed:

> I think most teachers will tell you, you've got a class in front of you. You don't have a class of Asian kids, you don't have a class of Sri Lankan kids, you don't have a class of Korean kids, you've got a class of kids, and maybe you have to sometimes sit back and say, Well, what backgrounds do you have in there? Let me think for a second. There's Chris, there's John, there's Thomas, there's Doug, that's how you go.... It's a routine. You know there's no categorization. (Interview #4163 / W-M)

To acknowledge or recognize race for these participants is perceived as being unnecessary and irrelevant. However, there is a difference between attributing negative meaning to race and denying racial differences when formulating policy for social justice. It is not the recognition of difference that is of issue but the interpretation of that difference (Dei, 2000). It may be difficult for whites to understand that equal treatment, a philosophy so often espoused as one that is more equitable than formal policies, can be discriminatory. On the other hand, it may also be difficult to understand that the differential treatment of individuals is not necessarily showing a preference but may in fact be correcting a legacy of historical injustices (Sue, 2004). It is therefore essential to consider difference but to do so by historicizing, contextualizing, and politicizing it, especially as it relates to racialized groups in Canada.

Whites often believe that fostering a notion of sameness will foster better race and ethnic relations and contribute to the disappearance of racism. If I tell myself that you are no different from me, then systemic oppression that produces difference and marginalization is non-existent. It is in this moment, however, that whiteness and its normalizing effects emerge and that its power continues to remain invisible, at least for whites. I say that it remains invisible at least for whites because I tend to question, much like Frankenberg (1997), whom whiteness is invisible *to*. Although works that look to expose the invisibility, including those of Frankenberg, are essential to better understanding how whiteness operates, she herself questions her own assertions on this issue after having read hooks's (1992) chapter, "Representation of Whiteness in the Black Imagination." In this chapter, hooks repeatedly shows how "*uninvisible* white people were to her and her kin and community" (p. 116, emphasis added). Does making the claim of the invisibility of whiteness, as emerging when the myth of sameness is invoked, not negate the concrete effects of whiteness on racialized peoples? What kinds of studies would be most effective in denaturalizing whiteness? This is the difficulty of doing this type of work. On the one hand, much of the work that is currently out there that looks at how whites understand whiteness and white privilege is not new information for racialized peoples. Therefore, whom are these works intended for? Do we need more research like hooks's to understand the significance of whiteness from the perspective of racialized peoples? I fear, however, that this once again will enable whites to escape interrogation, and it is imperative that we better understand how those who oppress make sense of their power as well as how they speak about those who oppress (Hurtado, 1999).

In addition to the practice of discounting difference through racelessness, many participants simply felt that diversity did not need to be "dealt with," addressed, or considered since there was no evidence of discord among groups.

> I don't address that [diversity] at all. I go in the class, I teach. And we're all there. We talk. There's nothing to be said about it [diversity]. One just goes in and does a regular schoolday. Because the groups aren't fighting, so there's nothing to address. If groups were fighting, well then there'd be something that would have to be dealt with, but when everyone's getting along, you just proceed ahead. (Interview #4184 / W-M)

> Students are really, really good. I mean, I find it a really good school here as far as student behaviour goes. And one of the rugby players on the bus, he asked me to mention that you don't see any problems among different backgrounds at [the name of the school]. It's a diversified school, and it really seems like everyone gets along, and everyone is very accepting of other cultures and backgrounds, and I think it's a very good school. Very multicultural, and there doesn't seem to be any racial conflict whatsoever. … I've never seen any racial issues in any of my classes, the kids really just

get along and they really don't care about skin colour. It doesn't matter to them. (Interview #4166 / W-M)

The fact that students are behaving suggests that racism is non-existent. Not hearing or seeing any sign of "bad conduct" or conflict meant that all was fine. These understandings of racism on the part of the teaching personnel also imply that it would primarily manifest itself between students as opposed to all levels of interactions, including that of teacher and student. As educators we need to better understand the ways in which power works, in particular as it relates to race. Without such understanding, we simply infer that if we do not see or hear anything that everything is fine. Ignoring race does not mean that racism is not occurring (Hurtado, 1999). It is often this misguided rationale that perpetuates the silence and negation of racism. Furthermore, equality and social justice cannot simply be addressed or enforced when there are visible conflicts. They must be practised at all times and in all levels of work and activity.

Although student diversity was most often described as harmonious, some participants did speak of racial conflicts that had emerged in their schools. Somewhat of a surprise, however, was how experiences of racism were described as over-exaggerations on the part of students. This understanding, according to Frankenberg (1993), reflects how whites understand racism and their role in the sustaining of it differently than the recipients of racism.

> In previous years, there's been some use of the word *racism*, but I think, again, it's been used by students who really are pretty insecure and that's the only way they can sort of put a boundary up, or not a boundary but more of a defence mechanism. Why are you picking on me, because I'm black or ... but I think there's pretty good respect, both among staff and students. (Interview #4138 / W-M)

Racism is a heavy burden that is not fully understood by those who are able to escape the stigma (Hurtado, 1999). Here, experiences of racism are pathologized and rendered as student misunderstandings and as ways for them to gain attention. Also evident is a form of disembodiment from the white teacher, a strategy that Moon (1999) identifies under bourgeois decorum. Although I will discuss this strategy and its many levels further on in the chapter, I felt it appropriate to refer to it here, as it also emerged when this second question was asked. The disembodiment of subjects, a manifestation of Whitespeak, is represented as "anonymous agents who are ultimately responsible for the perpetuation of racism. These unmarked bodies make life difficult for the rest of us good whitepeople" (p. 191). When the participant above makes note of the fact that there was *some use* of the word *racism*, we get the impression that it was present, although seemingly very minimally. It is distant anonymous agents that are responsible for the perpetuation of racism. As such, whatever may or may not have happened in the past does not reflect on the good relationships that are present now. Kendall (2001) critiques whites' lack of desire to take racism seriously and says that racism, for whites, more resembles an intellectual exercise that can be addressed in a very methodical way. The privilege for whites, who are able to live their lives knowing very little of the experiences of people of colour, is their ability to move on from racism as opposed to having it be a central part of their lives. The temporality of racism expressed here makes it but a fleeting experience. I do not use temporality as Levine-Rasky (2002) does to mean social history but a particular temporary moment. The following example is also descriptive and exemplifies two aspects of Whitespeak: the subjectification of racism defined as when agency is bestowed on race and racism, "forcing them to perform as the 'subject,' and at the same time, removes human agency and responsibility from the discussion" (Moon, 1999, p. 188) as well as the disembodiment of the subject.

> Last year we had this conversation [on diversity and conflicts]. I think I would probably have had a certain amount to say because *it* was an issue. There was a group of five or six girls who really stuck together and really thought and looked for areas where *perhaps* they *might* have been treated differently. And *it* was a very public thing all the time *with them*. And they were all part of the community centre that was children, with probably mixed backgrounds but South American or the Islands, who really stuck very closely together and had a bit of a chip on their shoulder and maybe *went looking for it*. With the group this year, *it's* just such a non-issue…. They'd [the girls from the previous year] also gone through a very, very tough year. It probably stemmed after an incident at the community centre where one of their counsellors was gunned down. He was somebody who was very close to their hearts, and it was in the media a great deal, and the fact that he was black played into it. So I think that *it* was sort of a beginning with the kids questioning more of that and noticing differences perhaps or looking for differences, and this *particular* group tried to use their colour to question everything or to try to explain why things happened for them or didn't happen. (Interview #4146 / W-F, emphasis added)

Racism, here, is never mentioned and is only referred to as "it." We are also not clear in some instances on what "it" means, especially when the participant says that the girls went looking for "it." Does "it" here mean conflict, trouble, or that the students "went looking to identify racism"? What is happening here for Moon is the subjectification of racism, which bestows agency on race and racism, removing responsibility from whites. Subjectification "allows whitepeople to enter disengaged discussions of race and racism in ways that clearly communicate that these topics have little to do with them. This disengagement allows whitepeople to deny their own complicity in relations of racial dominations as well as any awareness or understanding of the historical legacy of white supremacy" (p. 189). The disembodiment of subjects, meanwhile, is apparent when there is mention of the killing of a counsellor. This event is completely removed from the daily realities of the violence blacks experience as a result of systemic racism. Furthermore, we also see the removal of agency in the use of the phrase "perhaps they might have been treated differently." Finally, there is once again a temporality here as well as a specificity and particularity that is given to racism. It is not persistent and pervasive but experienced by a particular group of five or six girls. This reminds me of how white racism is often reduced to a particularity, where we often hear that it is the result of a few bad people. If it is understood as being the result of a few bad white people, it must therefore only be subjected toward a few racialized people. Racism in the lives of racialized students goes largely unnoticed or unacknowledged in its complexities. It is not surprising, therefore, that racialized students harbour a great deal of animosity, distrust, fear and dismay at school officials. Evidence of despondence or lack of engagement is more readily attributed to family deficiencies than systemic racism that plagues school systems. We see the failure in acknowledging systemic racism, when those who feel marginalized and oppressed are told that it is simply a question of not being included, represented, or celebrated enough. I do not wish to minimize or trivialize teachers who are helping students cope on a day-to-day level, but to stress that racism and its complexities cannot be underestimated and celebrated away.

The following section describes the third strategy of whiteness, that of exoticizing the Other. Here I look at when and how the discourse of diversity and the notion of "inclusiveness" were invoked by participants and once again recentre whiteness as the norm.

Exoticizing the Other

The celebration of diversity was the most consistent answer given by most participants when asked what helped them to deal with diversity. Many spoke of the beauty in ethnic and racial diversity and of the wonderful colourful rainbow effect that it provides to schools and classrooms. Diverse student ethnic clubs were said to be popular and desired on the part of many students. The most prominent practice of "inclusiveness" was multicultural nights and events. Of the five discourses of whiteness that I identify in this chapter, the one that most perpetuates the national and official education discourse is that of exoticizing the Other. The central goal of multiculturalism especially as defined in the 1971 policy was to develop and maintain cultural identities of Canada as a pluralistic culture as opposed to one of a melting pot (Abu-Laban & Gabriel, 2002; Li, 1988). Although less emphasized in the revised policy of 1988, this perspective nonetheless has been prominent not only as an official policy at the federal level but also at provincial and local levels. In Ontario, the notion of diversity and the celebration of pluralism are reflected during the Ontario Heritage Week, where there are various cultural displays/events/activities that take place that during the third week of February (Government of Ontario, 2005). The Ministry of Education, schools boards, and schools themselves are also supportive of these types of practices and celebrations. The reflection and support of diversity are reflected in policy, practice, and curriculum.

Bedard (2000) provides three critiques against education through cultural understanding. In a sense, these multicultural events are perceived as being sufficient to the much-needed radical changes to Eurocentric curriculum. What evolves for Bedard is an "us" and "them" dichotomy where whiteness is naturalized as the norm and Others are relegated to the margins. What is also an issue with many of these cultural events is the "static and outdated images of non-White cultures" (p. 52). This, on the one hand, negates the dynamic changing nature of culture but also perpetuates the idea, as Razack (2002) notes, that progressiveness and evolution are traits inherent in whites. Third, trying to solve racism through the understanding of cultural difference fails to challenge whiteness as a hegemonic system of oppression. Therefore, to challenge stereotypes that rely on white essentialist notions of the past strengthens those very stereotypes (Bedard, 2000). Furthermore, the emphasis on cultural diversity results in what Razack (1998) notes in citing Mohanty, as "a harmonious, empty pluralism" (p. 9). Constructed notions of homogenized essentialized cultural communities with very restrictive notions of culture, tradition, and religion are contradictory from immigrant's actual immigration histories, cultures, and values. The various groups that are in Canada are not only distinct politically, socially, and culturally from one another but are also internally heterogeneous (Bannerji, 2000). Therefore, are schools simply extensions to what is produced in society at large? Are we encouraging manifestations of insulated communities in schools that are depoliticized and homogenized? These are all questions that future studies on schooling and the creation of enclave ethnic clubs would need to address.

The strategy of whiteness identified by Nakayama and Krizek (1999) that corresponds to the power relations that operate through the discourse of multiculturalism is when whiteness is defined as a negative, where it is defined not in what it is but what it is not. In citing Ball (1993), the authors assert that this negation "demonstrates how white people only appear after subtraction. The cultural markings of everyone else are spun out, separated, and identified in the statistical centrifuge, leaving only ... pure whites" (p. 98). Whiteness, therefore, is only "marked in reverse" (p. 98). When marked in reverse this means that power is unevenly distributed. When racialized people are on display, we must ask ourselves where the gaze is coming from. More importantly, what is the gaze of the Other constructing and sustaining? The intensity of the restrictive gaze toward racialized peoples produces a sense of oddness, "differentness," and as them being exceptions and deviations from the norm. The norm, defined as white, is rendered natural, ordinary, and universal (Harper, 2002). At the micro level, there is something more problematic with the practices required in the celebration of diversity. These events and practices often require that students, in particular racialized students, not only engage in theatrical performance as well as culinary and clothing displays but must also engage in the sharing their "stories," as expressed here:

> You just have to let everyone kind of tell their stories. Everyone learns from each other's stories, and just kind of celebrate it, and I noticed that kids like to learn about other cultures.... It's important to incorporate it, and celebrate that, that's why Canada is so multicultural and this is what makes it a good country to live in. (Interview #4124 / W-F)

> It's a celebration of our diversity and a sharing of each other's cultures. There's a great two-way street of learning from the students. You're not just being the teacher, sometimes you're the student as well. (Interview #4134 / W-M)

The assumption is often that storytelling in all contexts is positive and that power and oppression between teller and listener are non-existent. It is also rare to question who is made to tell their stories and what such practices induce and produce in the classroom. Storytelling and the sharing of experiences often befall on non-whites who are perceived as deviating from the norm (Razack, 1993). This practice, especially when directed at non-whites, continually perpetuates the idea of foreignness.

In addition to creating alienation, essentially what is removed from these "Disneyfied" stories is a complicated, rich history or philosophy that is worth exploration (Bissoondath, 1994). Not only is difference de-politicized, de-historicized, and de-contextualized but going back to the notion of the gaze, we also cannot forget the history of the commodification and exotification of the Other (hooks, 1992). What emerges in storytelling is a form of specialness that "can serve the dominant groups as entertainment, as 'that voice difference likely to bring us *what we can't have* and to divert us from the monotony of sameness'" (Trinh, 1989 as cited in Razack, 1993, p. 66, emphasis in original). Part of understanding the complexities of racism rests on understanding which bodies have continuously been objectified, essentialized, and exoticized. This also means to understand the norm to which the exoticized Other stands in relation.

The formal multiculturalism policy has been criticized by many as reflecting diversity in a superficial fashion. In questioning or critiquing the perpetuation of these practices at the school board and school level, it is also a critique of the official policy. A fourth strategy of whiteness that emerged when participants were asked how they would describe this ethnocultural diversity is what duCille (1994) refers to as the "Driving Miss Daisy Syndrome."

Driving Miss Daisy Syndrome

In these instances, participants described ethnocultural diversity as being equally represented by all groups. Whites were often said to be minorities in classrooms and schools. This identification of whiteness is completely different from the first strategy of whiteness identified by Nakayama and Krizek (1999), which ties the category *white* "closely to power in a rather crude, naked manner" (p. 96). When students in their study were asked how they defined the category *white*, one replied of it being the "majority" and another as symbolizing "status." Whiteness, as a category, authors argue, has not been "entirely hidden from view, which is crucial if it is to function as powerful" (p. 97). That is, whiteness as a system that provides privileges is somewhat visible and known to white people. What I observed in this project is somewhat different from what these authors discuss. Since this research project did not have whiteness and white privilege as central focuses, I did not find any instances when whiteness was identified as a system of oppression. A few participants in this study did identify whiteness as being a racial category, as two of the quotes below reveal:

> I thought back to that article earlier [that the participant read] where you know by the year 2000 and whatever that white Anglo-Saxons will be part of a minority, and that certainly was reflective. It's a very mixed population of all kinds of ethnic backgrounds. (Interview #4130 / W-F)

> We have mixed ethnicity. We don't have one particular group, but we have students from all over the world, and our Anglo-Saxon population would be relatively small at this point in time. (Interview #4183 / W-F)

The identification of whiteness as a racial category and the context for which this fact emerges reveals a different understanding of whiteness than that which is identified by Nakayama and Krizek (1999). Although we are made aware in the first two responses that whites are in fact present, what is most telling is when this category emerges. We see here that whiteness emerges when it is perceived as being under siege or overwhelmed by a "crowd" of recent immigrant children. Whiteness is only defined or recognized when it is de-centred and when the privileges that it awards are perceived as being threatened or lost (Hurtado, 1999). We are reminded that no one dominant group is represented.

> Oh, I think there's over 100 of them [ethnic groups]. There's just so many. … We put a big mural in front of our school with all the different countries that were represented within the school, and it was just filled, countries that I didn't even know existed…. There's not really one dominant group in my class. (Interview #4135 / W-F)

> We are a very mixed school. I wouldn't say that one culture dominates at all. It's a really healthy mix. We have kids from all over the world and, as well, different economic backgrounds. So it makes it interesting that way, and I hope the kids learn to appreciate one another and maybe feel grateful for what they do have. It makes it a lively school. (Interview #4141 / W-F)

The presence of whites, described as diminishing, is a deceiving claim in that we are made to believe that whiteness as a system of oppression is non-existent. Whiteness, and the privilege it accords to whites, is understood simply in ethnic/racial terms and less so in the power that is embedded in this category. The quantification and the positing of a numerical "equal" representation of different groups obscure the systemic ways in which dominance and power operate. The fact that whites are less represented numerically is said to imply that they are racially non-dominant and simply a racial group as any other. Again, this falsehood negates the ways in which the hegemony of whiteness is continuously in operation regardless if whites are represented as a racial majority or minority. One needs only to look at South Africa and apartheid as an example. DuCille (1994) refers to this understanding as the "Driving Miss Daisy Syndrome," whereby transformation of power, oppression, and race relations "make best friends out of driver and driven, master and slave, boss and servant, white boy and black man" (p. 615). This false assumption is perhaps most difficult to challenge as whites cannot see how white racial oppression can manifest itself in these circumstances. It is equally difficult to see this within the teacher–student dynamic, where a white teacher may see herself/himself as a racial minority in relation to racialized students and therefore cannot see how whites might racially oppress their students. We must be better able to challenge how power and oppression are conceptualized. In leaving the Driving Miss Daisy Syndrome intact, whiteness is again unchallenged in the ways that it systemically operates and in the privileges it accords to whites regardless of their smaller numerical representation. Furthermore, this furthers the discounting of oppression and marginalization of racialized people.

I now wish to examine in greater detail the final strategy of whiteness, which, in borrowing from Moon (1999), I identify as the larger strategy of bourgeois decorum, which is where "white solidarity and supremacy are discursively reproduced through bourgeois communication practices" (p. 183). It primarily operates in two ways: by euphemizing white racism and hyperpoliteness. The category of euphemizing white racism is defined as a type of coded speak or Whitespeak that manifests itself in three ways: the subjectification of racism and race, the erasure of agency (passive voice), and the disembodiment of subjects. Hyperpoliteness signifies an excessive concern with language forms.

Bourgeois Decorum

When we asked participants the question of whether they could talk about a recent event in which they adapted a practice due to ethnocultural diversity, most had difficulty answering the question. I believe the question was trying to determine if teachers felt the need to adapt curriculum to represent a more racially and ethnically diverse student clientele. A small number replied on occasion when teaching about particular foods or animals predominantly found in Canada, that they altered them in order to make them relevant to their students. Another practice was encouraging and strategically organizing students to work with other students with whom they might not have normally associated on a daily basis. Interestingly, it is the students who are made to question their assumptions about particular groups and are made to leave their comfort zones. For many researchers, however, much work needs to be done on the part of white teachers to question their own subject positions and their participation in whiteness (Bedard, 2000; Dei, 2000). Apart from substitutions and commingling, the performance of whiteness manifested itself in three specific ways when asked about adaptation of practices: the euphemizing of white racism, the use of a passive voice, and hyperpoliteness. Euphemisms, Moon (1999) contends, "are commonly utilised in everyday white discourse around racialized issues such as affirmative action, welfare reform, family values, reverse discrimination, and immigration" (p. 187).

She gives the example of whites often articulating that African Americans attended "separate" as opposed to segregated schools or that the Japanese were "relocated" as opposed to imprisoned during the Second World War. A similar practice was employed by this teacher:

> Religion is part of what we teach during the day, and very often, at certain times of the year we may talk specifically about certain events in the Bible. At Christmastime, we read a lot about the birth of Jesus and where Joseph and Mary were going and why they were going to a specific place … it's a very important figure in our program so we have to talk about the Egyptians and the slavery of the Jews in Egypt. We have a high population of Egyptian children, so we have to be very careful in how we present that because we do not want to offend the children who have that heritage. So we have to not alter but be very sensitive about the kind of language we use and the tone that we use when we present these stories.… It's that idea of, in terms of the Egyptians, trying not to make the Egyptians sound cruel and mean and, you know, they had slaves and it's just that idea. (Interview #4150 / W-F)

Although this participant is speaking of oppression committed by a racialized group as opposed to whites, it nonetheless reveals that oppression is perceived as having to be diluted. There is a difference, however, between offending and looking at agency and responsibility on the part of all involved. When looking at how whites discuss issues of race, it is important to note how euphemisms are continuously deployed and how they allow for a more sanitized discussion of seemingly offensive or distasteful subjects and negate agency (Moon, 1999).

> You know what? No. I don't think I have [adapted teaching or lesson] because as long as I've been here, I've had a very multicultural classroom in front of me so I think you're always aware of who's in front of you. And if you're teaching history, you're trying to draw attention to maybe a group of people that have been *put down* or *discriminated against* and show them that it *happens to everybody* and you have to learn from that and not repeat it. So, you know what, I don't think I've changed anything just because of who's in my room. (Interview #4141 / W-F, emphasis added)

For Moon (1999), euphemisms "work to mask the facts of domination, rendering them 'harmless or sanitized,' thereby obscuring the 'use of coercion' … [and] cloak racist expression with a veneer of 'bourgeois civility/gentility,' while enabling whitepeople freely to express racism—in coded ways—as a signal of white solidarity" (p. 188). The comment that domination happens to everybody and the need to remind students that histories of domination cannot be repeated negates the ways in which oppression, against Aboriginal peoples for instance, is ongoing and ever present. White people, when discussing issues of race, often linguistically shift, according to Moon (1999), into a kind of "white code" that allows them to discuss race issues in ways that maintain the status quo, removes them from complicity, while also securing approval from other whites. It would be interesting to do more research on how colonialism and slavery are taught by teachers. Since these systems of oppression in Canada are to this day still denied, when do teachers teach about them, and how is it done (Bannerji, 2000; Razack, 2002)? It is difficult to make specific claims here since there was less data to work with on this issue.

Another strategy utilized by participants that still coincides with the larger strategy of bourgeois decorum and in particular Whitespeak is the use of the passive voice, defined as when white people are able to recognize historical events, show a level of empathy and tolerance for racialized people, but repress any such history as being in any way related to them (Moon, 1999). Moon reveals that many of her participants had difficulties explaining and understanding the problems faced by communities of colour, noting that many focus on personal attributes versus a historical explanation. She gives this quote as an example: "I had a group of Native American kids come to campus for a tour. They were relatively intelligent kids, but had been cloistered on the reservation to the point that they were afraid to come to campus" (Moon, 1999, p. 190). She notes that in defining Native Americans as having been cloistered negates the responsibility of the agent in addition to the historical practices that contributed to such segregationist actions. Therefore, cloistering is understood as a problem whereas the history that produced such present-day cloistering is not. Something similar can be observed from the quote above where the use of the words *put down* or *discriminated against* are used as opposed to *oppressed* or *marginalized*.

In this study it also became evident that the use of a passive voice was a pervasive strategy deployed in discussions of what I call "racialized student dysfunctions," that is, from discussions on racialized students' academic achievement or level of performance.

> Their [racialized students'] environment at home, most of the time, contradicts the environment in the school. So at school there's a lot of structure in place, at home there seems to be very little, because parents are maybe working late shifts and they don't get to see their children any more. Who knows whatever it is, but this is what I'm hearing, that there's a lot of, for a lack of a better word, dysfunction within the family home life. (Interview #4125 / W-M)

> I think it's just a manifestation of something that these students have witnessed in their own culture. But now there are some difficulties that manifest more with parents. It's almost like real major difficulties. Again, this is a gross generalization, but a major issue we have there with Portuguese students is family break-up, divorce, and the major issue we have with Filipinos is the real difficulty of the family and/or the individual student making the transition from moving from the Philippines to Canada. (Interview #4138 / W-M)

In her analysis of her study participant's comment on Native American kids above, Moon (1999) contends that this participant was able to demonstrate racial tolerance, depicted as personal empathy, while still being able to avoid responsibility and awareness of the historical practices and power relations that have contributed to Native Americans' present realities. Similarly, teachers in this study were often empathetic to the students' situation but never pointed to any of the historical and present conditions that have and continue to structure these situations. What has been labelled a "dysfunction" is personalized as opposed to historicized in relation to globalization, racist immigration policies, and systemic racism. These understandings reveal that there is a lack of a critical focus on the complex socio-historical circumstances and material conditions that create students' "failure" and "success." Finally, perceptions of dysfunction are often coupled with "family issues"; however, there needs to be more discussions around what is being defined as "the family" (Dei, 1998). Moon provides another example where empathy is the only perspective given: "you're in a ghetto and nobody works because they are all on welfare. This is a broad generalization, but you're used to people in gangs, on dope, hanging out, and that's all you see. Would you get out of it? How would you get out of it?" (Moon, 1999, p. 190). A similar comment was expressed from the same participant quoted above:

> It's difficult. When I see a child come in with, I'll just give an example here, a piece of pizza that was obviously eaten before, wrapped up in a Canadian Tire flyer, your jaw just drops and your heart just wants to be out there for that child and the family, if it's what you can do. That's why our school was very instrumental in getting a breakfast program in here really quickly, and doing something to help these families.... Our hearts go out to these children. We know where they're coming from. (Interview #4125 / W-M)

I am not questioning here the teacher's or the school's motive and intentions in trying to help and provide support to marginalized children. The issue is in how the conditions with which racialized people live are de-historicized and de-contextualized, and much like Moon, I am questioning the lack of agency and responsibility on the part of whites and lack of understanding of how white privilege secures benefits and privileges not available to all. Moon's explanation of her scenarios directly speaks to the quote about the child eating out of a paper flyer. Although there is the recognition of the existence of reservations and the ghettos, how such sites came into existence is absent from her participants' frame of reference. Reservations and ghettos are de-historicized, and the power relations that have created such spaces in the first place are obscured. While reducing these debates to individualist terms allows both female participants in Moon's study to show concern, empathy, and tolerance for "dysfunctional" behaviour, it also enables them to remove or distance themselves from any involvement. Agency, social responsibility, and the privileges that have been gained from the very conditions that have produced such situations are absent. Again, economic and social hardship are recognized; however, the relational perspective of privilege is not. Both women are described as using the passive voice to indicate, according to Moon (1999), that "'something' happened to 'someone' (e.g., 'they' somehow ended up on a reservation or in a ghetto), without identifying the historical agents who conspired in these events" (pp. 190–191).

I recognize that we are not made aware of whether the child mentioned above is white or not. The purpose of including this quote was on the one hand to show how whites fail to historicize and contextualize conditions of oppression in relation to race. If the child was in fact white, it would still not prevent us from doing an analysis on race. Some may read the quote as testimony that the problem is in fact not race but class. When I hear the comment that everything is not race and that there are poor white children in schools, it tells me that once again, that whites are not seen as being raced. Interestingly for many white participants, class was in fact perceived as the most pressing issue as opposed to race. When the performance of racialized students is described as poor and weak, it is understood as being the result of poverty and not racism. It is easier to understand classism as being in operation as opposed to racism. We must acknowledge that poverty is racialized and gendered. The poorest people in Canada are more likely to be racialized women. The desire to relegate race to a subordinate position within an additive model negates the complexities of the organization of hierarchies (Razack, 1998). I therefore agree with Razack when she states that "if we take as our point of departure that systems of domination interlock and sustain one another, we can begin to identify those moments when we are dominant and those when we are subordinate" (p. 159).

Conclusion

There are several immediate things that can be done to further social justice and equality. For one, curriculum in Initial Teacher Education Programs needs to have a politicized focus that will enable students, willing or not, to engage with issues of race and white privilege (Harper, 2002). As part of the curriculum that is taught in Initial Teacher Education Programs, we also need to challenge the notion of the inaccessibility or "non-practical" nature of theory that is so often levelled by teachers. We may also need to think about the prerequisites for candidates. Programs should require students to have a minimum amount of credits in courses that take up the question of race and racism in Canada. Furthermore, in seeing that compulsory critical multicultural courses in Initial Teacher Education Programs are often met with great resistance on the part of white students (Schick, 2002), it is imperative that we have qualified, experienced individuals who are able to challenge the hostility and denial that emerges.

I also believe that in order to better understand the pervasiveness and the universalizing nature of whiteness, white teachers must question their own subjectivity and their role in this system of oppression. Whiteness as deployed by white teaching personnel is continually depicted as the norm, universal, and unproblematic, to the extent that racial identity is only something to be recognized by non-whites (duCille, 1994). Interestingly, learning, as it pertains to race, is continually framed in a singular direction: student to teacher. There is the perception that teachers will learn about race and racism from the children themselves, the problem here is that children are just that: children. Assuming that children will have the best way to deal with issues of racism is presumptuous and, secondly, again negates the ways in which systemic racism and white privilege plague the educational system.

Finally, within the actual school system, measures need to be put in place to allow teachers and administrators to attend conferences and symposiums on issues of colonialism, slavery, racism, and whiteness. I do not believe that we need to reorganize or create new programs in order to make this possible for teaching personnel. There are numerous local conferences and one-day symposiums that take place on a monthly basis throughout the Greater Toronto Area. Some have no costs while others are offered for minimal fees. Understanding that teachers are extremely overburdened and overwhelmed with issues, we need to find ways to "incorporate" these kinds of activities in their professional lives while not adding to their already hectic schedules.

The suggestions that I provide above are by no means exhaustive, and much work needs to be done on many different levels, including policy, curriculum, training, and so on if we are to achieve greater equality in schools.

This includes also looking at systemic racism in Initial Teacher Education Programs as well as in schools.

Notes

1. Hall (1997), who relies on Foucault, defines discourse as "a group of statements which provide a language for talking about—a way of representing the knowledge about—a particular topic at a particular historical moment" (p. 44).
2. Although this chapter is more specifically focused on race and ethnocultural diversity, the larger national project addressed other types of diversities, such as sexual orientation, gender, and so forth, which were taken up by other researchers in different sites.
3. The research project has an official website where more details on the study can be obtained—www.teachcan.ca.
4. Interviews are identified with an identification number, as white males (W-M) or white females (W-F).
5. As indicated above, this information was obtained from an Ontario School Board website. Although this information is public and accessible to anyone, considering the location of where interviews were conducted for this project, I am fearful that identifying the website would compromise ethical consideration and participant anonymity. I therefore prefer to simply indicate the reference as being from an Ontarian School Board website.

References

Abu-Laban, Y. & Gabriel, C. (2002). *Selling diversity: Immigration, multiculturalism, employment equity, and globalization*. Peterborough: Broadview Press.

Ball, E. (1993, May 18). The white issue. *The Village Voice*, 24–27.

Bannerji, H. (2000). *The dark side of the nation: Essays on multiculturalism, nationalism and gender*. Toronto: Canadian Scholars' Press.

Bedard, G. (2000). Deconstructing whiteness: Pedagogical implications for anti-racism education. In G.J.S. Dei & A. Calliste (Eds.), *Power, knowledge and anti-racism education: A critical reader* (pp. 41–56). Halifax: Fernwood.

Bissoondath, N. (1994). *Selling illusions: The cult of multiculturalism in Canada*. Toronto: Penguin Books.

Dei, G.J.S. (1998).The politics of educational change: Taking anti-racism education seriously. In V. Satzewich, (Ed.), *Racism & social inequality in Canada: Concepts, controversies & strategies of resistance* (pp. 299–314). Toronto: Thompson Educational Publishing.

Dei, G.J.S. (2000). Towards an anti-racism discursive framework. In G.J.S. Dei, & A. Calliste (Eds.), *Power, knowledge and anti-racism education: A critical reader* (pp. 23–40). Halifax: Fernwood.

duCille, A. (1994). The occult of true black womanhood: Critical demeanor and black feminist studies. *Signs: Journal of Women in Culture and Society, 19*(3), 591–629.

Fairclough, N. (2001). The discourse of new labour: Critical discourse analysis. In M. Wetherell, S. Taylor & S. Yates (Eds.), *Discourse as data: A guide for analysis* (pp. 229–266). London: Sage.

Frankenberg, R. (1993). *White women, race matters: The social organization of whiteness*. Minneapolis: University of Minnesota Press.

Frankenberg, R. (Ed.). (1997). Introduction. In R. Frankenberg (Ed.), *Displacing whiteness: essays in social and cultural criticism* (pp. 1–33). London: Duke University Press.

Government of Ontario. (2005). *Heritage week celebrates Ontario's diversity.* Press release, Feb 21, 2005. Retrieved February 15, 2007, from www.ogov.newswire.ca/ontario/GPOE/2005/02/21/c6639.html?lmartch=%E2%8C%A9=_e.html.

Hall, S. (1997). The work of representation. In S. Hall (Ed.), *Representation: Cultural representation and signifying practices* (pp. 13–74). London: Sage.

Harper, H. (2002). When the big snow melts: White women teaching in Canada's north. In C. Levine-Rasky (Ed.), *Working through whiteness: International perspectives* (pp. 269–288). Albany: State University of New York Press.

hooks, b. (1992). *Black looks: Race and representation.* Boston: South End Press.

Hurtado, A. (1999). The trickster's play: Whiteness in the subordination and liberation process. In R.D. Torres, L.F. Mirón and J.X. Inda (Eds.), *Race, identity, and citizenship: A reader* (pp. 225–243). Malden, MA: Blackwell Publishers.

Karim, K.H. (1993). Reconstructing the multicultural community in Canada: Discursive strategies of inclusion and exclusion. *International Journal of Politics, Culture and Society, 7*(2), 189–207.

Kendall, F.E. (2001). *Understanding white privilege.* Retrieved February 15, 2007, from www.alumni.berkeley.edu/Students/Leadership/Online_LRC/Diversity_Center/Understanding_White_Priveledge.asp.

Levine-Rasky, C. (2002). Critical/relational/contextual: Toward a model for studying whiteness. In C. Levine-Rasky (Ed.), *Working through whiteness: International perspectives* (pp. 319–352). Albany: State University of New York Press.

Li, P. (1988). *Ethnic inequality in a class society.* Toronto: Thompson Educational Publishing.

Luke, A. (1995). Text and discourse in education: An introduction to critical discourse analysis. *Review of Research in Education, 21,* 3–48.

Moon, D. (1999). Whiteness in U.S. contexts. White enculturation and bourgeois ideology: The discursive production of "good (white) girls." In T.K. Nakayama and J.N. Martin (Eds.), *Whiteness: The communication of social identity* (pp. 177–97). Thousand Oaks, CA: Sage.

Nakayama, T.K., & Krizek, R. (1999). Whiteness as a strategic rhetoric. In T.K. Nakayama and J.N. Martin (Eds.), *Whiteness: The communication of social identity* (pp. 87–106). Thousand Oaks, CA: Sage.

Razack, S. (2002). Introduction: When place becomes race. In S. Razack (Ed.), *Race, space, and the law: Unmapping a white settler society* (pp.1–20). Toronto: Between the Lines.

Razack, S. (1998). *Looking white people in the eye: Gender, race, and culture in courtrooms and classrooms.* Toronto: University of Toronto Press.

Razack, S. (1993). Story-telling for social change. *Gender and Education, 5*(1), 55–70.

Rich, A. (1979). *On lies, secrets, and silence.* New York: W.W. Norton & Company.

Shadd, A. (1991). Institutionalized racism and Canadian history: Notes of a Black Canadian. In O. McKague (Ed.), *Racism in Canada* (pp. 1–13). Saskatoon: Fifth House Publishers.

Schick, C. (2002). Keeping the ivory tower white: Discourses of racial domination. In S. Razack (Ed.), *Race, space and the law: Unmapping a white settler society* (pp. 99–119). Toronto: Between the Lines.

Solomon, P.R., Portelli, J.P., Daniel, B.J., & Campbell, A. (2005). The discourse of denial: How white teacher candidates construct race, racism and "white privilege." *Race Ethnicity and Education, 8*(2), 147–169.

Sue, D.W. (2004). Whiteness and ethnocentric monoculturalism: Making the "invisible" visible. *American Psychologist, 59*(8), 761–769.

van Dijk, T.A. (1993). Editor's forward to critical discourse analysis. *Discourse & Society, 4*(2), 131–132.

Wander, M., Martin, J., & Nakayama, T.K. (1999). Whiteness and beyond: Sociohistorical foundations of whiteness and contemporary challenges. In T.K. Nakayama and J.N. Martin (Eds.), *Whiteness: The communication of social identity* (pp. 13–26). Thousand Oaks, CA: Sage Publications.

CHAPTER 5

Student Diversity and Schooling in Metropolitan Toronto
A COMPARATIVE ANALYSIS OF THE DISCOURSES OF ANGLOPHONE AND FRANCOPHONE SCHOOL PERSONNEL

Diane Gérin-Lajoie

Multiculturalism in Canada has been part of the official discourse for more than 30 years now. Following the federal Commission on Bilingualism and Biculturalism at the end of the 1960s, a policy on multiculturalism was implemented by Prime Minister Pierre Elliott Trudeau at the beginning of the 1970s. In 1988, the Multiculturalism Act came into effect. Although it was a piece of federal legislation, its impact has also been felt in areas of provincial jurisdiction, such as education.

Provincial Ministries of Education across Canada developed specific guidelines in regard to the integration of immigrant children in their schools. In English Canada, the integration of immigrant children was defined as multicultural education, whereas in Quebec the official discourse referred to it as intercultural education. In the case of the former, the official discourse emphasized the recognition that all cultures are equal in Canada and as such should be respected and celebrated in the context of the linguistic and cultural duality of the country; meanwhile, intercultural education focused on developing a dialogue between cultures and integrating newcomers into the host society, as part of a project of creating a "new society" (Gérin-Lajoie, 1995). In both cases, the emphasis was on newcomer students' assimilation to the majority society.

The increasing racial, ethnic, and linguistic diversity among students has considerably altered the social mapping of the schools over the years. One must wonder how teachers and principals make sense of their working reality and how they adapt to the situation in order to answer the needs of all students—in regards to the curriculum, the pedagogical tools to be used, the languages and cultures to promote, and so forth. In Ontario, for example, do the Ontario Ministry of Education, faculties of education, and school boards provide school personnel with the appropriate support to accomplish a true integration of all students, as diverse as they are, in both anglophone and francophone school systems?

Recent works by critical theorists and educators, such as those of Ladson-Billings (2004), Popkewitz (1998, 2000), and Dei (1999) to name a few, have raised questions about the nature of racial, ethnic, and linguistic student inclusion in schools. In regard to French minority language education in Canada, my own research points out the shortcomings of a framework that ignores the complexities of the socio-political context in which French language schools evolve and the way that students are—or are not—positively integrated (Gérin-Lajoie, 2003, 2006). Following in these steps, I will attempt in this chapter to deconstruct the discourses of teachers and principals on the notions of racial, ethnic, and linguistic student diversity and inclusion in relation to the official discourse.

In recent years, education has seen teachers' and principals' positions regulated by the discursive formations of school achievement, accountability, and teachers' professionalization. Voithofer and Foley (2007), using Foucault's definition of discursive formation, explain how discursive formations shape subject positions in the following terms:

> According to Foucault (1972), a discursive formation is defined by how institutions regulate "truth" and contribute to the construction of subject positions, concepts and strategic choices. In other words, discursive formations shape subject positions for students and educators through concepts such as accountability, assessment, and standards that are dispersed through strategies including legislation, content, and performance standards, policies, pedagogies, and research funding. (p. 16)

Discourses represent ways of thinking bounded by shared assumptions (Niesz, 2006). In Ontario, educational policies and reforms have, over the past 15 years, reflected a paradigm shift of the official discourse toward a tighter regulation of teacher work and student performance. For example, the creation of the Ontario College of Teachers in 1997 and the provincial testing of Grades 3 and 6 students that began in 1993 demonstrate how the government position shifted toward instituting a more accountable educational system. Accountability has been at the centre of the official discourse in recent years. Consequently, students' racial, ethnic, and linguistic diversity and the inclusion of this diverse school population are no longer at the forefront of education politics in Ontario.

How then do teachers and principals take into account students' racial, ethnic, and linguistic diversity, and most importantly, how does student inclusion fit into the actual official policy discourse, which shows less concern about inclusive practices than it did in the past? How similar or different is the teaching reality in French minority language schools from the reality lived by teachers in the English language majority schools? How do school personnel make sense of their realities? To address such questions, I will present a comparative analysis of school personnel discourses on the notion of students' racial, ethnic, and linguistic diversity in English and in French language schools in Ontario. I will specifically examine whether teachers and principals who are working in French language schools share similar concerns to those of their English language counterparts, in regard to students' racial, ethnic, and linguistic diversity in their schools. The sociological analysis of teacher and principal discourses on the issue of student diversity will draw from the results of interviews performed with a sample of teachers and principals from Toronto who participated in Project 4 of a national study.[1] These interview participants work in the anglophone majority schools, as well as in the francophone minority schools in Metropolitan Toronto. I will illustrate how, in both school contexts, school practices are influenced by the presence of a significant ethnic, linguistic, and racial diversity among the students.

Before presenting the analysis of the results, I will locate the issue of students' racial, ethnic, and linguistic diversity in schools in examining the critical literature that highlights the shortcomings of neoliberal and neoconservative approaches to student diversity and to inclusion. Second, I will give an overview of the Ontario official discourse on students' racial, ethnic, and linguistic diversity mainly through its educational policies. In a subsequent section, I will briefly address the reality of French minority language education in Ontario, which is relatively unknown to the public. Then I will give a short description of the methodology used in this study. My analysis will then be divided into three main areas: 1) teachers' and principals' discourses on students' racial, ethnic, and linguistic diversity in their schools; 2) teachers' and principals' discourses on the impact of students' racial, ethnic, and linguistic diversity on their work and how well prepared they feel they are to accomplish that work, and 3) teachers' and principals' discourses on the notion of language.

Schooling and Students' Racial, Ethnic, and Linguistic Diversity

Over the years, the issue of student diversity in the school system has been examined from different angles and from different standpoints. Critical theory—the standpoint that I privilege for my analysis—questions how well racial, ethnic, and linguistic minorities are integrated in the school system (Dei, 1999; Henry & Tator, 1999; Ladson-Billings, 2004; Popkewitz, 1998, 2000; Sleeter & Grant, 1991; Solomon & Levine-Rasky, 1996). In an attempt to shed light on power relations, critical theorists demonstrate in their writings how minorities are denied equal access to schooling because of their location within the power structure. My own work in the area of French minority language education also points to an integration model that does not take into consideration the social, political, and economic context in which schools operate. Within the French minority language education context, a "majority"-oriented philosophy is at the very core of the official discourse (Gérin-Lajoie, 2002, 2003, 2006).

However, the notion of integration has been firmly inscribed in the official discourse in North America and around the world for some time now. The official discourse, grounded in a version of multicultural education that still promotes the celebration of difference, "understanding and respect" for students from diverse racial, ethnic, and linguistic backgrounds, remains the reference point for most teachers and principals. This discourse continues, nevertheless, to ignore social justice or equity issues. Furthermore, it is not uncommon to see race and ethnicity "ignored." The "colour-blind" approach denies that skin colour can matter and that racism can also exist in schools (Dei, 1999; Sleeter, 2004). Addressing the issue of multicultural education in Ontario in particular, Shaikh (2006) mentions the following:

> Over the last 35 years, multicultural education in Ontario schools for the most part, has superficially dealt with the cultural distinctiveness of various groups, choosing to focus on token recognitions commonly referred to as the "foods and festivals" approach (concept borrowed from Ladson-Billings, 1994). (p. 23)

Advocates for social justice claim that the educational system must go beyond simply recognizing differences among students. Anti-racism education looks specifically at how educational policies and practices contribute significantly to the reproduction of all sorts of inequalities, where race is central. As explained by Harper (1997) "anti-racist education examines issues of power and powerlessness in connection with how particular racial identities are produced as normal or aberrant in school contexts" (p. 201). The examination of racism, personal prejudices, and systemic discrimination is at the foundation of this approach. Similarly, critical multicultural education "challenges the traditional and cultural hegemony" (Henry & Tator, 1999, p. 98) of the school system. Critical multiculturalism, among other things, "focusses on empowerment and resistance to forms of subjugation; the politization and mobilization of marginalized groups" (Henry & Tator, 1999, p. 98). Contrary to multicultural education, where tolerance and accommodation are at the centre of its philosophy, critical multicultural education is concerned with justice and equity. Both anti-racism education and critical multicultural education call for a serious re-examination of how social practices are embedded in the power structure of the educational system and of the existing society, and of the impact of social practices of power on school practices.

As agents of social, cultural, and linguistic reproduction, teachers play a key role in the lives of their students. However, there is a common understanding among anti-racist and critical multiculturalist theorists that teachers are still not trained adequately to work with racial, ethnic, and linguistic diversity among students (Gérin-Lajoie, 2002; King, 2004; Mujawamariya & Mahrouse, 2004; Solomon & Levine-Rasky, 1996). Solomon and Levine-Rasky (1996) insist on the "urgent need for pre-service and in-service teacher education to integrate anti-racism into a pedagogy that does not separate or isolate it from other social and political movements" (p. 339). King (2004) explains that teachers have "limited and distorted understandings" about inequity and diversity (p. 72). She names it "dysconscious racism":

> Dysconscious racism is a form of racism that tacitly accepts dominant White norms and privileges. It is not the *absence* of consciousness (i.e., not unconsciousness) but an *impaired* consciousness or distorted way of thinking as compared to, for example, critical consciousness. Uncritical ways of thinking about racial inequity accept certain culturally sanctioned assumptions, myths, and beliefs that justify the social and economic advantages White people have as a result of subordinating diverse others. (King, 2004, p. 73)

Where dysconscious racism prevails, teachers' actual practices tend to maintain and reproduce inequity (Mujawamariya & Mahrouse, 2004). Teachers must commit themselves to the principle of social justice in their practices with students (Solomon & Levine-Rasky, 1996). As argued by Popkewitz (1998) 10 years ago with regard to the United States, teacher education and teaching must look for "new forms of socialization" (p. 121). Although some might say that progress has been made, training for diversity is not a priority in teacher education (Jones, 2000).

I would like to add to this discussion my own interpretation of the present situation of the inclusion of racial, ethnic, and linguistic minorities in the school system. Despite the fact that some efforts have been made to make diversity part of the official discourse for some years now, very little improvement shows in the area of student inclusion. In addition, the majority of the work on the issue of student diversity has been done in the context of Canadian majority settings, in schools where the language of instruction is the province's official language, the dominant language. In Ontario, English is the language of the majority. However, francophones, as an official minority in Canada, have the right to be educated in French under the Canadian

Charter of Rights and Freedom. As a consequence, French minority language schools, where French as the first language is the language of instruction, exist in Ontario. They, too, have a very heterogeneous school population in terms of race, culture, and language. In this school context, immigrant students become a "minority within a minority," which complexifies the work performed by teachers and principals. Minorization takes then a different meaning in this particular context of power relations, where the francophone host society is itself a minority within the anglophone Ontario context. The newcomers find themselves in a situation where they have to integrate into a community that is itself minoritized.

Student Diversity in the Official Discourse on the Ontario Educational Scene

With the 1971 Multiculturalism Policy, created by the Trudeau federal government, Ministries of Education across Canada were encouraged to define their own student inclusion guidelines in regard to an increasingly diversified population. Provincial and territorial governments needed to develop an infrastructure that would meet the needs of a new type of school population—that from immigration. Although not a reality everywhere in the country, school systems across Canada were expected to provide some guidelines for the inclusion of students from diverse racial, ethnic, and linguistic backgrounds.

In Ontario (the province with the highest number of immigrants in the country), the Ministry of Education and school boards, especially in urban settings, were attentive to the issue of student inclusion early on. In line with the Multiculturalism Act, the Ontario educational system promoted the recognition of cultures in the schools. Multicultural education in Ontario, as stated by the Ministry of Education and Training in 1992, in the 1980s meant "creating and enhancing understanding of and respect for cultural and racial diversity" (p. 35). However, as critiques have pointed out, this approach to inclusion was superficial; it has commonly been referred to as the "foods and festivals" approach (Shaikh, 2006) or, as explained by Harper (1997), "celebrating diversity." In 1987, a provincial advisory committee was struck to examine the issue of student inclusion in schools. The recommendations made by that committee led to the writing of the *Anti-racist and Ethnocultural Equity in School Boards: Guidelines for Policy Development and Implementation*, released in 1993 (Lloyd, 1998). However, the Conservative government that was elected in June 1995 never officially followed through with the implementation of these guidelines. It was left to the school boards to create their own inclusion policy. Consequently, the issue of anti-racist and ethnocultural equity in Ontario schools found itself in a grey zone.

Since the publication of these guidelines in 1993, the issue of immigrant student inclusion in Ontario schools has been relegated to a low priority in schools and school boards across the province, even in urban areas where most of the immigrant population is found. For example, in Toronto only, the number of new immigrants since 1991 represents 21 percent of the total population, and 43 percent of the population reported being members of a "visible minority." The top four visible minority groups in Toronto are South Asian, Chinese, black, and Filipino (City of Toronto, 2007). Today, it is not uncommon to find that in the majority opinion, racial, ethnic, and linguistic diversity is less of an issue in schools than before because it is not considered a new and high-priority phenomenon relative to other concerns (e.g., safe schools, standardized testing, etc.), unless diversity is seen to cause problems. In such cases, these problems are typically considered to require intervention oriented toward specific individuals, and to be resolved as quickly as possible.

However, in its *Report to the Government of Ontario* in 1994, the Ontario Royal Commission on Learning emphasizes the importance of serving all students in the province:

> The Commission takes with utmost seriousness the school system's mandate to serve all students. It means that the system needs to ensure that every school is welcoming to every faith, first language ethnocultural background, or colour. Ontario must not only build inclusive schools and curricula but, because a student can be formally included but still marginalized, the province must also create schools and curricula that place the views, concerns, and needs of all students and communities at the very centre of teacher's work. (p. 87)

Although a significant number of recommendations made by the commission were taken up by what was at the time the new Conservative government, student diversity, and most importantly, from the commissioners' point of view, students' equity was ignored by the government in power. From the government perspective, other issues have been considered to be more pressing. As a matter of fact, since the early 1990s, policies and school reforms in Ontario have focused mainly on three major areas: accountability, teacher professionalization, and governance (Anderson & Ben Jaafar, 2006). The issue of true student inclusion has thus been lost in a sea of prescriptive measures to make schools more accountable to diverse stakeholders, such as government representatives, policy makers, parents, and the population in general (Gérin-Lajoie, 2007).

All educational policies in Ontario apply to both English and French language schools. Both school systems must comply with the same Ministry of

Education requirements. One language planning policy, however, concerns only French language schools, which is the *Aménagement linguistique* policy. This language planning policy was released in 2004. Its objective is to help schools contribute to the maintenance of the French language and culture in Ontario. French language education in Ontario is much more than "teaching the curriculum in French." The province's francophone community looks up to its schools to protect, transmit, and enhance French language and culture. In this context, French language education is different from French immersion. French immersion serves children wishing to learn French as a second language. French language education serves children whose parents have a right to have them educated in the French language and culture. The *Aménagement linguistique*, or language planning policy, sets guidelines for all institutions in Ontario providing French language education. A strong emphasis is put on the process of identity construction among students. The school, with the family and sometimes in the place of the family, sees its role as one of agent of linguistic and cultural reproduction. We will see, however, in the next section, that this role is not always well understood by teachers and principals.

The Reality of French Minority Language Education in Ontario

Ontario has a total population of more than 12.5 million individuals, 2,153,045 of whom identified as a "visible minority" (Statistics Canada, 2001). The francophone population in Ontario includes 548,940 individuals and constitutes 4.8 percent of the total population of the province.[2] Among these francophones, 10.3 percent, or 58,520, are members of a "visible minority," a third of whom live in Toronto. The number of francophone "visible minorities" in Ontario has increased more than 40 percent between 1996 and 2001 (Office for Francophone Affairs, 2007). Consequently, the social fabric of the francophone community has changed considerably in recent years.

Not only has the francophone community become more multiracial in recent years, but its language practices have also changed significantly over time, due to the increasing influence of English language and culture on francophones' lives. However, changes in language practices occurred prior to the immigration wave. In the urbanization era, a significant number of francophones left their rural communities, which were mostly homogeneous in linguistic and cultural terms, to establish themselves in urban settings where English language and culture were predominant. Linguistic diversity was soon part of francophones' lives. They worked in English and interacted increasingly with the anglophone majority. Mixed marriages were more and more common, where francophones who were bilingual had to speak English because of the inability of their spouses to speak French. Crossing linguistic borders on a regular basis became the reality of a large number of francophones in Ontario. The influence of the anglophone majority had a tremendous impact on the francophones' individual and collective identity. Through these social, linguistic, and cultural changes, the school has nonetheless remained an essential institution for francophones living as a minority in Ontario.

The school, along with the family and the church, has contributed significantly to maintaining the French language and the French culture in this minority context. Over the years, education has played a political role in French minority language communities, as the sphere through which francophones gained rights. Francophones who live outside of Quebec are considered an official minority in Canada. They have the right to be educated in French under article 23 of the Canadian Charter of Rights and Freedoms, which guarantees—under specific criteria—children to be educated in the language of the official minority of the province or territory where they reside.

In Ontario, there are 397 French minority language schools, at the elementary and secondary levels, where the language of instruction is French as a first language. All courses are then taught in French, with the exception of the English as a Second Language subject. These schools are different from French immersion schools, where the student population is anglophone. French immersion schools are under the responsibility of anglophone school boards. French minority language schools are run by francophone school boards and must admit francophone students or students from a francophone heritage only.[3]

The student population in French minority language schools is, however, diversified in its capacity to speak French. Some of the students speak French fluently, but others have little and, in some cases, no knowledge of French when they start school. Even for those who speak French fluently, some prefer English or other languages to French. The linguistic heterogeneity in the schools arises from a large number of students from mixed-marriage families, where one parent is francophone and the other is a speaker of a language other than French. Even in families where both parents are francophone, in some instances, the language used at home is a language other than French, predominantly English. In addition, in recent years, a newly arrived immigrant student population from diverse linguistic, racial, and ethnic origins with ties to the French-speaking world raises the question of how to serve students best (Gérin-Lajoie, 1995, 2002). Teachers are then placed in a situation where they have to work with a very diversified school population and where language competencies vary depending on the family context in which the students live.

The language practices that take place in school reflect the duality of living continually in between two (or more) languages and cultures. Under these circumstances, students easily cross language borders. Yet French minority language school teachers face the challenge of holding the primary responsibility for reproducing the French language and French culture. Because of their direct contact on a daily basis with the students, French minority language school teachers participate actively in the students' identity construction process. In this social context, where the francophone minority counts on the school system to maintain the minority language and culture, teachers' work takes on new significance, especially when we compare this to the work performed by teachers in anglophone schools. Surprisingly though, this "added" responsibility is not always fully comprehended by teachers, and the political role of the French minority language school is rarely recognized by teachers (Gérin-Lajoie, 2001, 2002). In the present provincial social context, where notions of accountability, professionalization, and governance are front and centre, teachers are more concerned with the expectations brought about by educational reforms than with reflecting on their role as agents of linguistic and cultural reproduction.

After this brief overview of the francophone reality in Ontario, I will turn now to the analysis of the research results of the present study, which I will preface with a few words on the methodology used to collect the data.

The Methodology

The results used for the present analysis are drawn from the first set of interviews conducted in 2003 with 100 participants (teachers and principals) from the Toronto metropolitan area, in the context of Project 4—a longitudinal sub-study on school personnel practices. The interview was about the career path of the interviewees and included a final section about their actual work. In this section of the interview, the Toronto research team asked specifically about students' racial, ethnic, and linguistic diversity and its impact on their work as teachers or principals.

THE PARTICIPANTS

The participants from Metropolitan Toronto are teachers and principals who work in four school boards. Two of these boards are anglophone (one is Catholic and the other is non-confessional), and the two others are francophone (as well, one is Catholic and the other non-confessional).

Out of the 100 participants, 84 are teachers (70 anglophones and 14 francophones) and 16 are principals (12 anglophones and four francophones).

They were working in 15 different schools at the time of the first interview (some of them moved to new schools during the course of the study—we followed them in their new work environment). The majority—11—of those were English language schools: five non-confessional with two elementary and three secondary schools; and six Catholic schools with three elementary and three secondary schools. There were four French language schools: two non-confessional, with one elementary and one secondary school; and two Catholic schools, one at the elementary level and one at the secondary level.

THE ANALYSIS

In what follows, teachers and principals express their views on students' diversity and how prepared they feel they are to work with a diversified school population in both linguistic school systems. Finally, the notion of language was brought up by several participants and will be discussed. My intent is to critically examine these results within the socio-political context in which they take place, acknowledging that social practices are embedded in power relations, within the group itself as well as outside of its boundaries.

The Results

TEACHERS' AND PRINCIPALS' DISCOURSES ON DIVERSITY

All participants acknowledged the presence of a highly diversified school population in terms of race, ethnic background, and language; many of them were proud to mention the number of different minorities that were present in their schools. Being located in and around Toronto, the participants are working in schools at the centre of the immigration influx that Toronto has experienced in the past and present times in the anglophone majority, as well as in the francophone minority.

In the teacher and principal discourses, student inclusion means mostly celebrating diversity, as expressed by several participants:

> I think we try to assimilate them into Canadian culture as much as possible, and treat them fairly and equitably. Like this week, for example, we're celebrating multiculturalism by having every day a different nationality have some displays. During lunchtime we play games coming from different ethnic backgrounds. We pray in different languages. This week every day we have students praying in their own language. We talk about diverse cultures. Every year we do something different. Some years here they had multicultural night when they invited various ethnic groups,

> dance groups or singers, to put on a show. So in that respect we celebrate our differences by bringing out the most positive things from various ethnic groups, whether it's food or music or so, we allow them to play their music and share their books and their costumes. You know, to display their costumes, ethnic costumes at lunchtime, so other students can see. (Interview #4153, anglophone school)

> I am heavily involved with the annual multicultural night, which we just had last Friday, and it's a celebration of our diversity and a sharing of each other's cultures. There's a great two-way street of learning from the students. You're not just being the teacher, sometimes you're the student as well. They're able to teach you so much about what they've been through in terms of their immigration history. Their story of what caused their family to choose Canada. (Interview #4134, anglophone school)

> We acknowledge all the holidays. And there's always an assembly presentation. We do songs. We do poems. We do books. We do reading activities around all the cultural celebrations. So, it's just really nice. (Interview #4198, anglophone school)

The participants' discourse deployed here is in line with how multicultural education has been understood in the official discourse for the past 20 years. This notion of racial, ethnic, and linguistic integration refers to the celebration of students' folkloric origins, the "foods and festivals" concept as described by many (Harper, 1997; Ladson-Billings, 1994). Principles of social justice are not at the centre of participants' discourse, although each of them is empathic to the students' challenges as newly arrived in Canada. In this particular study, several interviewees have mentioned the fact that most of the immigrant children at their school live in poverty. In this context, not only do the students need to adapt to the school, but they need to have decent living conditions to help their inclusion process. As explained by these teachers:

> Most of them are from very poor families. A lot of them are still coming in coats that are too small, coats with zippers that are broken, winter boots they're just starting to get.... I would say most of my two classes are like that. (Interview #4195, anglophone school)

> A lot of them come from single-parent families. A lot of them come to school without lunch. Clothes are ripped. Not all of them, I think, some are okay, but the majority I'd say are in the low socio-economic range. Yes. (Interview #4124, anglophone school)

> These students are so needy. I don't know how aware you are of that? A lot of them are refugees and a lot of them live in one-bedroom apartments with up to sometimes 14 people. (Interview #4194, anglophone school)

Economic inequalities are persistent among visible minorities. In fact, we are in the presence of a colour-coded vertical mosaic, where a persistent gap remains between groups. With the presence of an increasing refugee population, the gap is not going to narrow soon. Referring to the cohort of immigrants who entered Canada in 1991, Chai and Zietsma (2003) explain that "the 1991 cohort, who arrived during a period of economic recession and who were more likely to be refugees than the other cohorts, had lower earnings and took longer to report having them than the 1981 cohort" (p. 28). Even with educational credentials, a lot of immigrants, refugees in particular, fail to get decent jobs. In the context of the schools that we studied, the harsh economic situation experienced by a lot of families is difficult to overcome, most particularly in the case of refugee families.

Another phenomenon, found mostly within English language schools, is that of the high turnover of minority students. This is another major challenge for some of the teachers and principals interviewed. Not only are students arriving at these schools at different levels than the other students in their class, but for some their stay at the same school is sometimes very short. Consequently, teachers must adapt to constant student population changes within their own classrooms, as explained by some of the participants:

> [We have] high turnover. Not last year but the year before we had a population of about 750. Well, 330 moved. And another 350 moved in to replace them. And it tends to be that the parents or families who are integrating successfully into Canada will move from here within a year or 18 months. So what that tends to do is to focus more and concentrate more in this school families who are not being successful. (Interview #4193, anglophone school)

> Before Christmas I lost four children, the first week back I got two, and I'm getting two more this week. So it's always you lose some, but then new ones come. Sometimes it's the same day. One goes out the door and two more come in, or two go out the door, one comes in, next week you get another one. I can tell you even in my school picture, the class photo, half of them—almost half of them in each class are gone to another school. So I find that very different. And I know it's not just kindergarten, it's all the grades. So I think in the higher grades that must be a big pressure. Just get the books, and they might be here a month. I had one child who came for two days and then was off to another school. Two days. Just got

> him in, got him his journal, he writes one thing, drew one picture, and then he wasn't here for three or four days, he came back one day to get his stuff and left. They're just coming in and going out. (Interview #4195, anglophone school)

The transience of the school population is presented more often than not as an issue for school personnel working in the outskirts of Toronto or in the inner city rather than in any other area of Toronto. School personnel and, mostly teachers, deal with a difficult teaching situation in some cases. They must adapt to continual changes in the social mapping of their classroom. This now constitutes their working reality.

Finally, a few participants mentioned the fact that they do not see any differences among their students that would be based on race, ethnicity, or language. For some of them, all students are the same. As expressed by the following participants:

> The school population is very diversified, but I have been in this for some years now, and there is no difference for me between the kids. (Interview #4110, francophone school, translated from French)

> It's very positive. I think most teachers will tell you, you've got a class in front of you. You don't have a class of Asian kids, you don't have a class of Sri Lankan kids, you don't have a class of Korean kids, you've got a class of kids, and maybe you have to sometimes sit back and say, Well, what backgrounds do you have in there. Let me think for a second. There's Chris, there's John, there's Thomas, there's Doug, that's how you go. (Interview #4163, anglophone school)

For these teachers, children are children no matter of their race. This discourse is not uncommon. Being "colour-blind" is not the exception among school personnel. Sleeter (2004), in a project of professional development with a group of white teachers over a period of two years, concluded the following:

> Faced with the paradox of liking and helping students of colour while explaining away the subordination of people of colour and adhering to social structures that benefit themselves and their own children, the White teachers I studied responded in patterned ways. Many simply refused to "see" colour. (p. 175)

"Colour-blindness" is found everywhere in society and represents a discursive form embraced by the majority. It is also interesting to note that the student names used by the teacher in the previous interview excerpt (John, Thomas,

Doug) are Anglo-Saxon, instead of using names that would be more representative of the student diversity in this classroom. In considering all students as equal, teachers and principals do not question how power comes into play in society and, most particularly, in school settings. In the school context, denying that differences exist treats inclusion as an individual process, with its success or failure (Harper, 1997).

TEACHERS' AND PRINCIPALS' DISCOURSES ON THE IMPACT OF STUDENT DIVERSITY ON THEIR WORK AND HOW PREPARED THEY FEEL THEY ARE TO ACCOMPLISH THIS WORK

Although government policy proposals and mandates call for equity in student learning opportunities and outcomes among all students (Ontario Royal Commission on Learning, 1994), much remains to be done to encourage teachers to take students' diversity into serious consideration in their practices (Harper, 1997; Jones, 2000; Mujawamariya & Mahrouse, 2004). Pre-service teacher training institutions have not systematically and deeply taken into account the issue of students' racial, ethnic, and linguistic diversity in their training with future teachers. As a result, most of the literature on the issue tells us that teachers are not always well prepared to face the challenge of a racially, ethnically, and linguistically heterogeneous classroom (Gérin-Lajoie, 2002; Sleeter & Grant, 1991; Sleeter, 2004; Solomon & Levine-Rasky, 1996).

Teaching can be challenging. Participants spoke out about the training, or the lack of training, they received to work with a diversified classroom in a teaching environment with increasing accountability expectations (e.g., assessment, reporting) associated with standards and outcomes driven curriculum policies. Nevertheless, some of the participants felt confident that they had what it takes to work with the student diversity of their classroom. For them, the need of training or support was not pressing, as one teacher mentioned:

> To me, I didn't need to be taught. I had a good handle on different cultures anyways, just through work. I mean, you deal with all kinds of different people. And, so it wasn't a stretch for me to find kids. And it was different for me when I went to high school. At [a large Ontario university], I graduated in 1989, and I graduated from a school that was probably 95 percent white, and still today is predominantly white. And I walk into here where the mix is like I've never seen before. You've got Eastern Europeans, you've got Asians, and Indians. The cultural mix here is something I wouldn't have believed. But I think it really works well. (Interview #4173, anglophone school)

Others expressed the need to prepare teachers better, especially in the area of language. One participant talked specifically about English as a Second Language (ESL) teaching skills, after being asked if there was a need for improvement in teacher's training:

> Yes. Absolutely, and I was just thinking about that when you were saying that, because I know what I do as an ESL teacher, and this is my first time teaching ESL in six years. So I'm still trying to learn and get my bag of tricks ready. But the poor kids come to me and they flounder in other classes because the teachers don't think to give them a vocabulary list. And I'm to blame too, because I don't do that in my other classes. You just are so inundated with the exceptional kids that sometimes the ESL kids are pushed aside, which is really unfortunate. But I think that's absolutely one of the best suggestions to do for a faculty, to make sure that everybody has a rudimentary understanding and some ESL strategies. (Interview #4187, anglophone school)

The students' language skills are considered to be deficient, and for some teachers and principals, the students' proficiency in the language of instruction presents the most challenging problem.

The same discourse takes place in French language schools about the perceived lack of training in the area of student diversity. In this particular context, the discourse is about two separate concerns. The first one is the fact that teachers do not know how to deal with diverse racial and ethnic students' backgrounds; the second concern relates to the difficulties encountered in their work because of the linguistic dominance of English in the school. The teachers' preoccupation with the latter is not a new phenomenon. Preoccupations with racial and ethnic diversity as part of the teachers' discourse, on the other hand, are relatively new and are mostly noticeable since the mid-1990s. As reflected in the following interview excerpts, attention to students' racial and ethnic diversity, in some participants' opinion, has not been integrated in teacher pre-service training programs.

> We had a little bit of training, I remember, at some point in time, during a professional development day, but nothing more than that. This is something you do as it comes. But I did not feel any big roadblocks, any big problems. I think the fact that we are in a small school helps tremendously. Communication among teachers is easier. It is easy to ask a question. (Interview #4117, francophone school, translated from French)

> It struck me when I was doing practice teaching, even with my colleagues, to see that the *francophonie*, the French language is different. That there

were a lot of flaws and that there was a pressing need to take care of it, I was surprised by that. Second, it was very much reflected in the classroom. Personally I was not trained to handle that, I had to adjust consequently. (Interview #4101, francophone school, translated from French)

The results from the interviews with these 100 participants indicate overall that in most cases, both teachers and principals felt that they were not adequately trained to face the multiracial, multi-ethnic, and multilingual classroom. The concerns raised were mostly about teaching, about their role as agents of knowledge transmission within the regulation of the provincial curriculum. Preoccupations from teachers, in particular, were about how to make sure that their students succeed in the context of the Ontario school system. These concerns lie within the scope of the official discourse that emphasizes the importance for schools (students as well as teachers and principals) to be accountable to the general public, what Ball (2004) refers to as "performativity in education" (p. 143).

These results support the conclusions of previous studies that pointed to the lack of awareness about social justice from teachers in the way they conceptualize diversity and student integration, which a lot of teachers and principals define as "multicultural education." Sleeter (2004) in her study of a group of white teachers in an Anglo-dominant context came to the conclusion that the ways these teachers construct the notion of race and make sense of it emphasize the notion of Otherness. As explained by Sleeter, "discussing race or multiculturalism meant discussing 'them,' not the social structure" (p. 175). King (2004) calls for the development of a liberatory pedagogy, but in order to accomplish that, teacher education must change. In their own study, Mujawamariya and Mahrouse (2004) came to the conclusion that the student teachers who were interviewed were looking more for teaching strategies than for an opportunity to examine closely the principles of social justice when talking about how to handle diversity in their classroom. Although not always very explicit regarding how it could be accomplished, critical educators and researchers insist on the need to transform teacher education to favour an anti-racism pedagogy (Dei, 1999; Solomon & Levine-Rasky, 1996). Critical educators acknowledge that the need for consciousness-raising among teachers and principals is real. Diversity must not be discussed only in terms of adapting the curriculum or the pedagogy, although this is also an important component of student inclusion, but first diversity needs to be examined within the existing power structure of our society.

TEACHERS' AND PRINCIPALS' DISCOURSES ON THE NOTION OF LANGUAGE

In the literature, diversity is often examined through race and ethnicity. Language is discussed, in most cases, in reference to the acquisition of a second language and/or in terms of school achievement—for example, the fact that ESL students experience more academic challenges than native speakers. Linguistic standardization and linguistic domination are seldom the focus of attention. In Canada, the presence of linguistic minorities is a social reality. As explained in a previous section, a substantial number of francophones live outside the province of Quebec, as well as anglophones in Quebec. In both situations, the minority language constitutes an important component in the maintenance of the community. It is mainly through education that linguistic rights have been gained over the years. Outside of Quebec, francophones rely on the school to help preserve the French language and French culture.

However, even if francophones have the right to be educated in French in a school system of their own, it does not mean that the influence of the anglophone majority stays at the school door when the students come in (Gérin-Lajoie, 2003). Consequently, linguistic diversity has been a major issue for a long time for the school personnel, even before facing racial and ethnic diversity.

In the French minority language schools, linguistic diversity exists among white students themselves. The influence of the language of the majority, English, is acknowledged among francophone participants as being omnipresent in their working reality. As stated by one teacher:

> Yes, I was surprised, because I did expect that francophones would better retain their language and culture. I was surprised to see the anglophone assimilation. (Interview #4105, francophone school, translated from French)

English is present in the classroom even though the school is a French milieu, where the language of instruction as well as the language of communication is French. In large proportion, students attending French language schools in Ontario live more in English than in French outside of the school. The use of English is then noticeable in a large number of French language schools throughout the province where students' competencies in French are unequal. Consequently, the situation sometimes presents a challenge for teachers. Students' language practices in the school are a reflection of the reality of living constantly at the border of two or more languages outside of the school. Teachers must then deal with a working reality where linguistic diversity is common and where students' language practices will be dependent upon language practices that take place at home, which themselves will be also greatly influenced by the anglophone immediate surroundings in which families live. You can imagine a circle composed of three rings, with the school in the most inner ring, the family in the middle, and the social environment at the outskirt of the ring. Schools, independently of their language of instruction, tend to forget about the influence of these two "outside" rings when it comes to linguistic diversity.

However, in regard to the language competencies in French, the situation is different with the students from non-white racial and ethnic origins enrolled in French language schools. Interestingly enough, overall these students have better language skills in French than their white counterparts do, as expressed by one francophone teacher during the interview:

> When I think of the students who have the strongest skills in French, they are from Arabic families, from Italian families, these are people that value languages in general. They will speak Italian, Arabic, English. (Interview #4113, francophone school, translated from French)

In several of my studies that have taken place in French language schools, I have observed the same phenomenon. In the Toronto area, it seems that, proportionally speaking, students from racial and ethnic minorities are more fluent in French than the rest of the students, especially for those who have been educated in French prior to their arrival in Ontario. Furthermore, they tend to speak a more standard French, the type of language in line with the normative French used in the school setting, compared to the other students who quite often speak a more vernacular French. This situation is most noticeable in high schools (Gérin-Lajoie, 2003).

What is fascinating, however, is the fact that the situation looks the opposite of what teachers and principals in English language schools say about racial and ethnic minorities' skills in English. In the latter, minority students are disadvantaged by their lack of language competencies in their second language to be successful in school. Francophone students' relatively strong French language proficiency levels might be explained by the fact that the students who enrol there have already received some education in French in their countries of origins. They could also be from countries where French is either the official language or the language of prestige that they were used to speaking.

This stands in contrast with the situation found in English language schools where most of the newcomers are taking English as a Second Language classes. Consequently, teachers in English language schools face the challenge of working with kids who often do not have a good grasp of English, as explained by some participants:

> It can be difficult. It is. It definitely is, and even this year my classes are an illustration of that. Yes, it does affect understanding; you know you're answering questions that in a less multicultural setting you wouldn't be answering. You're dealing with language problems that you wouldn't be dealing with. Sometimes here we get kids who are really still in the ESL program, but they're in a regular history course. (Interview #4172, anglophone school)

> [We have a] very high correlation of ethnics, so you find a lot learning issues with ethnic students in our school. They have language deficiencies. And so, part of that whole language [approach] that has shown that they're deficient in reading and deficient in writing [is] because of the language barrier. And, that's very common. (Interview #4158, anglophone school)

Here, the poor language competencies in English are seen as being deficient in relationship with the school standards. It is perceived that deficiencies must be treated. Principles from the old model of compensatory education are used in teachers' and principals' discourses in regard to solving "individual" problems. Students are seen as individuals lacking the necessary skills to succeed in school, to adapt to their new school environment.

Conclusion

The results presented in this chapter indicate that the study participants' discourses are in line with the prevailing official discourse on racial, ethnic, and linguistic student diversity and their inclusion in the Ontario school system, in English majority language schools as well as in French minority language schools.

When I compare the results between the two linguistic school systems, the only area where anglophones and francophones do not share the same views is about minority students' proficiency in their respective language of instruction. Nevertheless, even if francophone participants recognize that minority students in general have better skills in French than some of their other students, they still comment that they have to adapt their teaching to this segment of the school population. The notion of Otherness remains present in their discourse, as it does in the case of the anglophone participants. In the anglophone context, students whose origins differ from the white anglophone majority are often seen as disadvantaged children, with individual problems that need to be fixed. It does not appear, from the interview data, that school personnel make much attempt to be more critical of the situation by trying to locate these students within the context of their subordinated position and class location (van Dijk, 1993), and in so doing, students are framed as "victims" of class subordination rather than as subjects having agency. It seems that teachers and principals, although recognizing the challenges that some of their students face, look at them as subjects with no social history, subjects that are disconnected from the outside world, and subjects that only face individual challenges.

There is no doubt, however, that the participants in the present study have great compassion for their students. I, too, believe that changes such as better support and better training programs must be made to better meet the needs of these students. Nevertheless, I agree with Popkewitz (1998), who, discussing the US context, points out that

> the spatial politics of schooling is the production of a moral order that includes and excludes. My focus ... is not to argue against a curriculum that is more inclusive of groups represented. But I have been arguing that it is not sufficient to say that teachers need to believe in children as successful learners, that the school needs closer ties to the home, that the curriculum needs to be responsive to the diversity of the American population, or that schools need to be locally controlled—part of the mainstays of contemporary reform discussions. (p. 129)

Ministries of Education and policy makers must take a step further in trying to better understand the social context in which minority students live, in order to move away from simply individualizing students and seeing them as deficient. A closer examination of the social location of the student population (minority as well as majority students) would allow for a more genuine process of inclusion. From this perspective, anti-racism education continues to be much needed in our social context. Solomon and Levine-Rasky (1996) suggest that teacher education programs should adapt the following ideas to their respective needs: 1) study education in its social context; 2) critically examine all curricular practices; 3) integrate the study of social difference, race, and anti-racism into the mainstream of teacher education scholarship; 4) link teacher education to social action; and 5) develop a multi-dimensional critical reflective practice (pp. 352–353). Sleeter (2004) refers to this shift as "reeducation" (p. 176).

Although a step in the right direction, I question the feasibility of such a program in the socio-political context in which schools presently operate. How can this be accomplished in the highly prescriptive school system of today? There is a need to recognize that more often than not, discussions on the issue of racial, ethnic, and linguistic diversity in schooling take place within academia. Unfortunately, it does not always reach the public school classroom. What makes sense on paper might be difficult to implement. Social and educational practices are complex. This complexity is not always taken into account in theoretical discussions, however, as Niesz (2006) explains:

> In conclusion, the ways in which critical practice is produced in real schools are much more complex than the ways that critical theories of schooling are elaborated in the academy. Multicultural education, critical pedagogy, community service learning and other instructional practices advocated by critical educational theorists must be seen as subject to multiple potential interpretations. (p. 343)

There is a need to document actual school practices in order to see how these critical approaches to schooling are being implemented and what makes them work. Several of the studies cited in this chapter showed the difficulties involved in trying to use an anti-racist framework with teachers in pre-service and in-service training. This information is valuable as it shows what is working and what is not. I agree with Niesz (2006) when she comments that "educators appropriate pedagogical and curricular ideas from multiple places, blending and mixing to produce school practice" (p. 343). Lastly, as academics, we must keep in mind that teachers and principals cannot be taken to be solely responsible for the ills of our schools. Schools are sites of contradictions where complex social practices take place, influenced by an official discourse that continues to dictate the rules.

Notes

1. The national study called *Current Trends in the Evolution of School Personnel in Canadian Elementary and Secondary Schools* (2002–2007) was funded by the Major Collaborative Research Initiatives of the Social Sciences and Humanities Research Council of Canada. For a more detailed account of this national study, see Chapter 1 of this book. I would like to thank Denise Wilson, my senior research officer, and my research assistants Christine Connelly, Christine Lenouvel, and Mélanie Knight for their contribution to the data collection.
2. In Canada, there are one million francophones outside the province of Quebec, half of whom are living in Ontario.
3. Non-francophone students may in some cases be allowed to enrol in the francophone school if accepted by a special admissions committee, the *comité d'admission*, which evaluates the student's suitability for the francophone school on a case-by-case basis, according to criteria defined by the school board. Examples of admissions criteria include the student's proficiency level and motivation to learn French, his or her parents' commitment to French language education, the potential for the student to succeed in a francophone context according to the degree of support at home, among other factors.

References

Anderson, S. & Ben Jaafar, S. (2006). *Policy Trends in Ontario Education—1990–2006*. Toronto: OISE/UT.

Ball, S.J. (2004). Performativities and fabrications in the education economy. In S.J. Ball (Ed.), *The Routledge-Falmer Reader in Sociology of Education* (pp. 143–155). London: Routledge-Falmer.

Chui, T. & Zietzma, D. (2003). Earnings of immigrants in the 1990s. *Canadian Social Trends*, Fall, 24–28.

City of Toronto. (2007). *Toronto facts. Toronto racial diversity.* Retrieved July 20, 2007, from www.toronto.ca/toronto_facts/diversity.htm.

Dei, G.J.S. (1999). The denial of difference: Reframing antiracist praxis. *Race, Ethnicity, and Education, 2*(1), 17–37.

Gérin-Lajoie, D. (2007). Effets des politiques scolaires dans la pratique du métier d'enseignante et d'enseignant au Canada. In R. Malet (Ed.), *L'école, lieu de tensions et de médiations: Quels effets sur les pratiques scolaires? Actes du colloque international de l'AFEC, 22, 23 et 24 juin 2006* (pp. 395–405). Lille: Association francophone d'éducation comparée.

Gérin-Lajoie, D. (2002). Le personnel enseignant dans les écoles minoritaires de langue française. In D. Mujawamariya (Ed.), *L'intégration des minorités visibles et ethnoculturelles dans la profession enseignante: Récits d'expérience, enjeux et perspectives* (pp. 167–181). Montreal: Les Éditions Logiques.

Gérin-Lajoie, D. (2001). Les défis de l'enseignement en milieu francophone minoritaire: Le cas de l'Ontario [Electronic version]. *Éducation et Francophonie, 24*(1). Retrieved April 9, 2007, from www.acelf.ca/c/revue/revuehtml/29-1/02-Gerin-Lajoie.html.

Gérin-Lajoie, D. (1995). Les écoles minoritaires de langue française canadiennes à l'heure du pluralisme ethnoculturel. *Études ethniques au Canada/Canadian Ethnic Studies, 27*(1), 32–47.

Harper, H. (1997). Difference and diversity in Ontario schooling. *Canadian Journal of Education, 22*(2), 192–206.

Henry, F. & Tator, C. (1999). State policy and practices as racialized discourse: Multiculturalism, the charter, and employment equity. In P.S. Li (Ed.), *Race and Ethnic Relations in Canada* (pp. 88–115). Toronto: Oxford University Press.

Jones, B.M. (2000). Multiculturalism and citizenship: The status of "visible minorities" in Canada. *Canadian Ethnic Studies, 32*(1), 111–125.

King, J.E. (2004). Dysconscious racism: Ideology, identity, and the miseducation of teachers. In G. Ladson-Billings and D. Gillborn (Eds.), *The Routledge-Falmer Reader on Multicultural Education* (pp. 71–83). London: Routledge-Falmer.

Ladson-Billings, G. (2004). Just what is critical race theory and what's it doing in a nice field like education? In G. Ladson-Billings & D. Gillborn (Eds.), *The Routledge-Falmer Reader in Multicultural Education* (pp. 49–67). London: Routledge-Falmer.

Ladson-Billings, G. (1994). *The Dreamkeepers: Successful teachers of African-American children.* San Francisco: Jossey-Bass Publishers.

Li, P.S. (1999). The Multiculturalism debate. In P.S. Li (Ed.), *Race and Ethnic Relations in Canada* (pp. 148–177). Toronto: Oxford University Press.

Lloyd, T. (1998). *Planning and the politics of race.* Unpublished MA thesis, York University, Toronto.

Mujawamariya, D. & Mahrouse, G. (2004). Multicultural education in Canadian pre-service programmes: Teacher candidates' perspectives. *The Alberta Journal of Educational Research, 50*(4), 336–353.

Niesz, T. (2006). Beneath the surface: Teacher subjectivities and the appropriation of critical pedagogies. *Equity and Excellence in Education, 39*, 335–344.

Office for Francophone Affairs. (2007). Highlights from the general profile of francophones in Ontario. *Statistical Profiles 2005*. Toronto: Office of Francophone Affairs.

Ontario Ministry of Education and Training. (1993). *Antiracism and ethnocultural equity in school boards: Guidelines for policy development and implementation*. Toronto: Ontario Ministry of Education.

Ontario Royal Commission on Learning. (1994). Equity considerations. In *For the love of learning, Volume IV: Making it Happen* (chap. 16). Toronto: Queen's Printer for Ontario.

Popkewitz, T.S. (1998). *Struggling for the soul: The politics of schooling and the construction of the teacher*. New York: Teachers College Press.

Popkewitz. T.S. (2000). Globalization/regionalization, knowledge, and the educational practices. In T.S. Popkewitz (Ed.), *Educational Knowledge* (pp. 3–27). New York: State University of New York Press.

Shaikh, S. (2006). *Promoting equitable schools: The role of equity policies in Toronto-area schools*. Unpublished MA thesis, University of Toronto.

Sleeter, C.E. (2004). How white teachers construct race. In G. Ladson-Billings & D. Gillborn (Eds.), *The Routledge-Falmer Reader in Multicultural Education* (pp. 163–178). London: Routledge-Falmer Press.

Sleeter, C.E. & Grant, C.A. (1991). Mapping terrains of power: Student cultural knowledge versus classroom knowledge. In C.E. Sleeter (Ed.), *Empowerment through multicultural education* (pp. 49–68). Albany: State University of New York Press.

Solomon, R.P. & Levine-Rasky, C. (1996). Transforming teacher education for an antiracism pedagogy. *Canadian Review of Sociology and Anthropology, 33*(3), 337–359.

Statistics Canada. (2001). *Census of Population*. Ottawa: Government of Canada.

van Dijk, T.A. (1993). *Elite discourse and racism*. Newbury Park, CA: Sage Publications.

Voithofer, R. & Foley, A. (2007). Digital dissonances: Structuring absences in national discourses on equity and educational technologies. *Equity and Excellence in Education, 40*, 14–25.

CHAPTER 6

The Social Function of the School and the Work Performed by Montreal Teachers in the Context of Quebec Student Integration Policies

Louis LeVasseur

In recent years, the education system has been caught in a whirlwind of change that has affected many aspects not only of the system's configuration but also of the curriculum and pedagogy. Since the mid-1990s, the Quebec education system has undergone reform involving the enactment of legislation for decentralization; the merger and secularization of its school boards; the implementation of policies for the integration of students with disabilities, learning deficits, and behavioural problems; and the integration of students from immigrant families.

Given the scope of these changes, we need to ask whether the social functions of the school are also changing. Is the current focus on the integration of immigrant children and the integration of children who have traditionally been excluded from the mainstream classroom different from the focus on the democratization and modernization of society through education that we witnessed in the 1960s? And, in both cases, has the relationship between the school and society remained the same or has it changed?

When the reforms of the 1960s were implemented, the democratization of education quickly resulted in a phenomenon of massification, the differentiation of students, and the accommodation of new student clienteles with diverse profiles, few of whom would have stayed in school beyond grade school prior to the reform (Dandurand, 1990). Certain categories of students who have since had access to a secondary school education have had an antagonistic relationship toward school, which has made teachers' work considerably more complex (Lessard & Tardif, 1996). This was not the case prior to the reforms of the 1960s when students attending school pursued a classical education and attended university. With democratization came the need to manage student diversity.

Today, the phenomenon of differentiating between students is growing in some Montreal neighbourhoods due to the integration and francization of students from immigrant families, the integration of students with learning and behavioural difficulties into the mainstream classroom, and the emergence of a market model that has concentrated these students in one type of institution while concentrating "good students" in another type of institution. In spite of the fact that the social context has changed, we need to ask whether there are points of convergence between the notion of integration as practised in the 1960s and integration as practised in the year 2000 and beyond, and whether there are points of convergence between the management of diversity in the 1960s and today.

The purpose of this chapter is to describe the relationships between the social functions of the school, the changes in education policies, the heterogeneity of student clienteles, and the impact that these factors are having on the social function of the school, in particular on its integrative function and on the way in which teachers in Montreal's public schools talk about themselves and their work in such a context.

PART 1: The Social Functions of the School and the Issue of Diversity

What is meant by the "social functions" of the school? Isn't the core mission of the school to transmit knowledge or, as we would say today, to enable students to develop the skills they need to explore various fields of knowledge on their own? Without setting itself up in opposition to the existence of such a cultural mission, sociology, since Durkheim, has recognized that socialization is one of the basic functions of the school. The school transmits a set of values that must enable the student to "integrate" the world in which she or he lives and to function in it more effectively. As important as this function of socialization or integration is, it does not explain all of the social functions of the school. In an article on the social functions of the school, Martuccelli (2000) identifies, in addition to the function of integration, functions of domination or reproduction, modernization, and subjectivation.

Two comments about the concept of "function" are in order. First, based on what has just been said, the notion of the social function of the school cannot be reduced to the Durkheimian notion that there is a consensus around culture creating social ties and around the school playing a lead role in the integration of all members of society. Indeed, in addition to Durkheimian integration, Martuccelli (2000) associates reproduction with the social function of the school. Is this to say that culture and the institution of the school can only be seen from a structuralist perspective and can only fulfill a social destiny—that is, integration or, conversely, reproduction, which "determines" members of society *sui generis*? Not at all. Martuccelli (2000) also refers to the modernization of society through the school and to the function of subjectivation, by which subjects define themselves and the social actors in a more global fashion and give meaning to their actions in spite of the constraints associated with integration, reproduction, and the need to make strategic choices highlighted in the theoretical approaches of methodological individualism.

The second point to be made, in light of these distinguos, is that in the context of this chapter, the notion of the function of the school takes on the meaning of the relationships that exist between the school and society, not the Durkheimian notion of a role meeting a teleological necessity, that is, the integration of every member of society. Depending on the social and historical context, the school may indeed take on the function of integration or, through a set of education policies, promote the integration of every student in a context of great diversity. However, the school takes on other "social functions" that are likely to set up tension among one another. My goal is to show that, over and above the official discourse, various functions of the school—that is to say, various ways in which a school may exist in society (and which may consist of efforts at integration, democratization, the training of individuals, decentralization, etc.)—may have unexpected results. Thus, an education ministry's intentions to achieve integration or to manage diversity may lead to new forms of inequality, rather like a snake biting its own tail.

Martuccelli (2000) makes it possible to see, theoretically, that the school's place in society is multi-dimensional and that these dimensions can set up tension among one another. Without actually following Martuccelli step by step through the development of his theories, I will draw on them in developing a theoretical framework that reflects the socio-historical conditions that exist in Quebec schools today. Mainly, however, I will focus on the social function of the school as it relates to the issue of diversity.

THE FUNCTION OF MODERNIZATION

To the extent of its own self-modernization, education participated actively in the modernization of Quebec society, notably by training a skilled labour force and producing scientific knowledge. The *Parent Report*, Volume 1 (Government of Quebec, 1964a), contains the findings of a vast commission of inquiry into education reform. This report led to the modernization and democratization of the Quebec education system and made the development of human capital a priority of education. From then on, investments in education were perceived to be productive and profitable nationwide. Knowledge and training became necessary not only to the development of industry, but also to the development of the service sector (Government of Quebec, 1964a,

p. 70). In its modernizing role and through its contribution to economic and industrial development, what relationship does education have to diversity?

Beyond free schooling and the creation of new schools, the modernization of education took the form of a cultural revolution within the school itself. Making higher education universally available led to different expectations of education, a wider range of tastes, aptitudes, and aspirations, and a wider range of course offerings than had been available under the old system, which had primarily focused on philosophy and the classics (Government of Quebec, 1964a, p. 8).

Mass access to secondary and post-secondary education for new student clienteles did not, however, result in a true democratization of education; it led to forms of rejection and failure and streaming that was ineffective academically, professionally, and socially and made the management of diversity in the school more difficult. What if modernization and the accompanying management of diversity hide a function of domination?

THE FUNCTION OF DOMINATION

Domination and democratization are two sides of the same coin. Democratization is inevitably accompanied by a phenomenon of massification, which involves a form of academic exclusion exercised by the school itself (Dubet, 2000). In the 1960s, Quebec set itself the goal of democratizing education and ensuring that children stayed in school beyond Grade 5 or Grade 6. It passed legislation making it compulsory to attend school until the age of 16 and making education free. Enrolment exploded. These efforts at democratization were justified in part by a desire to reduce inequalities around education and to provide an entire segment of the population—the working class—with access to secondary and post-secondary education. However, "democratization" leads to new forms of inequality and dominance and even to rejection and resistive behaviour on the part of students or what French sociologists refer to as massification—the very opposite of democratization. In this way, democratization does not necessarily guarantee that all forms of inequality will be eliminated. Some critics claim that the school's function is not modernization or democratization but in fact domination (Althusser, 1970; Baudelot & Establet, 1971; Bourdieu, 1966; Bourdieu & Passeron, 1964; Bourdieu & Passeron, 1970; Bowles & Gintis, 1976). According to these critics, it is in the very "nature" of the school to create inequality and to maintain the distances that separate social groups. Quebec's transition from an essentially elitist education system to a universal education system with authentic mechanisms for social advancement did not succeed in eliminating all forms of domination and segregation.

In recent decades, sociology has shed light on aspects of the ways in which schools function as institutions that create inequality.[1] This reference to the school's function of domination and reproduction exposes the dark side of democratization that, from this theoretical perspective, is an illusion. Diversity creates risks for the dominant social groups—the risk of competition for academic titles and no doubt also the risk of pluralism that threatens the dominant culture. In the presence of such risks, the school must inevitably reject and exclude a large number of students, steering them toward devalued streams that offer no academic or social prospects. These streaming mechanisms are extremely varied and most often operate unbeknownst to educators. Paradoxically, however, the school continues to try to integrate all students. It subscribes to the idea—or perhaps the myth—of a common culture that unites all individuals and transforms diversity into a coherent, unified whole. What does this function of integration consist of? What relation does it bear to the issue of diversity?

THE FUNCTION OF INTEGRATION

The best description of the function of integration is the sociological definition provided by Durkheim in *Éducation et sociologie* (1989). All education systems come to rest on a common foundation (Durkheim, 1989, p. 49) that is comprised of the social, cultural, intellectual, legal, historical, and emotional information that education must impart to the next generation. And it is precisely this common foundation transmitted by education that ensures the very existence of society: "society can only survive if there is sufficient homogeneity between its members" (Durkheim, 1989, p. 50, translated from French). According to Durkheim, at the origin of the function of integration is the functionalist postulate of a correspondence between civilization and the individual. The development of the individual and his or her access to universal reason promote the economic and cultural development of society and vice versa.[2]

The function of integration remains central to the institution of the school, specifically in regard to its functions of socialization and the transmission of values. The social action of the school is even more closely related to this function of integration; however, the traditional modes of socialization are beginning to change. The subject, which is the main vector of modernity (Dubet, 1994; Dubet & Martuccelli, 1996; Martuccelli, 2000; Touraine, 1992, 1997), has caused new values to emerge that are weakening the traditional modes of socialization, in particular those of the school to which Durkheim refers when he describes the individual's internalization of the values at the foundation of society. Indeed, society is experiencing a major crisis in terms of its modes of socialization, grammars of communication, and ways of living in community (Bonafé-Schmitt, 1997). We are witnessing a decline of the institution (Dubet, 2002); traditional modes of socialization are being replaced by modes of socialization and the construction of societal norms in which the actor plays an active and determining role (de Munck & Verhoeven, 1997; Dubet, 1994; LeVasseur, 2003). In this way, diversity in the school poses a challenge to the institution itself, to its traditional modes of socialization, and to the function of integration that defines it. The integration of diversity has not been able to address, and no doubt will not be able to address, this challenge unless it shifts to new modes of socialization and, by extension, ceases to see the function of integration, as Durkheim defines this term, as the primary means by which the subject or the individual constructs his identity.

We shall now see that the school system is in fact criss-crossed by different forms of logic according to which the school should be doing everything in its power to integrate certain categories of students, whereas in fact, in the name of respect for diversity (taking into account parents' demands for diversity in learning, honouring local dynamics, adapting national policies at the local level, etc.), it is involuntarily creating exclusion.

PART 2: A New Social Function Centred on the Integration of Students from Immigrant Families and Students Traditionally Excluded from the Mainstream Classroom

Is the function of integration—which Durkheim conceives as establishing one education system designed for all students in order to create social beings rather than individual beings and which is the ultimate condition for social unity and cohesion—as meaningful in schools today as it was 50 years ago? Does the massification and heterogeneity of the school population make it necessary to transform the function of integration in order to take student diversity into account and, accordingly, to avoid socially excluding a certain category of students? We need to determine: 1) whether the function of integration as it existed in the 1960s in Quebec still exists or whether it has changed; and 2) if it has changed, whether this change has had an impact on the work of teachers. In order to determine whether the school's function of integration has changed, I will first provide a general outline of recent education policies in Quebec that are having an impact on student diversity and then describe their impact on the work of teachers in Montreal's public schools.

MULTI-ETHNICITY, MASSIFICATION, AND EDUCATION POLICIES RELATED TO THE MANAGEMENT OF STUDENT DIVERSITY

We can retrace the school's function of integration through recent education policies of a social nature introduced by the Quebec Ministry of Education (Ministère de l'Éducation [MEQ]). These policies are presented as integration policies (policy on the integration of students from immigrant families, policy on the integration of students traditionally excluded from mainstream classrooms). However, they are not the only policies that have had an impact on the school's social function. The recent policy on decentralization and some of the provisions for curriculum reform are moving the school's social function toward an increase in the management of diversity and integration.[3] In other words, policies such as those concerning francization, student integration, decentralization, and curriculum reform are increasing student diversity in certain Montreal schools and amplifying the school's function of integration.

The Integration of Students from Immigrant Families

The Montreal region in particular is affected by Quebec's policy on educational integration and intercultural education, entitled *Politique d'intégration scolaire et d'éducation interculturelle* (MEQ, 1998). This region accounts for more than 80 percent of all newcomers in Quebec and "is home to over 80 ethnic communities speaking more than 149 languages and dialects" (translation).[4] For example, the schools in the Montreal School Board [Commission scolaire de Montréal] almost single-handedly assume the roles of integration and especially the francization of students from immigrant families.

There is an important distinction to be made between the policy on educational integration and intercultural education and the policy for the integration of students traditionally excluded from mainstream classrooms. Students from families who have recently immigrated are not necessarily at risk of social or academic exclusion. The research tends to show, on the contrary, that many immigrant families see the school as a way of guaranteeing successful immigration (Quebec Ministry of Education, Recreation, and Sports [Ministère de l'Éducation, du Loisir et du Sport (MELS)],[5] 2006; Zéroulou, 1988). This is not to say that every student who has recently arrived in Quebec stands at the head of the class, however; as with the policy on integration, the idea is to get students integrated into the mainstream classroom as quickly as possible because it offers "richer possibilities for socialization" than the *classe d'accueil* (class for newcomers) (MEQ, 1998, p. 19, translated from French).

From a broader social standpoint, and in the context of linguistic, ethnic, cultural, and religious diversity, this policy is designed "to develop the ability to communicate with individuals with various referents and to develop attitudes of openness, tolerance, and solidarity" (MEQ, 1998, p. 2, translated from French). Rather than being an abrupt departure from the history of the management of ethnic diversity in Quebec schools, this is consistent with a series of changes subsequent to the waves of immigration that marked the late 1970s.

In the early 1980s, the Conseil supérieur de l'éducation (CSE, 1983) issued guidelines for Quebec schools with respect to multi-ethnicity, in particular a guideline for an approach called *accueil d'intégration* (welcoming immigrant students) with an emphasis on integrating immigrant students into the host society. Very quickly, the Chancy Report (MEQ, 1985) sharply criticized this approach, which required a major cultural change on the part of ethnic groups but not on the part of the dominant or host society. It proposed instead two objectives—the preservation of cultural features and the inter-penetration of these cultural features in order to create a culture of convergence. Pagé (1988) exposed the contradictions between these objectives. In 1987, the CSE proposed a resolutely relativist definition of culture and advocated openness toward the culture of the Other, toward difference, and toward a consideration of the relative and partial nature of one's own culture. This point of view requires individuals belonging to the dominant culture in a pluralistic society to step away from the centre. According to Pagé (1988), this CSE recommendation introduced an aporia or philosophical puzzle, namely, the challenge of maintaining a strong cultural identity while subscribing to the notion of cultural relativism requiring a critical consideration of one's own cultural identity. According to this notion of culture in a pluralistic society, ethnic groups that have recently arrived are able to preserve the unique characteristics of their culture, which suggests that integrating the core values of the host society is neither an obligation for them, nor a condition of living in community. In the 1990s, the CSE (1993) reintroduced the notion of a common culture to be shared by all and placed the focus once more on the obligation to integrate cultural communities. According to some critics, this hinted at assimilationism under the cloak of a common culture of citizenship. With the Proulx report (MEQ, 1999a), however, the notion of a common culture seemed to entail not the imposition of a cultural standard but the notion of a culture in the making. Culture is not simply a collective heritage; similarly, identity, although inherited, is constantly in the process of being reshaped.

The current policy on educational integration and intercultural education (MEQ, 1998) appears to avoid the pitfalls of an assimilationist political orientation and the creation of a cultural mosaic, which would result in an impasse on the issue of social connection or common culture.

> Collective heritage is a term that refers both to a memory, that is to say, a set of historical heritages and the contributions of all those who have lived and who now live in Quebec, and an undertaking in which modern citizens, in all of their diversity and with their particular allegiances, develop the contents that shape society together. (MEQ, 1998, p. 26, translated from French)

It is important to remember that this policy maintains the *classes d'accueil*.[6] These classrooms have never really been questioned and are clearly the most active school structure for the integration of students from families of recent immigrants. It is generally recognized that these classrooms are necessary transitional measures that promote the French language as the common language and that strive to ensure that cultural communities are present in every sphere of Quebec society.

The Integration of Excluded Students

The general philosophy underlying the policy on the integration of students experiencing learning difficulties—which is the other major education policy of a social nature—includes the massification of the school, the introduction of new student clienteles that did not traditionally attend school beyond Grade 7 or Grade 8, the need to offer newcomer students services to address their learning difficulties or behavioural difficulties, and the need to help an increasingly large percentage of students grappling with personal and social problems that are undermining their chances of academic success. In urban and rural communities across Quebec, some schools have a high percentage of underprivileged students (MEQ, 2004). Schools now have to contend with extremely challenging social realities: an increase in poverty, a weakening of the social fabric, family dysfunction (due to poverty, violence, drugs, and sexual abuse), and an increase in single-parent families. In recent years, immigration has changed the ethnic and cultural mix of many neighbourhoods and cities, and this is particularly true of the greater Montreal area. In some Montreal schools, the students come primarily from minority groups and cultures whose values around schooling and cultural capital are sometimes very different from those of the white francophone majority. Here again the school and its educators must offer these students special services and must support their integration. Not only teachers but also non-teaching professionals (NTP) such as school psychologists, psycho-educators, guidance counsellors, and speech therapists play a critical role in the support that is offered to a large percentage of the student population affected by these social transformations.

The first policy to integrate students experiencing learning difficulties or behavioural difficulties into the mainstream classroom was introduced in

1979, in the wake of the COPEX report (MEQ, 1976). This report advocated the integration of these students into the mainstream classroom in order to reduce the exorbitant costs of the existing approach, which essentially consisted of treatment delivered by an army of professionals. The policy on school adaptation, introduced in 1999 as part of the education reform undertaken by the *États généraux sur l'Éducation* (Estates General on Education) (MEQ, 1996), reaffirmed the principles underlying the 1979 policy, including the principle of integrating as many students as possible into the mainstream classroom (MEQ, 1999b, p. 17).

However, the current policy appears to go much further with integration than the 1979 policy (MEQ, 1979), advocating massive integration of students experiencing difficulties and substantially reducing classes designed strictly for this type of student. At the present time, in some schools, teachers do not have just one or two students who have an individual education plan and who are therefore working with a non-teaching professional because of their behavioural difficulties or learning difficulties, but sometimes as many as 10 or even 15 such students. This policy therefore has very serious consequences not only for the teachers who are required to welcome into the mainstream classroom students who were traditionally excluded for all sorts of reasons (serious behavioural problems, a wide range of learning difficulties, etc.), but also for the entire school system, which is now required to offer these students and their teachers services that are adapted to their special needs.

These two education policies—one geared toward the francization of immigrants and intercultural education and the other toward the integration of students with special needs—have transformed the institutional face of the public school. Although the public school still has a mission to educate, the various functions of integration that it assumes reflect a cultural mission that goes beyond the mere transmission of knowledge and straightforward learning activities. The social function of the Quebec school appears to be an extension of the integration of students from immigrant families and of the struggle against the exclusion of students who are academically and socially at risk.

It is important to point out that students from immigrant families are at the centre of both the policy on francization and the policy on the integration of students with learning difficulties or behavioural difficulties. Indeed, students from immigrant families have more academic ground to cover than Quebec students as a whole.

> Overall, ... the percentage of students from immigrant families with academic delays is higher than the percentage in the general student population. In 1994–1995, 27.4% of immigrant students had a delay in normal

academic achievement, compared to 21.6% of all students in the education system. In 2003–2004, these percentages had dropped to 19.9% and 16.7% respectively. The delay diminishes at all levels of education for all students. (MELS, 2006, p. 25, translated from French)

However, in reference to the differences in academic delays between students from immigrant families and students as a whole, the Ministry adds:

> The proportion of students from immigrant families with academic delays is greater than the proportion of students in the general student population with academic delays. This difference is only found in first-generation immigrant students; the percentage of second-generation immigrant students [with academic delays] is lower than the percentage of students in the general student population. (MELS, 2006, p. 30, translated from French)

These two education policies have resulted in a considerable increase in student diversity in certain settings. The decentralization policy of 1997 has had a similar—although unexpected—impact.

THE EFFECTS OF DECENTRALIZATION ON THE CONCENTRATION OF NON-INTEGRATED STUDENTS IN SCHOOLS

Although it is an administrative policy with no social agenda, the decentralization policy[7] has had important consequences for the management of students in need of special attention and students who, for various reasons, have difficulty adapting to the norm. Clearly, decentralization and the autonomy that it has granted to the institutions encouraged them to fly their local colours and to differentiate themselves, which in turn has encouraged differentiation in what they offered. Decentralization and institutional autonomy have been paired with a new regulation of the education system that provides much more latitude to local stakeholders. Through its decentralization policy, the government has been encouraging local pedagogical projects that reflect the needs of students and parents (MEQ, 1997; MEQ, 2003). They, in turn, have begun acting like consumers, which has led to the emergence of a market model with serious consequences for the concentration of students with special needs in certain institutions. Middle-class parents, who benefited the most from the democratization of the education system, have begun seeking ways to get around the effects of massification (the devaluation of diplomas, a real or imagined decrease in cultural content, and violence) and the more recent effects of the integration policy (MEQ, 1999b). The practice of avoiding institutions with the wrong mix of students has ultimately led to a concentration of "gifted" students in institutions whose "screening" practices keep students with difficulties or anti-school behaviour at a distance. These students are shunted off to other institutions.

Clearly, such changes in the composition of the student population of public schools, particularly in Montreal, has had a very strong impact on the management of diversity, on the school's integration function, and on the work of the teachers. Since the early 1990s, teachers have been calling for a new system of support for their students and themselves that they felt could not be offered by the professionals (psychologists, psycho-educators, social workers, etc.), given their small numbers and methods of working.[8] This system would need the ability to respond quickly to students who, for various reasons, required immediate assistance; often, the school professional is busy elsewhere, defining or evaluating an individual education plan with a student. During shortages such as the shortage experienced during 1995 budget crisis, the school professional was often working in another school. In response to difficult economic times, the education sector gradually began using technicians with college or secondary school diplomas. They were less well paid than the professionals and their job status was often precarious. Special education technicians (SETs) in particular have assumed the functions of school integration and social integration with the students who are most vulnerable economically, socially, culturally, and personally (LeVasseur & Tardif, 2005). Over the past 15 years, the number of SETs has increased by 260 percent. This has been the second largest increase of any group of education workers;[9] this group increased from 838.7[10] in 1990 to 3,019.5 in 2004. The work they perform amplifies and expands upon the socialization functions of the school; it literally takes an original form of struggle against exclusion (LeVasseur & Tardif, 2005).

What we have here are education policies that are working at odds. The policies on integration appear to be in conflict with the policy on decentralization and its segregationist effect which, involuntarily, are undermining efforts to create a common space for all students (LeVasseur, 2006) and, in some settings, are amplifying student diversity. The management of diversity includes both measures that reinforce the social function of integration and measures that reinforce the social function of domination. The school appears to want to include those that it is helping to exclude. How do the teachers who are required to manage this diversity perceive it and how does it affect their work?

PART 3: Teachers and Students: A Description of the Diversity of the Student Clienteles

Drawing on first-hand accounts, this section will show the social function of the school—the management and integration of different forms of diversity (social, ethnic, religious, linguistic, cultural, academic, etc.) as it comes across in the discourse of the teachers. The management of social practices and diversity presents constraints with which teachers must contend. In their discourse, the teachers do more than describe diversity. They show its impact on their work, their role, and their students. Their remarks provide a clear illustration of the way in which the school assumes its social function through the management of diversity.

I have hypothesized that the primary social function assumed by teachers working in public schools in Montreal is the management of diversity, integration, and the prevention of social and academic exclusion. However, not all forms of diversity represent the same degree of difficulty for teachers. Diversity itself is diverse; it has many different aspects. What the teachers see as a challenge is the co-existence in the classroom of these various aspects of diversity. For them, teaching a class that is ethnically diverse is not necessarily an insurmountable challenge that tests their professional and personal skills. In fact, many teachers value this type of diversity because it harks back to a time when students had respect for the teacher and took joy in learning. And ethnic diversity is not incompatible with either the school norm or a certain unity, although this seems completely paradoxical. As different as they may be in terms of their culture, ethnicity, worldviews, value systems, language, and religion, if students integrate the traditional requirements of the school (respect for the teacher's authority, discipline, hard work, effort, and industriousness) and respond positively to the school's expectations—even if the language barriers may adversely affect their academic learning and performance to varying degrees—compliance with the school norm offsets any differences. Consequently, diversity is not necessarily a destabilizing factor for teachers.

Diversity becomes a major challenge when there is a lack of unity in diversity or when diversity deviates from the school norm. What teachers tell us about diversity is that it becomes more complex when it takes on the more irregular aspects of non-standard, rebellious, unmanageable, untameable behaviour and when it is not matched with adequate resources for channelling it, giving it shape or remedying its most destabilizing aspects. Under these circumstances, diversity can then become a professional challenge for the teacher.

The comments from teachers that I quote below illustrate clearly the social function of the school or, rather, how teachers position themselves in response to the social function of the school. I present their comments on the impact of the education policies on their work. First, however, I will provide a brief description of the sample of teachers who took part in this research.

A FEW DETAILS ABOUT THE RESEARCH METHODOLOGY

In 2003, our research team interviewed 64 teachers in Montreal, 84 percent of whom were women and 83 percent of whom worked in elementary schools. In terms of their teaching experience, 12 percent had between one and four years of experience, 48 percent had between five and eight years of experience, 19 percent had between nine and 12 years of experience, 6 percent had between 13 and 16 years of experience, and approximately 14 percent had more than 17 years of experience. Their average age was 36 years. Approximately 86 percent worked in a francophone school and, of those who taught in anglophone schools, some taught French in immersion classes.

These interviews are part of Project 4 of a Major Collaborative Research Initiative (MCRI). This pan-Canadian initiative pursues various research objectives requiring the recruiting of participants based on number of years of teaching experience, level taught, and the geographical location of their work environment.[11] Part of the pan-Canadian research also involves school principals; however, for this chapter, I wanted to focus on teachers in Montreal who have to live with and manage student diversity on a daily basis. Here, the recruiting of research participants in urban centres takes on its full meaning.

POLICY ON THE INTEGRATION OF STUDENTS FROM IMMIGRANT FAMILIES

Not all schools are collapsing under the weight of their students' academic, behavioural, social, and psychological problems. And not all of the forms of diversity that the teachers encounter represent problems or challenges in their eyes. Generally, teachers view ethnic diversity extremely favourably:

> This is an underprivileged, very multicultural environment. I have 25 students. These are wonderful children who want to learn. I can talk to them about anything and they are interested. These are students who are keen. They have discussions, they talk, they are open, and they want to learn. It would be really nice to have a class like this every year.... I love working with these children because I feel as though I can give them something and really help them to learn. (Interview #5022, elementary level, translated from French)

However, developing a positive teacher–student relationship does not make their other concerns about the social and cultural challenges of language go away.

> The flip side of what makes multiethnicity interesting is the fact that the students have a lot of difficulty with French. It is their second, third, or fourth language. Many only speak French at school. Often, they only speak French in the classroom. Their inadequate French language skills follow them everywhere—to history, economics, and mathematics. (Interview #5020, secondary level, translated from French)

A lack of mastery of the French language and a predilection for English, which leads certain students to make English their language of use instead of French, are major concerns for teachers, although these concerns are tempered by the satisfaction they derive from establishing fulfilling teacher–student relationships with students who are recent arrivals to Quebec. Thus, ethnic diversity is not in and of itself a major pitfall of their work. However, there are other forms of diversity that pose major problems for them and they relate not so much to ethnic diversity as to the structures that have been introduced to manage ethnic diversity. For example, some schools that only receive a limited number of students from immigrant families have to group students together who are extremely diverse in terms of their age in a *classe d'accueil*; this can represent a major pedagogical challenge.

> I have had students ranging in age from six to 12 years in the same class. How can you sustain the interest of students who are so different in age? (Interview #5052, elementary level, translated from French)

Some institutions respond by integrating students who would normally be placed in a class for new immigrants directly into the mainstream classroom, which can considerably increase the academic gap between students.

> We no longer have *classes d'accueil* at the preschool level. Five-year-old children who come to us are placed directly into the regular Junior Kindergarten class. The JK teachers are starting to wonder how they will manage. Let's say I have 12 francophones in my class and eight immigrant children. What do I do? The 12 francophones are ready to progress more quickly. They sit there, looking at me. I can't just let them sit there doing nothing. Our speech therapy classes are bursting at the seams with children who were integrated into the mainstream classroom too quickly. (Interview #5074, elementary level, translated from French)

Generally speaking, cultural diversity and ethnic diversity are seen as assets, and students from immigrant families are perceived as respectful of the school system and, in many cases, imbued with an intellectual curiosity that comes close to the teachers' image of the ideal student.

What about the diversity that results from integrating students who have traditionally been excluded from the mainstream classroom? Is it also perceived positively by teachers or does it make their work more complex than ethnic diversity?

THE STUDENT INTEGRATION POLICY AS A GENERATOR OF DIVERSITY AND CHALLENGES

Clearly, the policy of integrating students who have traditionally been excluded from the mainstream classroom is one of the transformations of the Quebec education system that has had the most impact on student diversity in the schools. It must be pointed out that at one end of the education spectrum, there are schools, including public schools, which have become more homogeneous through practices that could be described as selective—practices that only allow in students who "perform." At the other end of the spectrum are schools that have tended to differentiate themselves by grouping together students experiencing difficulties of all sorts. At this end, the job of the teacher becomes considerably more complex. I will now describe this student diversity in the mainstream classroom, identifying the challenges that it presents for teachers.

Because the mainstream classroom now includes students who, until recently, were taught in special education classes, teachers face classroom management problems of unprecedented magnitude.

> I am dealing with a very wide range of difficulties. I have to manage behavioural difficulties. I have to get the attention of students with attention-deficit problems. I have to find ways to manage my hyperactive students. I have to reach my autistic student who is in his own world. It's a lot to think about at the same time. (Interview #5053, elementary level, translated from French)

Diversity that consists of both students with various deficits and students who function "normally" is the most difficult challenge facing teachers in the classroom; even one student can make the teacher's task so difficult that the most routine activities are difficult to accomplish.

> I had a student who was integrated into my classroom and I had to fight to get services. The board did not want to hire staff to work with him

> because he had not been identified with a deficit code. And so the principal had to hire a special education technician out of the school's budget. Initially, this technician helped me three times a week for an hour and a half. I managed to get her for five full mornings a week. This child cannot go to the washroom alone; he has to be reminded to go. I couldn't always think of this and so he wet his pants often and I had to change him. (Interview #5026, elementary level, translated from French)

While physical and mental disabilities add to the diversity of students in Montreal's public schools, major social problems often translate into behavioural problems or advanced forms of anti-school behaviour that affect other students in disadvantaged areas. The problems that these students face are extremely diverse in terms of their nature and their impact.

> Single-parent families are a major problem. Another major problem is low self-esteem. Also their inability to form relationships. Why would they trust adults? If they trust an adult, the adult immediately lets them down. And so why would they trust us? This is my sixth year here. The children know that I mean what I say; that I am always there for them; they know me. But when the children don't know us? Listen, I've seen drugs, I've seen prostitution, I've seen battered children.... I had not experienced street gangs before, but we try to reach the kids who hang around in gangs on the street because they need to build their self-esteem. I've had girls who had no self-esteem; their mothers were dancers. Some girls shoplifted. So what am I supposed to do? How am I supposed to find solutions? (Interview #5021, elementary level, translated from French)

Integrating students with various problems into the mainstream classroom makes it more difficult for the whole class to learn and progress at the same rate toward shared learning objectives. The differences between the students far exceed the age-related differences found in the *classes d'accueil*. We see diversity in terms of levels of schooling that is often accompanied by diversity in terms of levels of motivation. When students who are working hard are placed in the same groups as students who do not find school meaningful or gratifying and who are absent either once or repeatedly, the teacher's work is much more complex.

> In the mainstream classroom, you often have groups in which two-thirds of the students want to learn and one-third doesn't want to learn and becomes disruptive. They aren't against me. They aren't against the teacher. They're against the system. They are in revolt, they are constantly in reaction, and when they come to art class, they go wild. It was always

like that and it will always be like that. We need to reduce the number of students; the biggest problem is the number of students. (Interview #5033, secondary level, translated from French)

Diversity in Montreal's public schools has many facets and, most of all, hides realities that affect the teachers' work in different ways. The policy on the integration of students from immigrant families and the efforts to francize them definitely make the work of teachers more onerous because these students have varying levels of schooling to make up (see the section titled "Multi-ethnicity, Massification, and Education Policies Related to the Management of Student Diversity" in this chapter). However, it is important to remember that they do not necessarily have behavioural problems. The impact of the policy on integrating disabled students or students with adaptation difficulties and/or learning difficulties, on the other hand, makes it more difficult to manage the classroom. The diversity of problems becomes the daily lot of the teachers. In addition to the policies on francization and on integrating students traditionally excluded from the mainstream classroom, there are other institutional factors that accentuate the diversity of students in Montreal public schools and risk making the teachers' work more onerous.

THE IMPACT OF THE DECENTRALIZATION POLICY AND REFORM ON DIVERSITY

The decentralization policy (MEQ, 1997) is an extremely important factor in the differentiation of students in some Montreal schools. However, unlike the francization and student integration policies, the decentralization policy is not directly related to the school's social function. Rather, its goal is to change administrative practices in the Quebec education system, to redefine the government's role, to distribute the power to various education stakeholders, and to provide local stakeholders with an opportunity to define who they are in a way that meets the needs of their milieu, students, and parents. This policy constitutes a major departure in the administrative practices of the Quebec Ministry of Education that had focused on standardizing the curriculum since its creation in 1964.

A number of factors led the government to redefine its role in the management of public institutions, including educational institutions: doubt over the central government's management capabilities; the crisis in the Welfare State (Rosanvallon, 1981), and the search for management practices that were less bureaucratic, more dynamic, more participatory, and, above all, more cost-effective. Hence the importance in Quebec of the *conseils d'établissement* (school councils) that encourage parents and local institutional education stakeholders to participate in defining programs that meet the overall objectives of the provincial curriculum while differentiating themselves from these objectives in order to more fully meet the needs of local clienteles and the expectations of parents. This is also why, during the 1990s, we saw the proliferation of schools with special programs to attract target clienteles, often made up of gifted students, which made it possible to avoid the impact of massification and, more recently, to avoid the impact of the policies to integrate students with learning disabilities and behavioural difficulties into the mainstream classroom. This type of program constitutes an essential resource that middle-class parents can use in their strategies for educating their children.

These programs have a major impact on the distribution of high-achieving and low-achieving students in the various institutions. Although we do not have actual statistics on the movement of students within the territory, we do know that the best students have opportunities to "flee" institutions that have a bad reputation and to enrol in special programs in institutions with a better reputation academically and socially. The decentralization policy has contributed to the differentiation of students in some settings. For an institution, watching its best students leave for more attractive schools affects not only the dynamic in the classroom but also the dynamic in the school as a whole.

> The majority of our students are boys because there are girls' schools in the neighbourhood that take almost all of the girls. That changes the dynamic. (Interview #5035, secondary level, translated from French)

When enrolment declines, classes may be eliminated. The students from these classes are then divided among the remaining classes, increasing the workload of those teachers. In a setting with a highly diverse student population, increasing enrolment in one group can completely transform a teacher's daily work.

> Next year, positions will be cut and we will have bigger classes. But our students need speech therapy every day, not once a week. I have 21 students this year; I've never been able to help my children so much. But next year, they're going to eliminate a class. (Interview #5021, elementary level, translated from French)

The impact of the decentralization policy is augmented by the impact of some of the provisions of the reform. Two such provisions are the organization of education into two- or three-year learning cycles and the elimination of repeat grades. Students now have two years in which to cover the curriculum; this has resulted in a much higher automatic pass rate. For example, a student who is having difficulty in Grade 5 can now catch up in Grade 6. Students who would normally have had to repeat a grade move on to the next grade and only exceptionally are students required to repeat a grade. The teachers report that, because they have not acquired the prerequisites, many students are in programs that are too advanced for them.

> Previous measures, such as making failing students repeat a grade, are disappearing. What are we supposed to do with children who aren't really ready to take the plunge in Grade 1? Some would benefit from programs with more play. That's where they are in their development. More formal, systematic learning is not going to be easy for them. I'm concerned about that. (Interview #5077, kindergarten level, translated from French)

What do these various forms of diversity—ethnic, academic, behavioural, and social—and diverse physical and mental disabilities reveal about how institutions function?

INTEGRATION POLICIES AND LACK OF RESOURCES

The way in which schools function cannot be separated from all of the diversity they contain. When teachers have students in their class who have a limited knowledge of French, inadequate schooling, behavioural disorders, or physical or mental disabilities, they cannot teach as they would if they were in a homogeneous environment with students who were successful. In theory, integration policies are paired with substantial human resources. But do teachers feel they have the resources they need to carry out the Ministry of Education's ambitions for integration? In practice, the time and energy at their disposal are limited.

> The special education resource person we had was a gem. She supported me with the children who were experiencing difficulties; however, she is only here two days [a week] and she cannot perform miracles. By the end of the year, we both had burnout.... (Interview #5021, elementary level, translated from French)

One teacher was vehement in her criticism not of the principles or intentions of the student integration policy but of the ways in which it is being implemented.

> It's a trap. We want to integrate: i-n-t-e-g-r-a-t-e. But in the process of trying so hard to integrate every type of student we are de-integrating whole groups. If the teacher does not have the support of a speech therapist, he or she doesn't have time to work with a student with learning difficulties in a group of 32 or 33 students. And what happens is that this student

> drops out. If there was any way the government could create classes of 25, we would have the time to review the learning material with the children. Right now, the groups are being filled to over-capacity with just about anybody. (Interview #5029, elementary level, translated from French)

Many teachers reported that it was impossible to integrate students with diverse needs with inadequate resources. Often, services are delayed and when they do become available, the teachers only have very limited access to them.

The fact that the professionals who are supposed to help support students with learning difficulties are only there sporadically clearly illustrates the difficulties the teachers face in implementing the integration policies.

> This year, I have two kids who still can't read. And for me, it's very discouraging because I have 25 kids in my class. You want to help them all, but for these two particular kids I felt very [much like I was] drowning. I'm just treading water because they need such intense help and I can't give it to them because she [the teacher working with students with special needs] only comes in and out and her schedule is hectic, she is running all over the place, she has got all the other kids to help too. And we didn't really help them very much this year. That's the part that concerns me the most: how to help these kids who need it to that extent. (Interview #5084, elementary level)

The situation in Montreal's at-risk neighbourhoods is cause for concern. These neighbourhoods are home to more immigrant families because accommodation and general living expenses are cheaper there. At some schools, enrolment is constantly going up; given the lack of space, some schools will soon be turning students away. In this context, ethnic diversity is a major challenge to the Montreal school's function of integration and francization, not because of values or cultural conflicts but because of logistics.

DIVERSITY AND THE WORK AND IDENTITY OF TEACHERS

With diversity, there is an assumption that the education system will make accommodations, create policies, and promote certain values such as openness, the willingness to integrate, and the willingness to offer students traditionally marginalized from other students a chance to join the mainstream. Diversity not only forces institutions to question how they function and what values they are promoting, on an individual level, but it also forces teachers to redefine their roles. For some, it leads to a painful identity crisis.

When it comes to diversity, not all teachers are equal; there is an unequal division of labour. In resolutely interactionist terms, on a system-wide basis, the "dirty work" gets delegated (Hughes, 1996; Payet, 1997) to the public schools in at-risk neighbourhoods with high concentrations of students from immigrant families and students with adaptation and learning difficulties. On a school-wide basis, it is the new teachers who inherit what are familiarly referred to as "the grunt jobs."

> This is a difficult clientele. There are a lot of single-parent families, a lot of poverty. These kids aren't necessarily stimulated. In my class, only about one-quarter of the kids get their basic needs met. This is not an easy environment at all. Generally, when we post jobs, ours is the last school to be chosen. I wasn't asked if I wanted to be at School X or not ... because nobody wants to go to School X. (Interview #5060, elementary level, translated from French)

Our research team met with a teacher who was at the beginning of her career. She was fully occupied trying to manage her class, which was in survival mode in a difficult environment. She also had to support new teachers who were just starting out in spite of the fact that she barely had more experience or confidence than they did. However, there are teachers who are grappling with far more serious existential issues and who are wondering how to interpret the program, which parts to focus on, which culture to transmit to the students—the theoretical or the practical—and how fast to move the students along.

> My principal, who knows these students, told me to work at their pace. I am going to focus on learning that speaks to them, rather than on learning that is not all that important. On the other hand, there are students who are able to learn that the imperfect tense is written differently from the present or future tense. But these students form a "melting pot"; sometimes, I find it difficult to know what is most important for each student. (Interview #5040, elementary level, translated from French)

Other teachers are asking themselves whether certain students shouldn't be left behind so that the others will have a better chance of succeeding.

> Even when one child needs help because of his behaviour, which is a concern, you still have to look after the others. Sometimes you have children who pay for the other students who have behavioural problems. The energy that you put into that child—because there is no one else to look after him—is energy that you don't have for students with learning diffi-

> culies. They aren't getting the services they need either. It's a lot of things all at once. (Interview #5060, elementary level, translated from French)

Between their desire to take the students as far as possible in terms of learning and the temptation to leave some of them behind, teachers opt for a compromise, invoking the principle of the well-being of all students (Derouet, 1992). They focus their efforts on creating an atmosphere that is favourable for the children, especially for their personal growth. Their role is centred more on relationship than on the transmission of knowledge. At the very least, teachers work from the principle that knowledge can only be acquired if the student's well-being has been taken care of first.

> I find that the role of the teacher has changed a lot: it's not just teaching. You have a lot of students with big problems. They aren't just coming to school to learn things. (Interview #5087, elementary level, translated from French)

The notion that learning cannot take place without relationship is a recurring one in the discourse of teachers. Is this because they teach at the elementary level or because they work with students experiencing multiple difficulties? Regardless, their belief in the primacy of the children's well-being does not solve all of the problems in the classroom. And while it may reassure teachers in the choices they make, it does not necessarily obviate the need for deep reflection on their role as teachers.

PART 4: The Transformation of the School and its Social Function

Looking reflectively at the Quebec school system since the early 1960s, we see that it has continually sought to integrate students with extremely diverse academic, cultural, and social profiles by means of various education policies. The democratization of education in the 1960s promoted access to secondary and post-secondary education for the middle class. In this way, education was literally a springboard for a very large number of families and individuals (Robert & Tondreau, 1997). In the 1980s, we saw a new wave of integration. This time, it was the children of immigrants who were entering Quebec's francophone schools and who were being francized in *classes d'accueil*. The debate over the philosophical principles of integration has never ceased, nor has the debate over the role of the host society, its degree of openness to the Other, the degree of latitude that immigrants should be given, their responsibility to the host society, what constitutes successful integration, and so forth.

Should immigrants leave their cultural heritage behind and blend into the dominant culture or should they keep their heritage, forcing the host society to transform itself rather than imposing arbitrary cultural norms or policies of assimilation? Regardless of the outcome of these debates over the philosophical principles of the integration policy, in less than a decade, Quebec has succeeded in introducing francization structures in its elementary and secondary schools that make it possible for the children of immigrant families to get an education and to function in society in French.

This second wave of integration also includes efforts to integrate students traditionally excluded from the mainstream classroom. Since 2000, the integration policy has become radicalized. Many students in special education classes have been integrated into mainstream classrooms, as we have seen, with varying degrees of success. This integration has no doubt been difficult because of a lack of resources and certain shortcomings in the teacher training program, which focuses primarily on teaching under "normal" conditions in which students function relatively well. Many teachers lack experience when they start out and new teachers inherit the most difficult, if not the most thankless, tasks. It can also be said that integration has not been entirely successful for what are essentially social, cultural, and economic reasons. The weakening of the social fabric in some neighbourhoods, the fragmentation and impoverishment of families, and the major gap between the school culture and the students' culture of origin are also factors that explain why some students who are placed in mainstream classrooms have difficulty succeeding academically.

However—and this is one of the hypotheses raised in this chapter—the decentralization policy has resulted in destructuring effects in addition to those just mentioned. A school system driven by parents' demands rather than by a standard curriculum defined by the government runs counter to the policies on the integration of students, whether they are students from immigrant families or students traditionally excluded from the mainstream classroom.

And this is where the decentralization policy has a major impact on the transformation of the social function of the school, particularly on its integration function. Integrating all students into mainstream classrooms has resulted in an exodus of good students to good schools. At the secondary level, the exodus is most often to a private school. In order to avoid losing these good students to the private sector, the public schools have had to create elite classes starting at the elementary and in some cases the preschool level. Grouping all of the good students in certain institutions or classrooms inevitably leads to groups of students experiencing difficulties of all kinds in the other institutions or classrooms. The middle class, which derived the most benefit from the democratization of education in the 1960s in Quebec, is now abandoning the public system in greater numbers and adopting the behaviours of consumers of education services. How, then, can the school continue to assume its function of integration—creating social beings and cultural homogenization and imparting the references that make up the common culture—if children from different social classes are being educated in different institutions with different mission statements? In good institutions and good classrooms, the emphasis is on instruction. In the others, the emphasis is on socialization, education, and the avoidance of academic and social exclusion of the students.

In this way, the social function of integration of the Quebec school appears to have changed. In the 1960s, integration in Quebec took the form of a promise of upward mobility. At the present time, integration is focusing more on countering certain forms of social, cultural, and economic devaluation. The goal is no longer to reach the top of the social pyramid regardless of one's origins. The goal is to avoid a situation in which a large number of students languish in different forms of marginality. The school has a social function of reproduction that is disguised as making the public school more dynamic and making the education system more liberal.

All of these considerations of the social function of the school are more than simply theoretical. Integration, the management of diversity, and the struggle against exclusion refer to social and academic contexts, and to different public and political and academic actions. The struggle against exclusion may look like the integration of the 1960s; however, there are some important differences. Derouet (2000) states that the struggle against exclusion, which constitutes one of the means of managing diversity, assumes that there is a different model of society than the model that existed in the 1960s, as well as a different relationship between the school and society than the relationship that existed in the 1960s, when the school focused on achieving a model of equal opportunity in education. In Quebec, the education reform of the 1960s was designed to give every student, without distinction, an opportunity to rise to the top of the education system and society. At the present time, efforts in education focus on helping the weakest and most vulnerable avoid academic and social failure. As we have seen, the reform of the 1960s was led in the name of modernization. It was believed that modernization could stamp out the old social order with its inequalities and forms of poverty and indigence. We no longer believe that globalization, the new face of modernization, can solve all of the social problems that come with poverty.

Conclusion

By way of a conclusion, I would like to mention that the social function of the school is no longer defined in reference to a cohesive social entity to which it will give a definitive form. Nor, as we have just seen, is it defined in reference to an ideal of equal opportunity. The education system is structured in such a way that, upon graduation, good students have an opportunity to enter the cultural, social, and economic networks of globalization, whereas less successful students risk being shunted off to the margins of society, and eventually, rejected from society. If this happens, they will join the ranks of a sub-proletariat (Dubet, 2003) that exists beyond the reach of various forms of social security while depending on them permanently, with few opportunities to re-enter the world of production or the world of material and cultural consumption. In short, they join the ranks of a sub-proletariat that does not "have a place" in society and that cannot make plans based on a vision of the future or on an income that would enable them to escape abject poverty. Increasingly for these students who risk belonging to or who already belong to these groups of the excluded, the social function of the school appears to take the form of an action of socialization that replaces instruction, and the notion of equal and universal access to a common culture appears to be compromised.

In this way, what the Quebec Ministry of Education calls "integration" more closely resembles a struggle against the academic and social exclusion of students. This has consequences for the work of teachers. The diversity or heterogeneity of students, the difficulty of managing this diversity, and the introduction of education policies that provide the principles and structures to accommodate various forms of diversity are all major challenges for teachers, not only in their daily practices but also in the definition of their professional identity. The roles and values that guide a teacher's actions are not givens; a teacher must engage in an individual process of discovering what these are (Dubet & Martuccelli, 1996). On a more fundamental level, for the future of the profession, teachers must engage in this as a collective process of discovery.

Notes

1. Many different theories have expanded on the work of these critics, exploring the school's function of domination either through the determination of content based on the students' social group (Bernstein, 1975; Forquin, 1989; Young, 1971); the pedagogical relationship between teachers and students (Anyon, 1980; Becker, 1952; Keddie, 1971; Sirota, 1988); guidance, selection, and classification (Duru-Bellat & Mingat, 1999); and student grouping (Masson, 1999; Payet, 1995). Mention should also be made of trends in sociological theory with respect to the analysis of the processes that lead to racial inequality (black studies),

ethnic inequality (ethnic studies), and gender inequality (gender studies). An example is A. Van Zanten's meta-analysis (1996) of multiculturalism in schools in the United States and Great Britain, which deals extensively with studies on the social relations of ethnic and racial minorities.
2. The same postulate of complementarity between society and the individual supports the argument that is made for the modernization of society and the education system in the *Parent Report* (Government of Quebec, 1964b, p. 13; LeVasseur, 2000).
3. The school assumes another social function—the subject's construction of himself. However, it is less relevant than the three preceding functions for the purposes of this empirical study on the work of Montreal teachers in a context of diversity.
4. See the website of the Commission scolaire de Montréal at www.csdm.qc.ca/Csdm/ Administration/default.asp?csdm=mosaique consulted on May 1, 2006.
5. The Ministry of Education changed its name to the Ministry of Education, Recreation, and Sports with the Cabinet shuffle on February 18, 2005.
6. The function of these classrooms is to teach the French language to students who have recently immigrated. As soon as these students have acquired the rudiments of the French language, they are transferred to a mainstream classroom. Generally speaking, students spend an entire year in a *classe d'accueil*.
7. Bill 180 (An Act to amend the Education Act and various legislative provisions) was adopted on December 19, 1997. It defined the parameters for the decentralization of the Quebec education system; see also www2.publicationsduquebec.gouv.gc.ca/home.php# 1997, c. 96. The basic purpose of this decentralization policy was to give more decision-making power to the institutions so that the curriculum could be adapted to the needs of students and parents. However, the autonomy they were given came with a new type of management centred not on compliance with the curriculum programs but on an obligation to achieve results.
8. In the context of research on technical staff in Quebec schools, we met with many teachers, school principals, and human resources directors at the board level who confirmed the need for technical services, in particular the services of special education technicians. Special education technicians provide services that complete those provided by professionals such as psycho-educators; they do not replace these services. Whereas a professional makes a diagnosis, a technician works "on the ground," responding to emergencies, supervising students who have been expelled from the classroom, and so forth.
9. During this period, the only group to experience a larger increase—663.4 percent—was childcare workers employed in schools.
10. Data in full time equivalents. There are close to 11,000 specialized education technicians.
11. For more information on the research methodology, see Chapter 1 of this book, the MCRI website at www.teachcan.ca, or Riopel et al. (2007).

References

Althusser, L. (1970). Idéologie et appareils idéologiques d'État: Sur la reproduction des conditions de la production. *La Pensée*, June, 3–21.

Anyon, J. (1980). Social class and the hidden curriculum of work. *Journal of Education, 162*(1), 67–92.

Baudelot, C. & Establet, R. (1971). *L'école capitaliste en France*. Paris: Maspero.

Bernstein, B. (1975). *Langage et classes sociales: Codes socio-linguistiques et contrôle social*. (J.-C. Chamboredon, Trans.). Paris: Éditions de Minuit.

Becker, H.S. (1952). Social-class variations in the teacher-pupil relationship. *Journal of Educational Sociology, 25*(8), 451–465.

Bonafé-Schmitt, J.-P. (1997). La médiation scolaire: Une technique de gestion de la violence ou un processus éducatif? In B.J.-C. Charlot (Ed.), *Violences à l'école: État des savoirs* (pp. 255–282). Paris: Armand Colin.

Bourdieu, P. (1966). L'école conservatrice: Les inégalités devant l'école et devant la culture. *Revue française de sociologie, 7*, 325–347.

Bourdieu, P., & Passeron, J.-C. (1970). *La reproduction*. Paris: Éditions de Minuit.

Bourdieu, P., & Passeron, J.-C. (1964). *Les héritiers*. Paris: Éditions de Minuit.

Bowles, S., & Gintis, H. (1976). *Schooling in capitalist America*. New York: Basic Books.

Conseil supérieur de l'éducation. (1993). *Pour un accueil et une intégration réussis des élèves des communautés culturelles*. Quebec City: Government of Quebec.

Conseil supérieur de l'éducation. (1987). *Les défis éducatifs de la pluralité*. Quebec City: Government of Quebec.

Conseil supérieur de l'éducation. (1983). *L'éducation interculturelle*. Quebec City: Government of Quebec.

Dandurand, P. (1990). Démocratie et école au Québec: bilan et défis. In F. Dumont & Y. Martin (Eds.), *L'éducation 25 ans plus tard! Et après?* (pp. 37–60). Quebec City: Institut québécois de recherche sur la culture.

de Munck, J., & Verhoeven, M. (1997). *Les mutations du rapport à la norme*. Paris and Brussels: De Boeck & Larcier.

Derouet, J.-L. (2000). La sociologie des inégalités d'éducation à l'épreuve de la seconde explosion scolaire: Déplacements des questionnements et relance de la critique. *Éducation et Sociétés, 5*(1), 9–24.

Derouet, J.-L. (1992). *École et justice. De l'égalité des chances aux compromis locaux?* Paris: Éditions du Métailié.

Dubet, F. (2003). La société et ses stratifications. Inclus/exclus: une opposition pertinente? *Cahiers français, 314*, May/June, 47–52.

Dubet, F. (2002). *Le déclin de l'institution*. Paris: Seuil.

Dubet, F. (2000). L'école et l'exclusion. *Éducation et Sociétés, 5*(1), 43–57.

Dubet, F. (1994). *Sociologie de l'expérience*. Paris: Seuil.

Dubet, F., & Martuccelli, D. (1996). *À l'école: Sociologie de l'expérience scolaire*. Paris: Seuil.

Durkheim, É. (1989). *Éducation et sociologie*. Paris: Presses universitaires de France.

Duru-Bellat, M., & Mingat, A. (1999). Implications en termes de justice des modes de groupement des élèves. In D. Meuret (Ed.), *La justice du système éducatif* (pp. 99–112). Paris: DeBoeck.

Forquin, J.-C. (1989). *École et culture. Le point de vue des sociologues britanniques*. Brussels: DeBoeck Université.

Government of Quebec. (1964a). *Rapport de la Commission royale d'enquête sur l'enseignement dans la province de Québec (rapport Parent), Volume 1*. Quebec City: Government of Quebec.

Government of Quebec. (1964b). *Rapport de la Commission royale d'enquête sur l'enseignement dans la province de Québec (rapport Parent), Volume 2*. Quebec City: Government of Quebec.

Hughes, E. (1996). *Le regard sociologique*. Paris: Éditions de l'École des Hautes Études en Sciences Sociales.

Keddie, N. (1971). Classroom knowledge. In M.F.D. Young (Ed.), *Knowledge and control* (pp. 133–160). London: Collier-Macmillan.

Lessard, C., & Tardif, M. (1996). *La profession enseignante au Québec 1945–1990: Histoire, structures, système*. Montreal: Presses de l'université de Montréal.

LeVasseur, L., & Tardif, M. (2005). L'essor du travail technique en milieu scolaire et son incidence sur l'organisation du travail. *Recherches sociographiques, 46*(1), 97–118.

LeVasseur, L. (2006). *Décentralisation et concurrence dans le système d'éducation québécois et leurs effets sur le travail des enseignants*, CDHEP, Haute École de Pédagogie, Hep-Bejune, Switzerland, 15–28.

LeVasseur, L. (2003). Transformations culturelles et normatives dans le système d'éducation au Québec. In P. Beaucage & J.-P. Dupuis (Eds.), *Des sociétés en mutation* (pp. 201–225). Quebec City: Éditeur Nota Bene.

LeVasseur, L. (2000). La dérive instrumentale de la formation générale dans les collèges du Québec. *Sociologie et sociétés, 32*(1), 197–211.

Martuccelli, D. (2000). Évolution des problématiques. Études sociologiques des fonctions de l'école. *L'année sociologique, 50*(2), 297–318.

Masson, P. (1999). *Les coulisses d'un lycée ordinaire. Enquête sur les établissements secondaires des années quatre-vingt-dix*. Paris: Presses universitaires de France.

Ministère de l'éducation, du loisir et du sport. (2006). *Portrait scolaire des élèves issus de l'immigration: de 1994–1995 à 2003–2004*. Quebec City: Government of Quebec.

Ministère de l'éducation du Québec. (2004). *Indice de milieu socio-économique par école. Indice du seuil de faible revenu par école. Données 2003–2004*. Quebec City: Government of Quebec.

Ministère de l'éducation du Québec. (1999a). *Laïcité et religions, (rapport Proulx)*. Quebec City: Government of Quebec.

Ministère de l'éducation du Québec. (1999b). *Une école adaptée à tous ses élèves. Politique de l'adaptation scolaire*. Quebec City: Government of Quebec.

Ministère de l'éducation du Québec. (1998). *Une école d'avenir. Politique d'intégration scolaire et d'éducation interculturelle*. Quebec City: Government of Quebec.

Ministère de l'éducation du Québec. (1997). *L'école, tout un programme. Énoncé de politique éducative*. Quebec City: Government of Quebec.

Ministère de l'éducation du Québec. (1996). *Les États généraux sur l'éducation, 1995–1996. Rénover notre système d'éducation: dix chantiers prioritaires*. Quebec City: Government of Quebec.

Ministère de l'éducation du Québec. (1985). *Rapport du comité sur l'école québécoise et les communautés culturelles* (Committee Chair: Max Chancy). Quebec City: Government of Quebec.

Ministère de l'éducation du Québec. (1979). *L'école québécoise. Énoncé de politique et plan d'action*. Quebec City: Government of Quebec.

Ministère de l'éducation du Québec. (1976). *L'éducation de l'enfance en difficulté d'adaptation et d'apprentissage au Québec: rapport du Comité provincial de l'enfance inadaptée (COPEX)*. Quebec City: Government of Quebec.

Pagé, M. (1988). L'éducation interculturelle au Québec: Bilan critique. In F. Ouellet (Ed.), *Pluralisme et école* (pp. 271–300). Institut québécois de recherche sur la culture.

Payet, J.-P. (1997). Le "sale boulot." Division morale du travail dans un collège de banlieue. *Les Annales de La Recherche Urbaine, 75*, 19–31.

Payet, J.-P. (1995). *Collèges de banlieue. Ethnographie d'un monde scolaire*. Paris: Méridiens Klincksieck.

Riopel, M.-C., Gérin-Lajoie, D. & Grimmet, P. (2007). Étude longitudinale du cheminement professionnel d'enseignants et de directeurs d'écoles primaires et secondaires. *Formation et profession, Bulletin du CRIFPE, 14*(1), 23–26.

Robert, M., & Tondreau, J. (1997). *L'école québécoise: débats, enjeux et pratiques sociales*. Montreal: Centre éducatif et culturel.

Rosanvallon, P. (1981). *La crise de l'État-providence*. Paris: Éditions du Seuil.

Sirota, R. (1988). *L'école primaire au quotidien.* Paris: Presses universitaires de France.

Touraine, A. (1997). *Pourrons-nous vivre ensemble? Égaux et différents.* Paris: Fayard.

Touraine, A. (1992). *Critique de la modernité.* Paris: Fayard.

Van Zanten, A. (1996). La scolarisation des enfants et des jeunes des minorités ethniques aux Etats-Unis et en Grande-Bretagne. *Revue française de pédagogie, 117*, 117–149.

Young, M.F.D. (Ed.). (1971). *Knowledge and Control. New Directions for the Sociology of Education.* London: Collier-Macmillan.

Zéroulou, Z. (1988). La réussite scolaire des enfants d'immigrés. L'apport d'une approche en termes de mobilisation. *Revue française de sociologie, 29*(1988), 447–470.

CHAPTER 7

Marking Bodies
INHABITING THE DISCURSIVE PRODUCTION OF OUTSTANDING "CANADIAN EDUCATION" WITHIN GLOBALIZATION

Christine Connelly

At its core, globalization, and thus also education, has a dual nature. It is the majoritarian processes and effects of homogenization, assimilation, and regulation aligned with the expansion of production on a global scale (Ghosh, 2004, p. 88). At the same time, it is also all that exceeds the reductions of capitalism, moving alongside coloniality (Benítez Rojo, 1996; Farris Thompson, 1983). The work of schools straddles and sometimes reconfigures these two logics.

In terms of majoritarian logics of globalization, the past decade has seen the implementation of a number of educational and social reforms in Canada aimed at eliminating high dropout rates, declining economic productivity, poverty, and a lack of functional literacy (Apple, 2000, p. 57). These factors have been presented as barriers involved in the declining ability of Canadian society to stay at the forefront of the emerging information age. Proponents of this movement share the common assumption that "change is unavoidable" and that "individuals, families, schools, firms and nations" must adapt to the new conditions of modern life characterized by new technologies, the reorganization of labour and trade relations, evolving communities, and changing social roles (Statistics Canada, 2005). Such notions privilege the goals of economic development, fiscal growth, and the accumulation of capital through increased productivity and consumption. The intensification of globalization in late capitalism has meant a reorganization of power where the future of local and national prosperity is predicated on the degree of one's alignment with the actors, interests, and ideologies of trade liberalization in the multinational corporate economy. The role of the nation in this social order is one of complicity, aiming to construct and reproduce domesticity and citizenship in convergence with the goals of sustaining the global market, especially in characterizing society as a "knowledge economy" in the "global village" aligned with technology (Drucker, 1969). In this context, the value of the individual is primarily that of his or her contribution to the greater value of economic growth and the global expansion of capital (Evans & Ayers, 2006). Implicit in the emphasis on individual participation in the global economy is the importance of a moral order of individual independence and responsibility in which individuals are expected to pull their weight, to earn their place in society, and to participate to their full capacity in capitalism in return for its wealth, particularly in a world of scarcity. Jordan (2001) defines five principles involved in defining education reform in terms of economic accountability and market-driven demand: 1) diversification; 2) decentralization (distributing responsibility for implementation, decision making, and funding and outsourcing tasks); 3) contestability (competition for resources); 4) prescription/surveillance (through standards-based reform); and 5) accountability to parents (pp. 350–351). Canadian classrooms, oriented toward the knowledge and skills required in the private sector, have been in the process of implementing revised standards of education as a means of ensuring the nation's status as a strong, efficient, unified, productive society where students, especially citizens aligned with the "first world," count as capital.

With the heightened emphasis on promoting education and skills development as an extended individual and collective responsibility to keep up with social change through lifelong learning, educational reform implies new mechanisms of social surveillance, regulation, monitoring, and discipline. One Canadian study, the *Adult Literacy and Lifeskills Survey* (ALL), notes "significant numbers of adult Canadians with low-level literacy skills that constrained their participation in society and in the economy," estimating that 15 percent of Canadians fail to meet the minimum competency requirements "for successfully functioning within the emerging knowledge society and information economy" (Treasury Board of Canada, 2005). By contrast, other recent reports, such as *The State of Learning in Canada: No Time for Complacency*, indicate the improved academic performance of high school students and increased enrolment in post-secondary education, but sound the alarm with respect to increasing poverty among children and continued gaps between socially advantaged and socially disadvantaged groups, particularly the poor, women, the elderly, Aboriginal peoples, and recent immigrants (Canadian Council on Learning, 2007). Another report, *Promoting Adult Learning* (Organisation for Economic Co-Operation and Development, 2005), highlights the importance of upgrading the skills of disadvantaged groups as a means of ensuring that all populations have equally developed skills, thus raising the overall economic performance and preventing further socio-economic and cultural "exclusion."

Yet, by some measures, educational reform predicated on the transmission of the majoritarian terms of the emerging economy has not been sufficient to produce the sort of substantive change that would eradicate poverty, illiteracy, or other markers of marginality. There is also mounting evidence that such initiatives exacerbate existing gaps between the privileged and the underprivileged, especially without substantively redressing the root causes of social bifurcation. Recent scholarship in a number of sub-specialties in social theories of education has taken issue with the terms of excellence that come to define the knowledges considered worthy of excellence, merit, and inclusion (sub-specialties such as critical theory, women's studies, queer theory, anti-colonial theory, and Aboriginal studies, among others). Critics have warned of the devaluation of indigenous knowledges (Apffel-Marglin, 1998; Tuhiwai-Smith, 1999) and the further alienation of those whose lived actuality has never been defined in terms of capitalism as the basis of inclusion, sustainability, and survival (Arguedas, 2000). Scholarship has for some time addressed the fear that with the expansion of elite power, the perpetuation of the values and representations of consumer culture will come to dominate in the transmission of knowledges, superimposing a homogenized worldview that advances a narrowed sense of what counts as legitimate (Baudrillard, 1988; Jameson, 1991).

However, the persistence of diversity across global social contexts continues to challenge the dominance of majoritarian power. Globalization is also seen as a site of instability where the governing structures of nation-states and their instruments of social control and reproduction are faced with the unexpected. The stability, uniformity, and sustainability of national identities is under siege, subject to a constant traffic of new identities formed with multiple, shifting allegiances on the nomadic terms of an informal realm of power and sociality beyond the jurisdiction of nationality or citizenship. The classroom, with its terms of privilege, as a site of hybridity can hardly contain the multiple identities of its diverse student and teacher body.

This chapter examines how teachers and principals engage the work of schools within such a framework of education at this current moment of globalization. In particular, how do teachers and principals imagine the work that they do in relationship to the terms of recent educational reform with its emphasis on excellence? How do educators make sense of their responsibilities and the possibilities of engaging in socially transformative ways in the context of diverse or historically asymmetric student populations?

Methods

In the discussion that follows, I will review the construction of education and social difference through the lens of interview data collected by a team of researchers in conversation with teachers and principals in Vancouver (1XXX-encoded series interviews), Toronto (4XXX-encoded series interviews), and Montreal (5XXX-encoded series interviews), in attempt to denote the premises given weight in the current discourse of educators in this particular historical moment of globalization and education.[1] In particular, for the purposes of this chapter, I will address select comments of teachers and principals in response to questions posed in Interview 2 in Year 3 of the study, in relation to curriculum and accountability, which were framed in terms of inviting teachers and principals to talk about their perceptions of ethnocultural diversity in their school context. The term *ethnocultural* diversity might seem euphemistic to English speakers since it eclipses the significance of race as a framework of analysis; the term *ethnocultural* is commonly used as a referent in French, though without a radical problematization of whiteness or racialization. Some questions in the Year 3, Interview 2 sequence sought information about how they as individual teachers and principals had rearticulated their practices to correspond with their student body and whether official texts had played a role in framing their work. Other questions inquired about the significance of province-specific policies regarding accountability, provincial testing, and curriculum reform to their individual practice as teachers or principals. The subtext of these questions is that education arises in a context of reform situated within globalization processes that result in increasing immigration and thus the increasing ethnocultural diversification of schools.

Homogeneity, Diversity, and Educators' Discourses in Canada

In spite of official policy advocating for equity approaches to education (Ontario Ministry of Education, 1993), the structuring of school and society also continues to be informed by a deficit-oriented approach to newcomers' knowledges, consistent with a long tradition of remedial education that privileges "norms" associated with a white, male, able, "northwestern," Euro-American standard of superiority, civilization, achievement, and excellence, against which the difference of recent immigrants' under-recognized background knowledges is perceived in terms of a potential weakness that threatens to diminish the standing of the target society. Despite the liberal human rights values promoted in official multiculturalism, the homogeneous society has often been invoked as the emblem of success. The Canadian school is no exception to this thinking. A homogenous school is considered apt to success, while a school with a high proportion of "underperforming" recent immigrants is seen as having a handicap in the race to the top in a school system designed for accountability to the reproduction of standards associated with white Euro-American heteropatriarchal capitalist notions of progress, modernization, technologization, and development.

The debate regarding mainstreaming versus ability grouping has a long history in Canadian schools. Research has shown that certain groups of students, including blacks, minority language students, recent immigrants, and students from single-parent or working-class families, have historically been overrepresented in special education programs (Curtis, Livingstone & Smaller, 1992; Dei, 2000). The production of a society marked by an elite leadership and a supporting underclass has long been justified, as with the educational policy advocacy of Durkheim (1969), through ability grouping and streaming, as an instrument of broader social meritocracy. "Steamer classes," for example, in early 20th-century Ontario were developed as "special education" units that would segregate, contain, and reform immigrant children from working-class backgrounds, with an emphasis on a psycho-medical deficit approach to educational remediation that would result in the children's assimilation to a white Anglo/Euro-American-centred "Canadian" model of social participation (Bélanger, 2003; Marshall, 1990). "Special needs students" continue to be defined relative to the notion of a homogenous, stable, Canadian population tied to a white Anglo/Eurocentric heteropatriarchal capitalist origin.

The impetus to produce student capital for the ends of the private sector means honouring certain forms of rationality, reason, or models of knowledge production aligned with objective, empirically observable scientific method and oriented toward a singular truth, at the expense of other knowledges or ways of knowing judged to be superfluous. Performance assessment, as with mandatory standardized testing, is not questioned for its terms of legitimate knowledge, nor is the washback effect that such measurement has on the way in which content is selected and delivered—often in a conventional teacher-directed, teacher-centred, transmission-oriented approach, with emphasis on discrete knowledge, seen as more efficient given the strict time constraints for curriculum delivery.

In a system that values diversity insofar as it is consistent with elitism or competitive advantage, but generally rewards normativity, a school's status, and thus its students' general performance, depends on how well individual students distinguish themselves in terms of the official norms encoded as school membership. Students entering the school as "different," or viewed as "poorly prepared," are met with judgments of inadequate performance or expectations of assimilation to the norm—for example, to act like other students, to demonstrate an average level of competency, or to dress or look like other students. In principle, the logic of sameness, coherence, and unity functions on a gross level as the ethos and telos of the school, and as the condition for its presence and the impetus or hope for its future. Such a climate inscribes teachers in a particular logic of education that means reproducing in each student the same exit profile: the universal values of a same education for all, where hope lies in the promise of cohesive schools and a unified society.

Assimilation Discourse

The production of a universal education for a diverse body of students presents educators with the conundrum of a paradigm which, following Lather (1986), brings individuals to inscribe themselves into an a priori logic of foundational schemas established to reduce "science" to objects that reproduce themselves according to tautological frameworks. Positivist discourse marks an attempt to filter out subjectivity and to reduce the ambiguity of what Lather (1986) refers to as the "essential indeterminacy of human experience." Similarly, a foundationalist discourse is one in which identity is defined in relationship to a static and knowable origin and group characteristics reframed as legitimate in opposition to atavistic origins; that a fixed and knowable law governs identity in terms of principles or values associated with the work of the school, as with its society. In this paradigm, the notion of a "common" education for all overrules "diversity" in superimposing a knowledge paradigm that presupposes the stability of knowledges and bodies.

In the data emerging in the transcripts of the interviews with teachers and principals in Vancouver, Montreal, and Toronto, it was particularly striking to read the extent to which the discourse on immigrant children as the Other was made present in relationship to a society taken for granted to be majoritarian. At the risk of reproducing a problematic dominant discourse of naming/reiterating marginalization, I take time here to unpack how the Othering of immigrant children takes effect; these narrative structures are inherent to a homogenizing discourse of globalization and education.

School discourse simplifies student identities into the terms of "group identities"; in this view, difference is collapsed around particular attributes (e.g., country of origin), with the erasure of other attributes representing complexity (e.g., length of time in Canada, nature of the individuals' sociopolitical relationships within the country of origin). Such elisions make social difference knowable, stabilized, and thus "manageable." Prevalent in this study is an overarching awareness on the part of some educators of the transformation of metroregions that, as other studies have observed, have become "increasingly economically, racially, ethnically and culturally heterogeneous and socially differentiated" (Lipman, 2005, p. 141). "Ethnocultural diversity" in the context of demographic change is often understood in binary terms as denoting people of colour relative to an invisible "whiteness" that is represented as a foundational and uniform presence associated with "true" Canadianness. Often the educators' language around naming difference in these interviews falls into a language of "helping others," or the binary opposition of "us and them" articulated in static terms, as in the language of this Toronto-based teacher:

> First it takes a committee to welcome those people, to make them understand the context. So to do that we set up partners, even with the parents; we put together a peer mediation team and we put into place a project against bullying. Because those people arrived from different regions ... in particular, last year we experienced problems between the Hutus and the Tutsis, even though they are the same colour, but they had major intestine wars, even at school. (Interview #4101)

Differences within what in the dominant logic constitutes "ethnocultural groups" are elided in terms of abstracted generalities. The categorization of students in fixed and knowable terms finds its expression in the assertion of school authority to engage what Coco Fusco has referred to as "managing the other" (Fusco, 1990). One teacher in Vancouver, for example, reframed the question about the existence of official policy in terms of "dealing with" difference in terms of Canadian values:

> Are we taught how to deal with the cultural customs, for example, of people coming from different areas? No, we aren't. We just try to use our own Canadian decorum and, hopefully, we treat people correctly. (Interview #1109)

"Canadian decorum" is presented as the fixed and knowable reality in the domain of educators and a corrective framework for encountering difference. This discourse also implies the stability of the educator's identity, uninfluenced by the Other. The fiction of national identity is not called into question (Anderson, 1991), nor is the notion of "culture" problematized as a construction in the sense suggested by Glissant (1997) that culture is "the precaution of those who claim to think thought but who steer clear of its chaotic journey" (p. 1).

The way in which the educator's identity and the school's official knowledges are established relative to those of immigrant students depends on the way in which the educators' discursive framework is aligned with a logic that associates difference relative to a normative structure as something requiring the educator's intervention. In considering what constitutes "good" relative to "bad" students, evaluation and selection criteria for admission to elite programs is determined according to a neoliberal logic of "colour-blindness."

> Students in the vocational program are identified by the Grade 8 school from our catchment area, and so they're just sending students who iden-

tified by percentile scores on intelligence tests. So regardless of cultural background, I'm looking at scores and determining whether this student meets the profile or not, and then they're in or they're not. (Interview #4177)

Here, the signifier of "ethnocultural identity" is both inscribed in hierarchy and emptied of histories of subjectivity/objectivity. In this perspective, taking the intelligence test to be the most neutral measure of merit, all students are considered to have equal rights under the common conditions of "education for all"; standardized testing is similarly taken to be the best possible measure of students' relative performance under the same controlled conditions of the classroom. Such a framing—an expression of students' equality—masks a normative, deficit discourse that certain students are considered to have earned access to resources that less capable children cannot appreciate to the same extent. The discrepancy between student test results is attributed to individual causes—for example, a second language deficiency, or a knowledge deficiency as a result of lack of exposure to the "Canadian" education system, low ability, inability to function in the regular classroom, or the need for access to resources.

Not only does the educational project become defined as the production of a sort of school success defined by normative outcomes, but with the ongoing reallocation of resources to special education and language remediation, whether through "mainstreaming" or segregation models of inclusion, education and the sustainability of the school is represented more in terms of the prevention of school and social failure. In some contexts, "special education" is extended to "all children" within a particular, essentialized population. For example, in one francophone school in Toronto described by the principal as "very multicultural," the school has implemented a new special program to prevent student failure on the new provincial testing, especially in mathematics:

> With last year's math tests—Grade 9—we realized that in applied math, there was a mark that really didn't meet my expectations. So, this year we put the accent on getting back those kids who had difficulty, which has meant that in some respects I have had to change the whole format of my math department, requiring attendance at regular meetings—once a month, all my math teachers have meetings during school hours, so we have to find substitutes for them. They have to submit reports to me. We did practice tests with all the Grade 8 and 9 students. That's a big deal—supervision, preparing the tests—practice tests that will help them to understand how it works—we went through the Grade 9 EQAO test

to highlight the elements from Grades 7, 8, and 10. So, you see, it is a whole structure—it's major. (Interview #4101, translated from French)

In other contexts, children identified as "at risk" as immigrant students from working-class communities have tended to become highly represented in special education programming. Special classes are created for such students to provide students identified as "having special needs," and non-identified students, with "access to education" that they would otherwise not have.

> We have three district programs here at the school. One for students who have FASD: Fetal Alcohol Spectrum Disorder. One for students in the ICAP Program and one for students in the life skills program, which is—what's turned into or become, in our school district—students with severe autism. And then what we have moved toward is what we call "the learning clusters," which is to break down the staffing barriers between the [name of school], the various other district programs that were strictly just around education, like students who would be functioning three to four grade levels below. This breakdown creates groups based on academic need and then also opens it up to students who haven't been able to get in because they've been on a district wait list and, therefore, have jumped through lots of hoops to get service. So, our kind of our learning clusters incorporate everybody between life skills and the regular stream. (Interview #1018)

One teacher frames this institutional structure as a means of "integration" to prevent "dropout":

> They also decided that we have, in the school, two clusters of fetal alcohol kids ... staying on track, staying in school, there's a program for that. (Interview #1019)

Where schools in some districts have become, as these Vancouver teachers describe, defined in relationship to the marginality of their student populations—marked, for example as working class or newcomer populations (with no explicit mention of racial profiling, but referenced in terms of "ethnic diversity")—schools are also vying for "model" students to reassert their legitimacy as a "better choice" for enrolment among available local schools.

> In my elective area, in my area in music, we lost three or four of the best kids from my previous school because their parents sold their houses and bought another house in another catchment area. It was that bad, and that was before the act was passed. The effect is to ghettoize schools

> because the mobile parents, the parents who are interested in their kids' education, will move them. Without the better students, it's resulted in academic magnets.... (Interview #1019)

In order to preserve its status as a "good school," the administration of another school in Toronto implemented an elite International Baccalaureate (IB) program with the intention of improving the school's public standing, the secret to its success being the blending of low-achieving, poor children with high-achieving children from well-off families.

> There was a recent document, a social index factor, that did a survey of, I think, about six, seven, or eight social factors of the families in the ... board, which included single-family homes, families living on government assistance, recent immigrants, highest level of education in the home, earning capacity, language spoken, a number of things like that. They came up with what they considered to be a risk factor. And because they determined that families with high-risk factors had low readiness to learn, the children had low readiness to learn. So they felt it was important to know how this was affecting schools. The biggest secret is we are one of the five neediest high schools in all of 43 on a social risk factor. When you bring in an IB program to a school, you bring in very, very educated families—families that have a high educational standard, right? You blend them with all kinds of kids. If you take a look at [a nearby street], all of those buildings along [that nearby street] are all high-rise buildings and they all have families that have a different earning capacity. So you take a look at this school in this community and you think, we have a really intriguing blend of low socio-economic, low performing, high performing, low needs, high needs. But to be ranked one of the top three neediest high schools in 43.... I mean, we see some really needy kids in this school and then we see some really, really high-performing kids in the school, and they're all blending together. Plus all the different cultures. (Interview #4170)

In the above example, the prevention of school failure is explicitly articulated as a socio-economic endeavour to raise the standards and commensurately also the standard of living of the school population. In Montreal, when one principal of a francophone school described the impact of the gentrification (the production of conditions of upward class mobility in a formerly subordinate socio-economic context) of the school catchment area on the homogeneity and whiteness of the schools, he noted that it would be "difficult to gentrify" or eradicate that which was referred to as a strong presence of visible minority of Haitian, Jamaican, Afro-American, and Asian students who constituted 15 percent of the student population (Interview #5003). In another school, a teacher describes the virtue of a "well-blended diversity" without "a predominant culture":

> Well, there are largely the same groups, although I think the movement is to Southeast Asian. And the students call themselves brown, so I'm wondering if that might pose a problem in the future because the great thing with the school is that it has such a well-blended diversity and it doesn't really have a predominant culture. But I sense that there's a little increase that way. And a bit of vocalization of some of that. (Interview #4171)

In effect, the predominant culture is the target culture to which students are expected to assimilate, as seen in this example in a less diverse area of Montreal:

> Twenty-five percent are children of ethnic origin, and there is a great variety of origins. So 25 percent of the children are well integrated. Some have difficulties because they speak English when they arrive at preschool, and they have never spoken French. There is an integration of these children in our contexts; for some children it works, and for other children we send them to specific classes for newcomers, where they present problems, even in their languages of origin, and there you must detect those children. But generally they're well integrated because one child in five is from an origin other than Québécois francophone. So, does it have a major impact? I am prepared to say that it does because the majority speak French and are integrated. I'd say that in a school where it would be 75 percent allophones and 25 percent Québécois, well, that would be a whole other dynamic. (Interview #5001, translated from French)

Where the norms of the school and its broader society arise in disjuncture with the everyday norms of its subjects, the threat of rupture is seen in majoritarian discourse to require mechanisms of social order to reiterate the sort of unity able to preserve the continuity of a fragmented society. The dissimilarity of student values with those of the school is often cited as a source of disruption, for example, in the language of one teacher describing a Roma student as lacking certain values required in the Canadian context concerning individual and collective responsibility:

> Resp.: Well, with Roma children, for example, the big thing is to talk to them. I find it's important to talk to them and to talk about their culture, and let them try to tell you why they're here, and how they're treated elsewhere. And ask them why do they think they're being treated that way.

> Now as kids, they don't have the first concept of why they should not be preferred, okay. They grow into accepting the values of the community amazingly well. Which is almost anti-societal in many ways.
> Int.: But it seems to be if they grow up with a family and in a culture that instills those values, it's hard to go against those, right?
> Resp.: Yeah. But they don't see any comparisons. It blinds them, because of the limited ability to be out of that community. They have nothing to compare it with. So they never see it as wrong. They never see it as non-growth producing, or a disadvantage. (Interview #4129)

Here, educator discourse emerges as an essentialized set of values appropriate to the school context, in opposition to essentialized student values, with the sense that the student must move beyond what is construed as a field of vision circumscribed by identification with a community of difference. Faced with the demands of standardized curriculum, educators work to prevent the emergence of conflict by suppressing difference in the name of unity, sameness, and dangerous solidarities. One teacher performs herself as neutral and neutralizing in an erasure of difference:

> You see, I am a Christian, and the others are Muslim. When we talk about religion, I put the emphasis on faith and belief—spirituality; I try not to dissociate religions from our broader religion because I know that it is faith that is important. So although the children are in a Christian and Catholic school, I try to talk about faith while mixing and showing the children that Christian faith cannot be dissociated from human faith. It's human faith that brings a person to Christian faith. Because if you humanly live something else, you would not tell me from a spiritual point of view that there is something else that makes you who you are as a person. But I don't place emphasis on these things to say that no, I don't like Muslims. There are times where the students state their opinions, especially in Grade 12 with the great religions and Islam, which we saw in the history of civilizations. Students raise opinions by saying, Muslims are like this. I listen to them—we talk about American politics, we talk about world politics—but at some point I try to remain neutral, because I cannot give my opinion. So there I say: That is what you say, I think that you must have a reason. (Interview #4104)

School authority functions to dismantle and reorient the power of the critical mass of minority groups as a marked presence with the potential to disrupt school unity. Several educators expressed concern about the potential problem of children communicating with one another in South Asian languages not understood by school officials:

Resp.: Yeah, well that's a good question. If it's just a little idle chat before the start of a lesson, that's okay, but we we try not to have conversations where we don't know what's going on. I mean, they could be talking negatively about somebody.... So yeah, English is what's expected. (Interview #4171)

Transformative Discourse

In the aforementioned examples, educator discourse on diversity reproduces the notion that minority and immigrant populations represent a barrier or even a threat to the status of a school; this orientation finds its pragmatic expression in reform at the local level in attempt to "compensate" for perceived deficits.

The deficit discourse is not the only discourse, however, in circulation. Documents such as the *Plan of action for educational integration and intercultural education, 1998—2002: A new direction for success* (Ministère de l'Éducation du Québec, 1998), articulate the need for "zero exclusion" (p. iii). In anglo-dominant economic contexts, documents emerged organized around liberal discourse of "inclusion," such as *Language education in BC Schools* (BC Ministry of Education, 1996) or *Diversity in BC Schools: A framework* (BC Ministry of Education, 2004), revised from its former 2001 edition to reflect greater awareness of sexual diversity, socio-economic background, and "an increasingly diverse population" (though this is presented as an "ongoing challenge" rather than an asset) (p. 9). Often, there are contradictions between policies advocating for barrier-free environments and those imposing social order (e.g., "official languages" framework as the modus operandi despite students' and educators' multilingualism). Yet, in the interstices of social regulation, schools as spaces of diversity also suggest the possibility of meaningful engagements with popular culture that exceeds the tight scripts of hegemonic discourses.

In some school contexts, diversity was interpreted in "additive" terms as a strength. For instance, in one Toronto francophone school, the principal describes a situation where the school has in principle adapted to the reality of language diversity by relaxing its discipline over language use while struggling to maintain the status of French as a language of social engagement in an anglo-dominant environment.

> Although we had untreatables in terms of English, I think we reached a mutual understanding. More and more, people seem to be interested in speaking French, knowing that economically, culturally, it is possible. Whereas before it was a big battle between us. We sense that with globalization, people speak several languages. So, without saying that it's in fashion to speak French, there is an interest in speaking French on the

> part of students and even parents. We feel it—even the third language, which is Spanish—our courses are full in Spanish because everyone wants to go. So, there is that interest, whereas before we were feeling offended, we resisted. On our behalf, I think English is more accepted too because we feel less threatened, our school boards are more solid in terms of their structures—the school, the parents, the environment—we feel stronger, more solid. I think we are capable of *coping* better with that aspect, and I find that positive … I would dare to say that there has been a beautiful pedagogical evolution and a good French/English integration now. (Interview #4101, translated from French)

Similarly, in another bilingual school in Montreal, an additive bilingualism approach to language diversity meant a positive view of language diversity and an acceptance of the students' multilingualism.

> It's not very visible here because most of the children seem so comfortable in English. French is spoken in their French classes, that is insisted upon, and they're doing very, very well. However, when they're playing outside, they're welcome and that's not an issue. We don't have to deal with it. They're more than welcome. We're intrigued. We ask them to tell us what they're saying. We joke with them. We learn from them. They enjoy telling us things and laughing at our pronunciation. It is not an issue. It's part of growing. (Interview #5086)

In other schools, an inclusive education mandate is given priority, in terms of the establishment of "unity" between students in spite of the hierarchies established through provincial standardized testing:

> We don't ignore [ethnocultural difference], but we call ourselves a community and we've worked on that since Grade 8. The kids that I have in my school come from very tight family groupings, and we typify that family grouping as a small culture or a small community. And my class is another community that comes together, and we spend six hours a day together, we talk with one another, we go to class with one another. So I told my students, "Well, the school is being profiled"—we get profiled quite a bit and usually we have mostly positive results with how well we do with government exams. All the kids sighed, "Awww." And all these kids are good kids, they've got fairly good marks, and I said, "What is wrong?" and one student said, "Well, [Teacher], what about the community?" And I said, "You know what, guys, you are perfectly right. We are about community, we do very well in government exams and when I

give this report, I am going to say schools are more than just government exams," and that was part of the focus. (Interview #1032)

Here the teacher finds herself in the pivotal role between mediating "community" despite the accountability measures reiterating the disparity between "good students" and "bad students" within a context of ethnocultural diversity.

ACCOUNTABILITY

In an era of increased emphasis on the accountability of schools to the public, schools conversely also exercise greater control over the documented student/teacher/administrator activities. Educators' discourse on diversity thus attributes a new role for the school that, while empathetic, draws on the importance of being fully accountable for each student, to the extent at times of presuming to intervene as a substitute or extension of parental authority or responsibility, to ensure that no students are beyond the jurisdiction of school authority as a means of socialization. One teacher in Toronto conveys her sense of responsibility to intervene:

> I'd rather do failure prevention. And when you talk about kids that leave and kids that do drugs. I've got a kid living in a car. I've got kids in the homeless shelter that I've registered. You want to tell me about normal things with them? I've got kids whose parents are dying. I've got kids from war-torn countries and I need time and people to help them. So that to me is a policy piece that's really hard. Although I understand and I respect the concept that health services should be doing the health component and we should be doing the education component; it's really hard to teach a kid who hasn't had breakfast, or who has slept all night in a car. You know I've got to feed the kid, make sure he feels warm, and then he'll learn, you know. In one case, the kid was having a hard time at home and was going to leave. He came to us to ask what we could do for him, and my best advice was to go to the shelter because the shelter has all kinds of social services and I have nothing. The government is looking at the new policy on experiential work, it's something called Pathways, which is the idea of the International Baccalaureate, for example, as a designated program. You must do this. Why is it that our brightest kids take a designated program, but our most at-risk kids don't have a designated program? They could choose whatever they want, and so starting down the line from the government and other boards and soon to come to my school and my board; we're going to start; we have a brand-new headship next year called Head of Alternative Programs. And we're going to get him

> to look at designating a program. So we're going to say, "You have to take this." Now if they fight us, we can try to change it, but kids are getting at the end sort of not knowing what they're doing. And the families aren't really capable of helping them. They're usually families who are struggling in a number of ways. So we're going to try it. (Interview #4170)

The administrator's omniscient discourse on the "at-risk child" reveals the degree to which the apparatus of school authority has gained access—and presumed the need—to enter the student's private realm. The boundary between school and extracurricular involvement is blurred in such encounters. Such mechanisms of surveillance have been described elsewhere as in terms of the micropolitics of disciplinary power (Foucault, 1973, p. 123), where the school institution can assume the therapeutic functions of a "normal family." The right to continue to manage one's own affairs as a family is carefully monitored by school officials, who must be prepared to assume the duty of care of involving appropriate specialists and state agencies to remand custody of children "neglected" through "improper" guardianship. A hegemonic discourse of surveillance operates here in a way that individuates blame, especially in the context of those under the gaze as "Other." A Toronto teacher expresses her presumption that aggression arises from a racialized cultural context:

> Sometimes I find that the way a child is raised is a bit aggressive, but the child won't talk to you about it, but maybe there is physical abuse, maybe, in terms of the culture that comes from Africa or in the schools, it is still possible to hit the child. I perhaps have a sense of what is happening at home, but the child comes to school and doesn't tell you about it, you don't see any marks, you don't have any proof, but you ask yourself ... I don't know. It's not the majority, but it's a few cases. (Interview #4108)

There is a need here to interrogate how the identification of "at risk" is established in the relations of power constructing the divide between school officials aligned with the dominant and racialized students constructed as marginal.

Meanwhile, the surveillance discourse that objectifies "at-risk" students also works to subject the school to intensified accountability structures, in principle creating means to involve parents more intimately as observers with access to information about the ways in which teachers and principals construct the processes of inclusion and exclusion at the heart of school life. In one Toronto francophone school, the principal found that the call to accountability and transparency had generated significantly different relationships among school staff, parents, and the school community, leading to positive outcomes such as increased parental involvement, whether or not that was what the school administrator and educators supported.

> I find that the major change I've experienced over the past five years is the imputability to which everyone is subjected. And this transparency with the EQAO testing, which goes through the board, and the parents who are there, and with the budget, for which we are accountable ... there is that aspect to everything: from the school rules, where you must always take account of your activities. I find that to be new, whereas before we were behind closed doors. The parents didn't appear, you only reported to your superintendent and that was hidden and all that. Now you have the Ministry—it's public—your results go on the Internet so you're judged in some way, and they are even in a position to ask you what your plan is to rectify the situation ... we weren't used to dealing with those people. And often I will receive phone calls saying, "I have the right to know this—why do you function like this?" and with reason. So, that's new. And the structures weren't yet in place, so there were parents who were really waiting for that, so from the first years, they were very aggressive because they really wanted to know everything. Now I think it's faded because it's better managed, it's better framed. Personally, I think that there is a better cooperation among all the actors—the board, the school administration. So I think that has been the major aspect to change. Once again, as I say, in terms of policies, it's putting into place the provincial testing and all that. And there, we are judged on that, whether we like it or not. (Interview #4101, translated from French)

Along with the mobility of its transnational population, the Canadian school, like other institutions, has become subject to intensified processes of managing difference. With recent educational reform reflecting renewed emphasis on administrative and teacher professionalization and accountability, schools are entered into the new mechanisms of surveillance, regulation, monitoring, and discipline (e.g., policies on zero tolerance and so forth). In the official context of the regulated worlds of school authorities in Vancouver, Toronto, and Montreal, the viability of mechanisms of ensuring the proliferation of social order through the reproduction and reiteration of official knowledges depends on the alignment of those (e.g., principals, teachers, students, parents, and support staff) concerned as an embodied extension of the state's disciplinary function (Foucault, 1977; Gramsci, 1971), and thus the meaningfulness of discourses of productivity, such as in the demands on teachers to keep up with requirements for professional development, function not only with material consequences, but also on a micropolitical level as an appeal to the value of a teacher's passion for "lifelong learning."

Yet, Morrow and Torres (1995) reminds us in recalling the discursive strategy of critical pragmatism that "social and educational discourses result from the exercise of power and the security of establishing a sound, normative, and foundational ground for scientific analysis may be illusory at this point of human history" insofar as the meaning of history and its social objects is open to ongoing refiguring.

Reading educator discourse regarding student diversity as a sociological "object" begins from the very paradox of official discourse, in the sense that students and educators are represented as artifacts of political and pedagogical intervention rather than agents of social change, people with active strategies and personal histories. A different set of questions—such as *Describe your relationship with your students this year; How do you relate with your students? How do you make sense of your race/ethnicity in relationship to your students?* or *Tell me about the dynamics of your classroom?*—might have yielded a different sense of possible responses and analyses that would perhaps have provided insight into moments of detour, transgression, and transformation in educators' own subjectivities and the ways they imagine their students. It would be of interest to read educators' discourses more closely in terms of the interrelational contexts in which they articulate themselves, in particular with an eye to examining how some discourses and not others come to be invoked in one context and not another. In particular, it would be interesting to invite and support further conversations with educators around the ways in which they come across transformative possibility beyond a normative "integration" model of student diversity. Further research is required to pursue how the emptied, commodified signifier of diversity in neoliberal discourse on schools might be refigured with possibility.

Note

1. For more information on the research methodology, please see Chapter 1 of this book, or the MCRI website at www.teachcan.ca.

References

Anderson, B. (1991). *Imagined communities: Reflections on the origin and spread of nationalism.* London: Verso.

Apffel-Marglin, F. (1998). *The spirit of regeneration: Andean culture confronting western notions of development.* London: Zed Books.

Apple, M. (2000). Between neoliberalism and neoconservatism: Education and conservatism in a global context. In N.C. Burbules and C.A. Torres (Eds.), *Globalization and education: Critical perspectives* (pp. 57–77). New York: Routledge.

Arguedas, J.M. (2000). *El zorro de arriba y el zorro de abajo.* Paris: ALLCA XX.

Baudrillard, J. (1988). Simulacra and simulations. In M. Poster (Ed.), *Jean Baudrillard: Selected writings*. Stanford: Stanford University Press.

Bélanger, N. (2003). Des steamer classes à l'enfance en difficulté: création de la différence. In N. Labrie & S. Lamoureux (Eds.), *L'éducation de langue française en Ontario: enjeux et processus sociaux* (pp. 109–126). Sudbury, ON: Les Éditions Prise de Parole.

Benítez Rojo, A. (1996). *La isla que se repite: El Caribe et la perspectiva postmoderna*. Hanover, NH: Ediciones del Norte.

British Columbia Ministry of Education. (2004). *Diversity in BC schools: A framework*. Retrieved February 19, 2007, from www.bced.gov.bc.ca/diversity/diversity_framework.pdf.

British Columbia Ministry of Education. (1996). *Language education in BC schools*. Retrieved February 19, 2007, from www.bced.gov.bc.ca/diversity/diversity_framework.pdf.

Canadian Council on Learning. (2007). *The state of learning in canada: No time for complacency: Report on learning in Canada 2007*. Ottawa: Canadian Council on Learning. Retrieved July 17, 2007, from www.ccl-cca.ca/NR/rdonlyres/5ECAA2E9-D5E4-43B9-94E4-84D6D31BC5BC/0/NewSOLR_Report.pdf.

Curtis, B., Livingstone, D.W., & Smaller, H. (1992). *Stacking the deck: The streaming of working-class kids in Ontario schools*. Montreal: La maîtresse d'école.

Dei, G.S. et al. (2000). *Removing the margins: The challenges and possibilities of inclusive schooling*. Toronto: Canadian Scholars' Press.

Drucker, P. (1969). *The age of discontinuity: Guidelines to our changing society*. New York: Harper and Row.

Durkheim, E. (1969). *L'évolution pédagogique en France, 2ᵉ édition*. Paris: Presses universitaires de France.

Evans, T. & Ayers, A.J. (2006). In the service of power: The global political economy of citizenship and human rights. *Citizenship studies, 10*(3), 289–308.

Farris Thompson, R. (1983). *Flash of the spirit: African and Afro-American art and philosophy*. New York: Random House.

Foucault, M. (1977). *Discipline and punish: The birth of the prison*. London: A. Lane.

Foucault, M. (1973). *Le pouvoir psychiatrique: Cours au Collège de France (1973–1974)*. Paris: Gallimard.

Fusco, C. (1990). Managing the other. *Lusitania, 1*(3): 77–83.

Ghosh, R. (2004). Globalization in the North American region: Toward renegotiation of culture. *McGill Journal of Education, 39*(1): 87–101.

Gramsci, A. (1971). *Selections from the Prison Notebook*. London: Lawrence and Wishart.

Glissant, É. (1997). *Poetics of relation*. (B. Wing, Trans.). Ann Arbor: University of Michigan Press.

Jameson, F. (1991). *Postmodernism, or the cultural logic of late capitalism*. Durham, NC: Duke University Press.

Jordan, A. (2001). Special education in Ontario: A case study of market-based reforms. *Cambridge Journal of Education, 31*(3), 349–371.

Lather, P. (1986). Issues of validity in openly ideological research: Between a rock and a soft place. *Interchange, 17*(4), 63–84.

Lipman, P. (2005). Metropolitan regions—new geographies of inequality in education: the Chicago metroregion case. *Globalisation, Societies and Education, 3*(2), 141–163.

Marshall, D. (1990). *The education of exceptional children in the public schools of Ontario: A historical analysis*. Unpublished doctoral dissertation, University of Toronto.

Ministère de l'Éducation du Québec. (1998). *Plan of action for educational integration and intercultural education, 1998–2002: A new direction for success*. Quebec City: Government of Quebec.

Morrow, R.A. & Torres, C.A. (1995). *Social theory and education: A critique of theories of social and cultural reproduction*. Albany, NY: State University of New York Press.

Organisation for Economic Co-operation and Development. (2005). *Promoting adult learning*. Paris: Organisation for Economic Co-operation and Development.

Ontario Ministry of Education and Training. (1993). *Antiracism and ethnocultural equity in school boards: Guidelines for policy development and implementation*. Retrieved July 19, 2007, from www.edu.gov.on.ca/eng/document/curricul/antiraci/antire.pdf.

Statistics Canada. (2005). *Learning a living: First results of the adult literacy and life skills survey*. Ottawa and Paris: Statistics Canada and the Organisation for Economic Co-operation and Development. Retrieved July 19, 2007, from www.statcan.ca/english/freepub/89-603-XIE/2005001/pdf/89-603-XWE-part1.pdf.

Treasury Board of Canada Secretariat. (2005). Canada's performance report 2005— Annex 3—Indicators and additional information. Retrieved July 19, 2007, from www.tbs-sct.gc.ca/report/govrev/05/ann301_e.asp.

Tuhiwai-Smith, L. (1999). *Decolonizing methodologies: Research and indigenous peoples*. New York: Zed Books.

CHAPTER 8

What Next?
OFFICIAL DISCOURSE AND SCHOOL REALITY

Diane Gérin-Lajoie

How can the findings and insights gathered on the issue of student diversity and student inclusion in Canadian schools in this book be useful? How can they inform the ongoing efforts of the school personnel and other education stakeholders to ensure that students from all backgrounds are fully and positively included in schools across Canada?

The results discussed in the previous chapters demonstrate that the discourses of our participants on racial, ethnic, and linguistic diversity of their student population share similarities in the interpretation of diversity. Diversity is mostly understood as an individual phenomenon characterizing students from diverse backgrounds. Students are often seen as having problems in school that need to be addressed. Students who adapt well to the school environment are considered like any other student, and teachers do not see them differently because of their race, ethnic background, or language. Elite students become racialized as passing for majority students insofar as their behaviour, their language and their cultural capital are considered to be consistent with those of the dominant discourse. Finally, in the participants' discourses, student inclusion is accomplished through the "celebration of differences," which is at the core of the multicultural education framework in the official discourse (Harper, 1997). These findings are in line, for the most part, with the way diversity and inclusion are understood by government officials and the general public, as a process of assimilation to the "mainstream or dominant state of affairs" (Ryan, 1999, p. 25).

The purpose of the present chapter is not to reiterate that school practices lie within the framework of racialized discourses, which "structure or filter in important ways the possible alternatives for interpreting race and ethnicity" (Ryan, 1999, p. 12). That has already been said in several of the previous chapters, with which I agree. Instead, I would like to talk about the work of school personnel with the students. We should wonder what it might take to succeed at supporting an increasingly diversified school population. Questioning the fact that teachers feel mostly like "rescuers" when it comes to student diversity and student inclusion, Dei et al. (2000) makes the following statement:

> Often when we discuss the role of dominant teachers educating across differences towards emancipatory outcomes, we inadvertently trigger notions of "rescuing the other." For example, teachers who regard themselves on a mission to "save" the underclass or disadvantaged only serve to reproduce the perception of inherent privilege accorded to those from the dominant culture who must "tend to the less fortunate." (p. 246)

Integrating students from all backgrounds represents more than supporting them to fit into the existing system, even in this present era of educational accountability. Dei et al. (2000), as well as other critical educators, suggests that teachers contribute to the empowerment of students instead. In order to do so, educational stakeholders (not only teachers) should be prepared to inquire critically about what needs to be done for the school to become truly inclusive of all students. For these students to be given the opportunity, schools must become sites of possibility, not "sites of disenfranchisement" (Dei, 1999, p. 270).

In order to accomplish the creation of sites of opportunity, first the educational community (government officials, school board representatives, principals, teachers, students and parents/guardians, caregivers, community support workers, etc.) needs to deconstruct the notion of student inclusion and to reconstruct it as a notion of possibilities. In short, the responsibility to get involved in the deconstructing process does not belong only to teachers, but to school stakeholders in general, and to school boards in particular.

Second, we need to recognize that what critical educators expect from teachers—becoming agents of change—can be interpreted as a contradiction in itself, given the fact that schools have always been sites for the social, cultural, and linguistic reproduction of existing social practices. Recognizing this contradiction does not mean that we should abandon the idea of transformative practices in schools. The potential for teachers to become agents of change still exists. It appears as essential, however, that critical educators take into consideration the complexity of the social practices, inside and outside of the school, that shape this institution. For teachers to engage as agents of change remains, nevertheless, a challenging task to accomplish in the present state of education.

Third, we need to pay more attention to the role of principals and to examine how they can provide, through professional development, a context more favourable to the accomplishment of better student inclusion. Despite a prescriptive work environment, principals have the potential, nevertheless, to "make things happen" in their schools, to revise some of the existing school practices in order to develop an inclusive school. The next pages will address these issues.

The Deconstruction of the Concepts of Students' Diversity and Student Inclusion

As mentioned in the introductory paragraphs of this chapter, interview results analyzed in the context of the book indicate that the concepts of student diversity and student inclusion articulated in the participants' discourses, across the country, are still mostly embedded in a multicultural education framework. In this framework, differences are celebrated through the recognition of the folkloric and cultural attributes (food, clothing, dances, etc.) of students from different racial, ethnic, and linguistic backgrounds. Our findings also indicate that student diversity continues to be interpreted as a reality to which teachers and principals must adapt, as if this were still a new phenomenon. Finally, our results point to the fact that a large number of participants see student inclusion as an individual process where students from diverse racial, ethnic, and linguistic backgrounds need to claim space. In the context of the official discourse on accountability that prevails across Canada, those who experience difficulties in the process of adapting to the school system are often perceived as having "problems." Language deficiencies, difficult socio-economic conditions, not being at the expected level of achievement or performance in the learning process are a few examples of how discourses from teachers and principals construct the notion of student diversity and student inclusion. To summarize, minorities and especially visible minorities are still considered "disadvantaged" students (van Dijk, 1993). Within their discourses, teachers and principals draw individualized pictures of their students' lived experiences and consider that most of them are "good kids" who have to struggle with a lot of challenges.

Obviously, no one would deny that minority students face the challenges reported in our discussions with the school personnel and stated in official documents in general. However, to present these challenges as individual experiences sends the message that students, because of an individual lack of performance, ability, effort, or interest, must be helped to catch up to fit into the existing prescriptive Canadian school model. This type of discourse fails to question the fact that Ministries of Education or school boards do not demonstrate the type of leadership and support needed for the development of a more inclusive school structure for students from diverse racial, ethnic, and linguistic backgrounds. More importantly, student diversity and student inclusion are not discussed in the context of social inequities.

There is a need to deconstruct existing notions of schooling to allow for a better understanding of the social practices that currently influence the fabric of the school and, in particular, the inclusion of students from diverse backgrounds. How can we do that realistically? What steps do we need to take to engage in a closer examination of the issues of diversity and inclusion, while at the same time, keeping in mind the existing prescriptive working environment of the school where these issues are dealt with? How can we, realistically, engage in a "language of possibility" (Aronowitz & Giroux, 1985) in the present state of education?

As reported throughout the book, teachers find themselves in a working environment where critical thinking and self-reflection are left with little room to grow. In these prescriptive times, racial, ethnic, and linguistic diversity, and student inclusion are no longer issues found at the top of priority lists in the official discourse. Right now, as I mentioned before, accountability, teachers' professionalization, and governance take centre stage in educational circles across Canada (Gérin-Lajoie, 2007a).

Nonetheless, schools are sites where students should be given tools to succeed as well as tools to develop their critical minds. Emancipatory pedagogy could accomplish this goal. As defined by Dei et al. (2000), "an emancipatory pedagogy is one where teachers are aware of the authoritative and social power they wield over students and must be willing to divest this power by restoring agency to their students" (p. 246). Despite the less-than-conducive existing context for inclusiveness—but perhaps because of it—critical educators continue to explore ways of establishing principles of equity and social justice in schools. These efforts are often drawn from an anti-racism education framework, which is often presented in opposition to the multicultural education model found in schools.

Arguing for an anti-racism pedagogy in the classroom, Solomon and Levine-Rasky (1996) explain the difficulties encountered to raise teachers' awareness in this area:

> Antiracism has been slow in achieving the objective of equalizing opportunities for racial minorities within institutions such as schools because of educators' ambivalence, contradictory responses, or outright antagonism to its concept, policy and practice.... Since teachers are strategically placed as school agents to effect change, their disengagement from antiracism severely restricts its transformative possibilities. (p. 338)

Critical educators encourage teachers to become agents of change in the school environment, because of the close relationships they have with students and their effect on one another. Giroux (1988) speaks of teachers as possible "transformative intellectuals," which he defines as "one who exercises forms of intellectual and pedagogical practice that attempt to insert teaching and learning directly into the political sphere by arguing that schooling represents both a struggle for meaning and a struggle over power relations" (p. 174). In the context of student diversity and student inclusion, critical educators have suggested that teachers use an anti-racism education framework to work with students. The notion of "agents of change" is promising. However, it contradicts the very essence of schooling, which is to make students the "good citizens" of tomorrow from a state point of view.

Teachers as Agents of Change: A Contradiction

Past studies have claimed, however, that teachers are often reluctant to embrace the idea of anti-racism pedagogy in their own practices (King, 2004; Mujawamariya & Mahrouse, 2004; Sleeter, 2004). In the present study, we did not directly ask participants if they considered themselves agents of change. Nevertheless, their alignment with the official discourse on diversity and inclusion suggests that, most likely, they would not see themselves as agents of change or transformative intellectuals, not at least as users of an anti-racism–oriented pedagogy.

It is important to point out, however, that teachers have their own histories. These histories have an impact on the way they define themselves as teachers or principals and on the standpoint they will choose to adopt in their professional lives. Sultana (1995) mentions the impact of teachers' social class on the way they view teaching. He explains that "it has been pointed out, for instance, that teachers tend to be overwhelmingly from a middle-class background, and that their contradictory class position in a stratified society means that they generally have little vested interest in promoting changes to the status quo" (Sultana, 1995, p. 135). He also points out that even those eager to promote justice and equality in their classrooms found themselves caught in a centralized, bureaucratic educational system that is not conducive to transformations (Sultana, 1995, p. 132). Should we then put the entire blame on teachers for the present situation in schools and hold them solely responsible for it, as it seems sometimes to be portrayed in the existing literature? Of course, the answer is no. Work performed in schools is mostly the result of top-down decisions, which do not give much room to the school personnel to deviate from a rather prescriptive working environment.

The notion of teachers as agents of change is also, to some extent, contradictory to the very essence of schooling, which, overall, is still to maintain the status quo of the existing social order. In their own work, teachers (and principals) find themselves caught between their respective subjective locations and the official discourse, which place them in a rather complex situation. This particularity must be kept in mind when researching ways of changing current school practices. I strongly agree with a statement made by Solomon and Levine-Rasky (1996) about their own work with students preparing to become teachers:

> Rather than restricting an understanding of contradiction to a standing problem in an orthodox research framework, when taken as an important analytical concern in itself, it furthers our purpose of exploring the complicated subjective, ideological and socio-political territory of teacher responses to antiracism pedagogy. The approach to interpreting teacher responses as reflecting contradictory positions, even contradictory identities situated in a particular social location in the world, is a vitally important one. (p. 339)

It seems apparent that teachers see their role with the students as mostly one of transmitting knowledge. Teachers' role in the transmission of social and cultural values, which some refer to as "socialization" and others as "social reproduction," is absent from their discourses, as if it were not a component of teachers' work. For example, in a recently completed study on teachers' work in francophone minority settings, I came to the conclusion that the teacher participants saw themselves primarily as agents of knowledge transmission. Even in the case of those teachers who manifested a political awareness about francophone linguistic minority rights, their discourse on teaching was limited to understanding their responsibilities in terms of teaching the prescriptive curriculum. These teachers did not see themselves as having the responsibility of going through a critical examination of minority issues with their students. This is an intriguing finding considering the fact that the purpose of French minority language schools is clearly stated in the official discourse as contributing to the maintenance of the French language and culture and to the process of student identity construction (Gérin-Lajoie, 2007b).

As indicated in the above study, even when the possibility is there for teachers to develop a more critical approach to their teaching, they are not taking the opportunity to do so in the context of their classroom, and neither do their principals at the school level. As in the case of English majority language schools, the French minority language schools represent the dominant model of schooling. Expectations are that when at school, students will shift their language practices to those of a francophone majority environment, even though the school is surrounded by the language and culture of the anglophone majority. In discarding the social milieu where francophones evolve, French language schools located outside Quebec become important sites of contradiction for the teachers as well as for the students.

The situation in the French minority language schools is not unique. Even in English majority language schools, there is a need for consciousness-raising among students. But as in the example presented above, there is a lack of awareness on the part of many teachers of the "political" role they play in the classroom, whether as agents of change or as agents of reproduction of the existing system. This lack of awareness is ingrained in the teaching culture itself and is a result of the way the official discourse portrays the role of teachers in our society.

Having raised the contradiction in the concept of "teachers as agents of change" does not mean, however, that we have to stop finding ways of making it happen. It remains essential to bring teachers to see their role through a more critical lens in regards to issues of equity and social justice in schools. The label to be given to this critical lens does not necessary matter, as long as we find constructive ways to do it. It could be named anti-racism education, critical multicultural education, or even multicultural education (not in the sense of the official discourse, though). A critical examination of these issues does not mean that it cannot be done through the existing curriculum. Such a re-examination of the curriculum would benefit the students, as well as teachers, in giving them the opportunity to examine critically existing social practices. Work needs to be done in the areas of pre-service teacher training, as well as in in-service teacher training, without, however, placing the sole burden of responsibility on teachers.

PRE-SERVICE TEACHER TRAINING

Teachers and critical educators agree that there is a lack of training in the areas of student diversity and student inclusion, especially in pre-service teacher training. However, the lack of training carries two different meanings.

In the study examined in this book, some teachers have mentioned never having received any training in preparation for a racially, ethnically, and linguistically diverse classroom. Their remarks refer to the lack of pedagogical tools or approaches to work with these students who often have poor language skills in the language of instruction. Teachers are preoccupied with knowledge transmission. In discussing the results of their study on anti-racism pedagogy conducted with student teachers and in-service teachers, Solomon and Levine-Rasky (1996) point out:

> Educators very often interpret antiracism as just another curricular innovation they are expected to add to their already full programmes, rather than an orientation to the teaching and the learning process that informs

their regular activities. In addition, it is seen within the pedagogic framework known as the transmission model of instruction, which dictates that the teacher be the distributor of knowledge, transmitting content to those without knowledge. (p. 342)

Critical educators, for their part, denounce the lack of training of teachers in the area of critical awareness, which impacts their potential role as agents of change. Critical educators are preoccupied with social change. As explained by King (2004):

To consider seriously the value commitment involved in teaching for social change as an option, students need experiential opportunities to recognize and evaluate the ideological influences that shape their thinking about schooling, society, themselves and, diverse others. The critique of ideology, identity and miseducation described herein represents a form of cultural politics in teacher education that is needed to address the specific rationality of social inequity in modern American society. (p. 80)

These two very different sets of preoccupations need to be reconciled in order to successfully transform schools into more equitable places for students. Critical literature tends to address mostly the issue of social change and the need to shift school practices from a domination-subordination *rapport* to an emancipatory-egalitarian one. As King (2004) states, "prospective teachers need both an intellectual understanding of schooling and inequity, as well as a self-reflective, transformative emotional growth experiences" (p. 72). Without embarking on a journey of critical reflection starting with their own experiences, it would be difficult, from the point of view of critical educators, for teachers to use emancipatory pedagogy with their own students.

From the perspective of critical educators, faculties of education must develop teacher training programs that will be preoccupied with equity and social justice. Equity and social justice issues should cross the entire preservice teaching program. One or two courses, sometimes elective courses, are not enough to give student teachers the opportunity to look at teaching through a more critical lens. They need a learning place where they get exposed to critical thinking in different ways. In their study on multicultural education in pre-service programs, Mujawamariya and Mahrouse (2004) explain the following:

Our findings ... provide further evidence that the multicultural education component of teacher education in general consistently falls short of the expectations of those for whom it is intended. According to our respondents, these shortcomings are mainly due to how multicultural education

> continues to be offered as a special-interest course rather than being an integral part of the teacher preparation curriculum. Many respondents were disappointed and frustrated with the paradox that in a system that professes to be equitable and inclusive, teacher education candidates who wish to engage with these issues in depth are often unable to do so because the program does not allow it. (p. 350)

These findings confirm what Giroux (1988) has claimed for some years now: that "schools of education rarely encourage their students to take seriously the imperatives of social critique and social change as part of a wider emancipatory vision" (p. 183).

Existing courses on multicultural education in pre-service teachers' programs might also reproduce dominant discourses through notions of multicultural education. As mentioned by Mujawamariya and Mahrouse (2004), "the challenge, therefore, is to consider how multicultural education might be reconfigured not only at a structural level, but also at a conceptual level" (p. 351). However, some examples of such a reconfiguration exist. Consciousness-raising work is performed on some occasions (King, 2004; Sleeter, 2004). For the participating teachers who get the opportunity to reflect on issues of equity and social justice, this critical reflection might be somehow disturbing in some cases, and might bring resistance on their part to change their views on their role as teachers.

IN-SERVICE TEACHER TRAINING

In the areas of student diversity and student inclusion, professional development should be envisaged under a school commitment in the form of a collective project under the principal's leadership, instead of expecting an individual commitment on the part of teachers. In-service teacher training should also go beyond one-day workshops. Schools need to articulate an action plan that will give the time and the space for teachers to think critically about equity and social justice, especially in the areas of diversity and inclusion. Such professional development initiatives would provide a terrain where ideas can be exchanged and debates take place. As we have witnessed through the book, at this point in time, student diversity and student inclusion is no longer part of any pressing agenda at the government level. The responsibility then comes back to school personnel to make sure that equity and social justice principles are a priority in their work environment.

Principals, because of their location in the power structure of the school, have a level of control that teachers do not have. Although principals cannot change all the rules due to the prescriptive reality of the school, they still have the power to prioritize what to emphasize in their own work environment.

As stated some time ago by Fullan (1992), "the principal is central, especially to changes in the culture of the school" (p. 145). I am in agreement with this statement. I think that the only way to develop any form of empowering pedagogy, and, to a certain extent, to work against the grain, is to install a climate of collaboration in the school. That can be more easily achieved under the leadership of the principal who will give directions and facilitate the change. In this instance, the role of the principal can be considered threefold:

1. To provide concrete support to teachers in their work with students from diverse racial, ethnic, and linguistic backgrounds.
2. To develop a climate of collaboration where teachers will think critically and work together toward the true inclusion of all minority students.
3. To help to promote a shared vision for the development of an inclusive school community.

As I have stated above, the critical examination of the work performed by the teachers in the areas mentioned previously could be accomplished through collaborative work. The notion of collaboration has become, in recent years, part of the official discourse about teachers' work in schools (Mitchell & Sackney, 2000). For example, the Ontario Ministry of Education has actively promoted the notion of professional learning communities, where teachers are strongly encouraged to work collaboratively toward a specific goal. In several Ontario school boards, this is now part of their yearly improvement plan. Hargreaves (1994) also mentions the emphasis in the official discourse on collaborative work in the context of school improvement.

> Collaboration and collegiality, then, form significant planks of policies to restructure schools from without and to improve them from within. Much of the burden of educational reform has been placed upon their fragile shoulders. School improvement, curriculum, reform, teacher development and leadership development are all seen to some extent as dependent on the building of positive collegial relationships for their success. (p. 187)

In the context of teachers' professional development, collaborative work appears to be a logical way to bring teachers together to do a critical examination of the school practices. In my opinion, this can only be accomplished if school principals show leadership in the areas of emancipatory pedagogy, equity issues, and social justice. However, are principals equipped to take on this leadership role? In my opinion, there is a need for research in this area. A lot has been said on teachers in the literature on multicultural education, and in particular in the writings on anti-racism education, as if teachers had full control over school practices. I think that we would benefit by learning more about school administrators and their views on equity and social justice principles, especially in the areas of student diversity and student inclusion.

Concluding Remarks

A lot has been said about teachers in this book. However, it is important to remind ourselves that participants' discourses on student diversity and student inclusion as well as school practices lie within the scope of larger school policies and reforms centred mostly on accountability, teacher professionalization, and school governance. Teachers' and principals' positions toward their work and toward schooling are highly regulated by these discursive formations. As an example, I can mention briefly the area of accountability and, in particular, standardized testing. A classroom with students who do not have the cultural capital or prior learning experiences required by the school to succeed presents a definitive challenge for teachers. For these teachers, school inclusion might be interpreted as being able to bring these students to the achievement level expected by the school. Within the present educational structure, teachers and principals face several demands and must act quickly to stay at the top. Changes within the school population, as illustrated in the results presented throughout the book, have a sizable impact on teachers' and principals' work. Social, economic, and political factors are not part of the equation in a context of standardization.

Teachers are overwhelmed, among other things, by the day-to-day responsibilities and by the increasing accountability expectations (e.g., assessment, reporting) associated with standards and outcomes driven curriculum policies. If proper pre-service teacher training and in-service teacher training are not provided, chances are slim that teachers will undertake a critical examination of student diversity and student inclusion on their own, given their work environment.

It is most important to remind ourselves that the primary responsibility of teachers is to care for their students, and it is evident that the teachers in our study do so. Is it enough, though, to give all students equal opportunities in school and, later on, in life? As researchers, we need to examine more closely what needs to be done to change the structure of the school system in a way that will benefit all students and especially ones from diverse racial, ethnic, and linguistic backgrounds. Pre-service and in-service teacher training, educational policies and school reforms, should all be concerned with the benefit of every student. Transformative possibilities exist in school, and school personnel should be trained to see which ones could be achieved in their respective contexts (Solomon and Levine-Rasky, 1996), within the limits imposed by the existing educational structure.

One objective of the book was to provide information on teachers and principals from across the country and from different linguistic school contexts. Results show that participants share a very similar discourse. This is an interesting finding, although not that unexpected when we look at schooling in Canada and the similarities between school policies and reforms in British Columbia, Ontario, and Quebec.

I hope the contents of the book will have provided readers with valuable new insights on teacher discourses and, to some extent, those of principals, on the issues of student diversity and student inclusion in the three major Canadian cities of Vancouver, Toronto, and Montreal. I also hope that it has raised questions to debate with colleagues, students, family members, and friends. Education is in the public domain. Issues of diversity, equity, and social justice in education should concern every one of us.

References

Aronowitz, S. & Giroux, H.A. (1985). *Education under siege: The conservative, liberal and radical debate over schooling*. New York: Bergin and Garvey.

Dei, G.J.S., James, I.M., James-Wilson, S., & Zine, J. (2000). *Removing the margins: The challenges and possibilities of inclusive schooling*. Toronto: Canadian Scholars' Press.

Dei, G.J.S. (1999). The denial of difference: Reframing antiracist praxis. *Race, Ethnicity and Education, 2*(1), 17–37.

Fullan, M. (1992). *The new meaning of educational change*. New York: Teachers College Press.

Gérin-Lajoie, D. (2007a). Effets des politiques scolaires dans la pratique du métier d'enseignante et d'enseignant au Canada. In R. Malet (Ed.), *L'école, lieu de tensions et de médiations: Quels effets sur les pratiques scolaires? Actes du colloque international de l'AFEC, 22, 23 et 24 juin 2006* (pp. 395–405). Lille: Association francophone d'éducation comparée.

Gérin-Lajoie, D. (2007b). Parcours identitaires et pratiques sociales du personnel enseignant dans les écoles de langue française en milieu minoritaire. In C. Gohier (Ed.), *Identités professionnelles d'acteurs de l'enseignement: Regard croisés*. Montreal: Presses de l'Université du Québec.

Giroux, H. (1988). *Schooling and the struggle for public life*. Minneapolis: University of Minnesota Press.

Hargreaves, A. (1994). *Changing teachers, changing times: Teachers' work and culture in the post modern age*. Toronto: OISE Press.

Harper, H. (1997). Difference and diversity in Ontario schooling. *Canadian Journal of Education. 22*(2), 192–206.

King, J.E. (2004). Dysconscious racism: Ideology, identity, and the miseducation of teachers. In G. Ladson-Billings and D. Gillborn (Eds.), *The Routledge-Falmer Reader on Multicultural Education* (pp. 71–83). London: Routledge-Falmer.

Mitchell, C. & Sackney, L. (2000). *Profound improvement: Building capacity for a learning community*. Lisse, Netherlands: Swets and Zeitlinger.

Mujawamariya, D. & Mahrouse, G. (2004). Multicultural education in Canadian pre-service programmes: Teacher candidates' perspectives. *The Alberta Journal of Educational Research*, *50*(4), 336–353.

Ryan, J. (1999). *Race and ethnicity in multi-ethnic schools*. Toronto: Multilingual Matters Ltd.

Sleeter, C.E. (2004). How white teachers construct race. In G. Ladson-Billings & D. Gillborn (Eds.), *The Routledge-Falmer Reader in Multicultural Education* (pp. 163–178). London: Routledge-Falmer Press.

Solomon, R.P. & Levine-Rasky, C. (1996). Transforming teacher education for an antiracism pedagogy. *Canadian Review of Sociology and Anthropology, 33*(3), 337–359.

Sultana, R.G. (1995). From critical education to a critical practice of teaching. In J. Smyth (Ed.), *Critical discourses on teacher development* (pp. 131–145). Toronto: OISE Press.

van Dijk, T.A. (1993). *Elite discourse and racism*. Newbury Park, CA: Sage Publications.